StarOffice 5.2

Writer

Handbook

NANCY D. WARNER

Sun Microsystems Press
A Prentice Hall Title

PH
PTR

The publisher offers discounts on this book when ordered in bulk quantities. For more
information, contact: Corporate Sales Department, Phone: 800-382-3419; FAX: 201-
236-7141; Email: corpsales@prenhall.com; or write: Prentice Hall PTR, Corp. Sales
Dept., One Lake Street, Upper Saddle River, NJ 07458

Editorial/production supervision: *Kathleen M. Caren*
Acquisitions Editor: *Gregory G. Doench*
Editorial Assistant: *Mary Treacy*
Technical Editor: *Bill Camarda*
Cover Design Director: *Jerry Votta*
Cover Design: *Bruce Kenselaar*
Manufacturing Manager: *Alexis R. Heydt*
Marketing Manager: *Debby van Dijk*
Series Design: *Gail Cocker-Bogusz*

Sun Microsystems Press:
Marketing Manager: *Michael Llwyd Alread*
Publisher: *Rachel Borden*

10 9 8 7 6 5 4 3 2 1

ISBN 0-13-029386-5

Sun Microsystems Press
A Prentice Hall Title

*I want to thank my partner Sid,
for his encouragement and support
while I wrote this book—even at 5 A.M.
when I was going to sleep
and you were going to work.*

Contents

Chapter   2
Working with Documents   27

Chapter   3
Editing Documents   53

Chapter   7
Working with Styles and Templates   139

Chapter 8
Working with Frames, Graphics, and Objects   163

Chapter   10
Reviewing, Collaborating, and
Merging Documents   233

Chapter   11
Working with Long Document Features   261

Chapter 12

Using Document Automation   307

Chapter   14
Customizing the Writer Environment   351

Appendix A
Writer Shortcut Keys   387

Index   395

Introduction

STAROFFICE WRITER HANDBOOK

Upon writing this book, individuals using StarOffice Writer on a daily basis were asked about the type of things that they wanted in a Writer book. The overwhelming response was, "Don't go into long explanations on what the features are, just give us an example and tell us the exact steps to perform the task." And accordingly, this is the fundamental precept for this book. You won't find lengthy explanations that don't get the job done; instead, you'll learn when a task should be performed and the exact steps to make it happen—fast!

For example, we all know what a table of contents is: you use it to locate specific places in your document according to main headings and other in-text references, such as tables or illustrations. As you might guess, this book explains how to open your document, perform the steps, and end up with a table of contents.

This example segues nicely into talking about the table of contents contained in this book. It is organized so that instead of having sections listed according to the menus or commands in the book, they are listed based on the task you want to perform. (Of course, they are arranged based on similar Writer features so that you don't have to look through the entire table of contents each time you want to find something.) For example, if you want to know how to create a new template, find the chapter on "Styles and Templates" and locate the section "To Create a New Template." It will be there, instead of being buried in an unrelated section as a fifth level header that, by the way, might not even get listed in the table of contents. Of course, you can and should use the index as well, but this book makes both the table of contents and the index a valuable resource for finding the tasks you want to perform.

In today's busy work-world, where things need to happen fast, *StarOffice Writer Handbook* will have you quickly working with even the most complicated tasks.

FEEDBACK

While every effort has been made to ensure that this book is accurate and timely, there is no doubt that some errors will be found or that information in this book will be overtaken by subsequent releases of StarOffice. If you find anything in need of correction, please let me know at warner58@home.com. I will ensure that the necessary corrections are made in future releases or in errata.

Acknowledgments

At Prentice Hall, much thanks to Greg Doench for all his guidance and patience throughout this project. Your level head and positive attitude made this enjoyable. I would also like to thank Kathleen Caren for all her hard work and expertise putting the book together and adding the final touches. In addition, a big thank you to Bill Camarda for making sure that the book was technically accurate and providing great suggestions.

I would like to thank all the folks at Sun Microsystems, especially Rachel Borden, for all her help making this project happen. In addition, I would like to thank Michael Alread for getting me feedback on StarOffice users, and Alex C. Dethier, Christina A. Galvan, Maureen Hands, and David T. Nix for being great interviewees.

Nancy Warner
November, 2000

chapter 1

Getting Started with StarOffice Writer

IN THIS CHAPTER:

Starting StarOffice Writer

You might have already noticed that you don't initially start Writer like you would an application in other productivity suites. You start StarOffice first, and then create or open text documents to gain access to the Writer application menus, commands, and features.

TO LAUNCH STAROFFICE

To launch StarOffice in the UNIX/Linux environment (for example, a Linux-based computer):

1   At the command prompt, use the cd command to move to the root/ office52/bin directory (or to the directory specific to your computer such as "username"/office52/bin).

2   At the prompt type ./soffice.

3   Press <Enter>.

StarOffice will open on your screen. In cases where you are running X Windows or a GUI based on X Windows, such as Gnome or KDE, you can typically start StarOffice from the Start or launch menu provided by the operating system.

To launch StarOffice in the Microsoft Windows environment (Windows 95, 98, NT, and 2000):

1   Click the Start menu button and point at Programs, then point at the StarOffice 5.2 folder.

2   On the cascading menu that appears, click the StarOffice icon.

You will find that whether you are working on a Linux-based computer or a Windows 2000 machine that StarOffice pretty much looks and behaves the same across the different platforms.

By default StarOffice provides a view of your desktop (Windows or other GUI interface provided by your operating system). This means that you have access to all the shortcuts or other items that you normally would on the desktop provided by your particular operating system. At the very bottom of the desktop you will find a Start button and a Taskbar. The Taskbar will provide you with buttons for any open windows that you may have open on the desktop, making it very easy for you to switch between various application windows.

The top of the StarOffice Desktop supplies you tools such as a menu system and toolbars that you can use to manipulate the desktop or launch StarOffice applications (by creating or opening a particular document type; in this case a document meaning a letter, spreadsheet, presentation, database, and so on).

The desktop also provides a URL locator in the Function bar. This allows you to browse the Web directly from the StarOffice Desktop. Below this command area is the Desktop workspace; this workspace will also serve as the application workspace, once you launch a particular application such as Writer.

TO USE THE MENU BAR

The menu bar provides you with easy access to commands related to the type of document or object that you are currently working on in the desktop workspace. As far as the StarOffice desktop goes, you will find that the menu system is fairly limited and provides commands related to creating or opening various file types, manipulating files or folders using edit commands, and customizing the view of the desktop. The menu system will provide a much more robust set of commands when you are working in one of the StarOffice applications like Writer. The menu choices on the desktop's menu bar consist of the following:

- File Menu—Allows you to open existing documents, spreadsheets or other files and begin new ones. You can either start new files by selecting a particular file type (such as text document in the case of Writer) or you can choose from a number of ready made document types using the AutoPilot.

- Edit Menu—Provides access to typical editing commands such as cut, copy, paste and select all. The Edit menu also provides a shortcut to your StarOffice Address Book, which can be used to quickly send emails or create a specific document type for someone in the address book.

- View Menu—Allows you to switch the default desktop view (the one you are looking at when you start StarOffice) and a full screen view that removes menus and toolbars from the desktop. You can also use the view menu to display items such as the Explorer and the Beamer (both of which are discussed later in the section "Exploring the Writer Screen").

- Tools Menu—Provides access to proofing tools, macros, as well as configuration and options settings that allow you to customize your workspace and default document parameters (more about customizing in Chapter 14).

- Window Menu—Provides you with a list of currently open windows that can be used to switch from window to window. The currently selected window is designated by a bullet.

- Help Menu—Contains commands related to the tips provided when you put the mouse on a particular toolbar tool and access the Help system by clicking the Contents command. The Help menu also allows you to activate the Help Agent, which can provide context sensitive help as you work in StarOffice.

To Start a New Text Document

1   Start StarOffice depending on the type of operating system you have.

    You will see the default StarOffice desktop.

2   Choose File, New, Text Document to begin a new text document.

To Turn the Integrated Desktop On

The Integrated Desktop allows you to toggle StarOffice between an integrated desktop and a window presentation; currently only available with the Windows operating system. When you have the Integrated Desktop activated, you will only see the StarOffice task bar (and buttons and symbols), but the Title bar will disappear. The following steps will not be available if you are not using the Windows operating system.

1   Choose View, Integrated Desktop.

    It is considered integrated because it automatically incorporates itself with your current operating system desktop.

    Repeat the procedure if you wish to turn the integrated desktop off again.

2   Double-click on the Title bar if you want to maximize the StarOffice desktop and the new text document to the full size of your screen.

    The Title bar lists the StarOffice version and the current document file name along the top of the window.

Exploring the Writer Screen

Because StarOffice allows you to create different types of documents without opening and closing different applications, once you learn the default features of the Writer desktop (toolbars, menus, and so on) you will know how to use them whether you are creating a text document, spreadsheet, or presentation.

The first thing you should know is how to turn off (and back on) some of the StarOffice features that take up a lot of desktop real estate.

To Use the Stickpin

The Stick icon, which looks like a thumbtack, resides on the border of the Explorer, Beamer, and Tip windows. You can use this icon to change these windows from a floating window (temporarily covers the other window) to a fixed window (both windows are placed next to each other on the screen).

1 Click the Floating button, which looks like a thumbtack stuck in the desktop (see Figure 1.1).

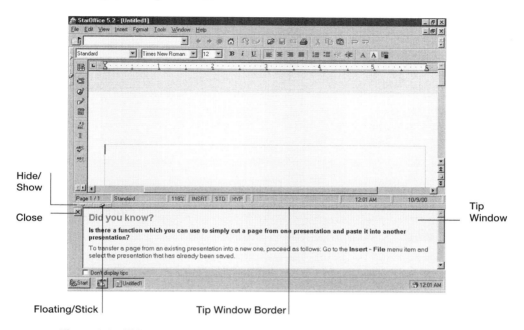

Figure 1.1   This is how a new text document appears in StarOffice Writer with the Tip window beneath the document window.

The Tip window will appear as if it is floating over the desktop and covering up some of the window (like a pinned note on a bulletin board would do).

2 Click the Stick button (as it is now called, looks like a thumbtack on its side) to display the Tip window along with the entire desktop window.

TO ALTER THE TIP WINDOW SIZE

1 Move the mouse pointer over the Tip window border so that it changes to a two-headed arrow with two lines in between.

2 Click and drag the border down to decrease, or up to increase the size of the Tip window.

TO HIDE AND SHOW TIPS

1   Click the Hide arrow button so the tips aren't visible on the desktop.

NOTE   If you have already turned the tips window off, in a previous section, the Hide and Show tips option will no longer be visible. So, instead, perform these steps on the Explorer window (choose View, Explorer if you need to open it first).

This is one of the best ways to eliminate the tips; otherwise, you must close the window completely, which will render them unavailable until you restart StarOffice again.

2   Click the Show arrow button to redisplay the tips.

It is identical to the Hide arrow button—just pointing in a different direction.

TO TURN TIPS OFF AND ON

1   Click the Close button (the X to the left of the "Did you know?" statement).

This will turn the tips off until you restart StarOffice again. If you prefer to disable them so that they don't display when you restart StarOffice, click the Don't display tips checkbox before you click the Close button.

2   Choose Tools, Options, General (in the Options window on the left side), and click Other.

3   Select the Show Tips checkbox and click the OK button.

The next time you start StarOffice, the tips will display. (The Show Tips checkbox will most likely already be checked because the default is to show the tips each time you start StarOffice.)

TO USE THE EXPLORER, BEAMER, AND THE GALLERY

The Explorer serves as the filing cabinet for the folder structure on your computer system, bookmarks to Web URLs, email outboxes, links to your database tables, and so on. You can use the Explorer to organize tasks, your work, bookmarks, and more. Simply click on the slider bar Explorer group you want to access.

Choose View, Explorer to display the Explorer groups (see Figure 1.2). If the Explorer command is already checked, click the Show button to the upper left of the Main toolbar to display the Explorer.

> **NOTE** If you are running StarOffice on a Windows-based computer, an additional group called My Documents (which provides quick access to the My Documents folder on your computer) is available in the Explorer window. If My Documents does not exist on your computer, this group will default to the folder StarOffice/user/work.

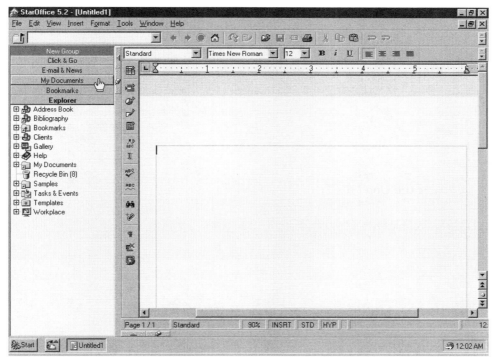

Figure 1.2 The Explorer contains slider bars that you can customize by dragging and dropping files.

You can right-click the New Group slider bar and select whether you want to create a new group as a folder or a link. In addition, you can drag commonly used files and links into a group for quick access. Click on the Explorer group slider bar and click on the + to the left of Gallery to expand the list of files. Double-click on the library list of files in the Gallery to see a thumbnail preview of a graphic or sound file in the Beamer (see Figure 1.3), which will display automatically. You can then click and drag a gallery file directly into a Writer document.

The Beamer displays the file names and subfolders of an Explorer folder. You can choose View, Beamer to display the contents of the selected Explorer group. The Beamer is particularly useful in cases where you wish to drag and drop a file such as a graphic from some location on your computer's hard drive (or network) into the document that you are currently working on.

Choose View, Explorer and View, Beamer again to hide them from the desktop. If you want to quickly access the Explorer or Beamer (or Gallery) in the future, click the Hide arrow button instead.

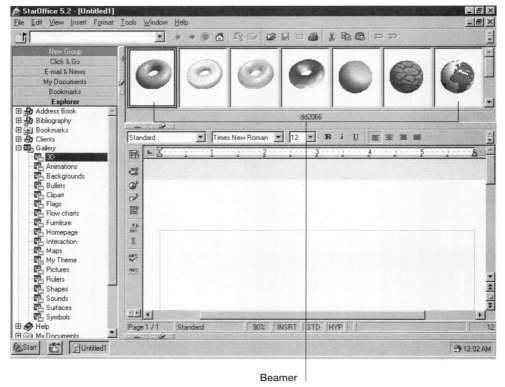

Beamer

Figure 1.3   Choose from the Explorer group what you prefer to view in the Beamer.

NOTE   For more information on the Explorer and creating new groups, see the section "Using the Explorer" in Chapter 13. In addition, Chapter 13 contains more information on using the Gallery and dragging and dropping graphics.

To Review the Writer Screen

Now that you can see more of the workspace, take a look at Figure 1.4 (and the corresponding Table 1.1) for a descriptive list of the Writer screen elements.

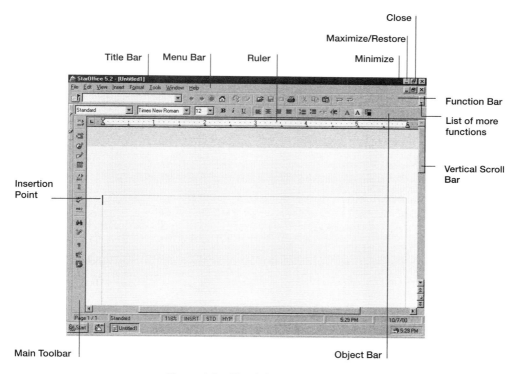

Figure 1.4 The default Writer screen.

Table 1.1 Writer Screen Elements

Element	Description
Title Bar	Lists the StarOffice version and the name of the current document. If you don't have a document open, it will display [Desktop]. If you have the Integrated Desktop activated, you won't see Title Bar at all.
Menu Bar	Contains application-sensitive menus and submenus that you can pull down (click on) depending on the type of document you are working with in StarOffice. You can access the menus using the mouse or pressing the <Alt> key in combination with the accelerator key (the underlined letter in a menu command's name).
Function Bar	A strip of buttons that are utilized within all StarOffice documents. For example, the Open File and Save Document buttons appear in the same location for a Writer document and a Calc spreadsheet. Choose View, Toolbars, Function Bar to toggle this on and off.

Table 1.1   Writer Screen Elements (Continued)

ELEMENT	DESCRIPTION
Object Bar	A strip of context-sensitive buttons that are displayed depending on the task you are performing within Writer. For example, if you are typing text into a document paragraph, you will see the text formatting buttons (for example, Bold, Italic, and Underline); if you are typing text into a table within a document, you will see table formatting buttons (for example, Insert Rows and Insert Columns). Choose View, Toolbars, Object Bar to toggle this on and off.
Main Toolbar	A strip of buttons on the left side of the screen that allows you to insert different types of objects and edit the document. If a button has a green arrow in the upper right corner, click and hold the mouse pointer on the button to see a display of more tools. The tool you choose will become the default option the next time you click on the button unless you hold the button down and again choose from the list. Choose View, Toolbars, Main Toolbar to toggle this on and off.
Hyperlink Bar	A strip of buttons and fields that allow you to insert and edit hyperlinks and URLs, as well as to search for keywords on the Internet. If you don't automatically see this toolbar, choose View, Toolbars, Hyperlink Bar.
Ruler	Displays tabs, indents, margins, and table columns. Toggle this on and off by choosing View, Ruler. You can right-click on the Ruler to alter the type of measurements displayed.
Insertion point	Indicates on-screen where you are located in your document. This also is where typed text will be inserted in the document.
Document window	Area where you work with your document.
Vertical Scroll bar	Used in conjunction with the mouse to move up and down in a document.
Scroll buttons	Used in conjunction with the mouse to scroll rapidly through a document.
Previous Page	Immediately moves to the page before the current page.
Next Page	Immediately moves to the page after the current page.
Navigation	Opens a floating toolbar of items you can use to move between objects in your document.
Horizontal Scroll bar	Used in conjunction with the mouse to move from left to right in a document.
Online Layout	Displayed on the Main Toolbar. Used to switch between the normal document view and Online Layout, which will display the document as it would appear as an HTML document.

Table 1.1   Writer Screen Elements (Continued)

ELEMENT	DESCRIPTION
Status bar	Displays the current page number, page style, page scale, insert mode, selection mode, hyperlinks in active or edit mode, whether changes to a document have been saved, and information about the active document (for example, the date and time).
Minimize, Maximize/ Restore, and Close buttons	Used to minimize, maximize or restore, and close the active document window. Cannot be used to exit StarOffice. You can double-click on the title bar of a window that is *not* maximized to increase it to the full size of the desktop.

NOTE   You might also see a Stylist window on your screen in Writer. This is where you can alter the styles of paragraphs, characters, frames, pages, and numbering in your documents. Refer to Chapter 7, "Working with Styles and Templates," for more information.

NOTE   To customize your individual toolbars, see the section "Configuring Toolbars" in Chapter 14, "Customizing the Writer Environment."

Customizing the Workspace View

You already learned how to activate some of the desktop features like the Tips and Explorer, but what about some of the more subtle workspace features?

TO ALTER VIEWABLE OPTIONS

The following list describes some of the additional workspace options available on the View menu. In order to toggle between showing and hiding each of these features, select the command from the View menu so that a checkmark appears to the left of the name:

- View, Text Boundaries—Activates the gray box around your text displaying the margins on your page (displayed by default).
- View, Field Shadings—Shades any fields that your text contains. For example, a date field would have a gray box around it (displayed by default).
- View, Fields—Displays the field name or the field contents. For example, a date field would appear as "Date (fixed)" if it were the field name; "09/27/02" if it were the field contents (not displayed by default).

- View, Nonprinting Characters—Displays symbols that exist in a document, but that will not print. For example, when Nonprinting Characters are shown, space characters between words appear as dots, and paragraph characters between paragraphs appear displayed with the paragraph symbol (¶) (not displayed by default).

- View, Hidden Paragraphs—Hides paragraphs of information so that it is out of view and unable to be printed. This is convenient when you have information in a document for personal reference, for example, an employee performance review (displayed by default). You can assign these hidden paragraphs when using conditional text, refer to the section "Working with Conditional Text," in Chapter 11.

- View, Full Screen—Allows you to view your document maximized to the size of your monitor screen, without all the menus and toolbars. The only button visible is the Full Screen button, which will return back to normal view (not displayed by default).

Entering Text Into a Document

When you are ready to enter text into your Writer document, simply begin typing. The default document template in Writer will appear with preset margins, fonts, and all the features available in the Standard document template. For more information on templates, see Chapter 7, "Working with Styles and Templates."

The document is named Untitled1, which is displayed on the Title bar. If there is no title bar, you are in the Integrated Desktop environment. To see the document name, choose the Window menu; there will be a black bullet to the left of the active document name on the menu.

> **NOTE**   Each additional new text document you open will increment automatically (Untitled1, Untitled2, and so on). If you close one of the untitled documents, StarOffice Writer starts over at the first available incremental number. For example, if you have Untitled1, Untitled2, and Untitled3 open, but decide to discard Untitled2. When you create a new text document, it will become Untitled2 again, not Untitled4 (as you might think).

TO ENTER TEXT INTO A DOCUMENT

1   Type the following text into the new document:

> This is your final notice that you have been pre-approved for the Spendalot Card, the card that believes in saving you money! With this card, you'll not only enjoy an APR as low as 1.9% on trans-ferred balances, you'll enjoy it for two weeks!

Notice that the text automatically wraps to the next line as you type (see Figure 1.5).

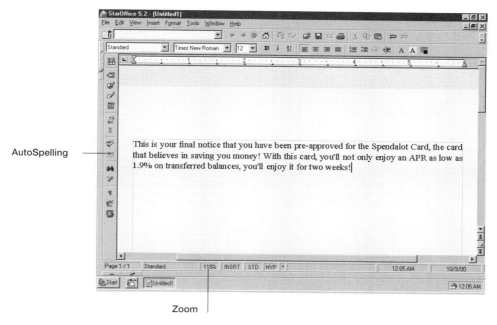

Figure 1.5   Text entered into a new document will automatically wrap to the next line.

2   Press the <Enter> key on the keyboard to end the current paragraph and begin a new paragraph.

If you wish to create extra blank lines, press the <Enter> key multiple times.

NOTE   Pressing the <Enter> key creates what is known as a *hard return*; pressing <Ctrl+Enter> creates a *soft return*. A hard return takes you to a new paragraph line; a soft return takes you to a new line in the same paragraph (without having to add text to automatically wrap to the next line). Understanding the difference between these two types of returns is important when you format your text, because formatting that applies to an entire paragraph will apply to text before and after a soft return. See the section "Inserting a Line Break" in Chapter 5 for more information.

3   Click the AutoSpelling button on the Main toolbar.

This button looks like a red, wavy line under the letters ABC.

4   Type the following additional text into your new document:

```
Along with this eceptional rate, you'll also receive a generous
credit line and won't pay an annual fee.
```

If you typed any of the previous text incorrectly (for example, "eceptional" is missing an "x"), you might have noticed that Writer automatically underlines the misspelled word with the red, wavy line. In addition, proper nouns will occasionally appear underlined (for example, "Spendalot"), because they aren't in the standard StarOffice dictionary.

To correct a misspelled word, click the right mouse button on the word and select the correct spelling from the shortcut menu.

To add a proper noun or a piece of commonly used jargon from your industry to the dictionary, click the right mouse button on the word, click the Add button on the shortcut menu, and choose the dictionary you are using (for example, the StarOffice dictionary soffice.dic).

5   On the Document window status bar, right-click the Zoom percentage.

This will allow you to view more or less of your document in the document window. Closing the Tip window will help as well, which was covered in the section "Exploring the Writer Screen."

6   Click to select a percentage from the shortcut menu.

Your document will resize automatically. If you prefer to specify a percentage that isn't displayed on the shortcut menu, double-click on the Zoom percentage in the status bar, select the Variable option on the Zoom dialog box, type in the exact percentage (or increase or decrease the percentage using the spin box controls), and click the OK button.

NOTE   The Optimal option on the shortcut menu or on the Zoom dialog box will size your document according to the amount of text that can be viewed to fit in your workspace.

Saving a Document

You should periodically save your text documents so that your edits and additions are stored either on disk or on a network. There are numerous ways to save and resave your documents; each will be covered in the following sections.

NOTE   To save documents automatically, you can activate the StarOffice AutoSave feature. Refer to the section "To Alter Document Save Options," in Chapter 14, "Customizing the Writer Environment."

TO SAVE A DOCUMENT THE FIRST TIME

1   Choose File, Save As (see Figure 1.6).

You can also click the Save Document button on the Function bar. This will open the Save As dialog box.

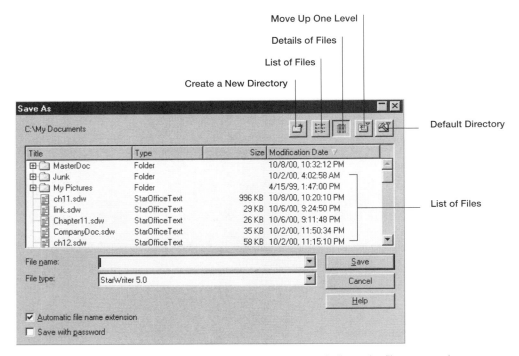

Figure 1.6   The Save As dialog box allows you to indicate the file name and
where you want to save the document.

2   Type the name of the document into the File name box (for example
Letter01).

3   Select from the following save options available on the Save As dialog
box:

- File type—Click this drop-down list to save the document as a previous
  StarOffice Writer version, a template, HTML, various text formats, or
  various Microsoft Word formats.
- Automatic file name extension—Select this to assign your Writer
  documents an .sdw file extension automatically (the Writer default). If
  you want to assign the File name a different extension (for example, to
  use the file in a different application), deselect this checkbox and type
  an alternative extension in the File name box (or you can just leave it
  blank; however, the file name won't display the Writer icon or indicate
  in any way that the file is a Writer file in Open dialog boxes or the
  Explorer).
- Save with password—Select this to assign a password that must be
  supplied in order to open the document. Check this option so when you
  save the document, you will be asked to type in a password and

password confirmation (it must be a minimum of 5 characters). Then, each time you open the document, you will be asked to type in a password. If you cannot remember the password, there is no way to open the document without it, so be sure to remember it.

NOTE   When in the Details view of the Save As dialog box, click any of the file detail headers (Title, Type, Size, Modification Date) to sort the files in ascending or descending order according to the header type (the little gray triangle will point up or down).

4   Click the Save button.

Now when you click on the Window menu, the active document has an assigned file name.

Keep in mind that you can always click the Cancel button on the Save As dialog box if you decide you don't want to save the document. In addition, if you forget to save the document and try to close it, you will be asked to save or discard your changes. Click the Save button to save changes; Discard button to close the file without saving the document; Cancel button to return to working in the document.

TO RESAVE A DOCUMENT

1   Choose File, Save.

You can also click the Save Document button on the Function bar.

TO SAVE A DOCUMENT WITH A NEW FILE NAME

1   Choose File, Save As.

This will open the Save As dialog box (refer to Figure 1.6).

2   Type the new name of the document into the File name box.

3   Click the Save button.

The new document name will remain open with the file name in the Title bar, and the original document will close.

TO SAVE DOCUMENT VERSIONS

1   Choose File, Versions to open the Versions of [filename.sdw] dialog box (where the filename is the name you saved the document as). This command will only be available on the File menu if you have previously

saved the document, if not, save the document now and then choose File, Versions.

The Version feature lets you save a document during different stages of completion. For example, if you are adding information to a document on a daily basis, you might want to keep track of where a previous day's information ended, in case you want to remove specific information that was added afterward.

2   Click the Save New Version button to open an Insert Version Comment dialog box (see Figure 1.7).

You can enter any comments necessary with regard to the current version of the document and click the OK button.

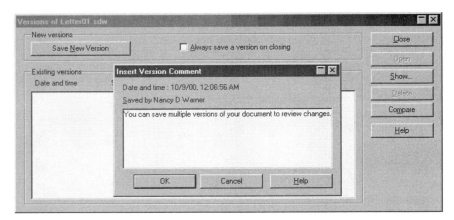

Figure 1.7   You can save multiple versions of your document to review changes.

3   Click the Close button when finished.

NOTE   If you want a version to be saved automatically each time you work in the document, select the Always save a version on closing the checkbox in the Versions of [filename.sdw] dialog box.

TO REVIEW DOCUMENT VERSIONS

1   Choose File, Versions to open the Versions of [filename.sdw] dialog box.

NOTE   If your comments are more extensive than the Versions of [filename.sdw] dialog box will display, click the version from the list and click the Show button to display the entire comment.

2   Click the existing version you want to review from the list and click the Open button (or double-click directly on each version of the document you want to review).

The version of the file will open in read-only format. You cannot make changes to the version; only review it. If you cannot readily see the difference between a particular version and the current version, click the Compare button.

NOTE   Once you compare two versions of a document, you can pick and choose which elements you want to retain because the differences are indicated as "changes" in the document. For more information on comparing documents, see the section "Recording Changes to a Document," in Chapter 10, "Reviewing, Collaborating, and Merging Documents."

3   Choose File, Close to close each version; click the Close button when finished.

TO RELOAD A DOCUMENT

1   Choose File, Reload.

The current document will be replaced with the last saved version of the document.

This is convenient if you don't want to keep the edits you made to your document, but prefer to keep working in the document.

TO SAVE ALL DOCUMENTS

1   Choose File, Save All.

This will save all the documents you currently have open in StarOffice. The Save All menu command will only be available on the File menu if you have multiple documents open (whether they are text documents, spreadsheets, or any other StarOffice document).

TO ADD DOCUMENT PROPERTIES

1   Choose File, Properties to open the document properties dialog box (see Figure 1.8).

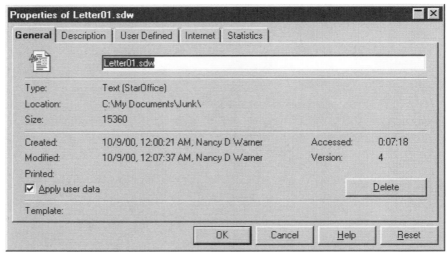

Figure 1.8   Save information about your documents.

2   Click any of the following tabs and enter the appropriate information:

• General—Lists the file specifications.
• Description—Enters a Title, Subject, Keywords, and any Comments.
• User Defined—Defines individual information text fields. For example, you can reference specific properties from a different application document (like Microsoft Word) that offers built-in fields that aren't available in StarOffice.
• Internet—Establishes whether the page will automatically reload, and if so, how often; also defines the URL and Frame location.
• Statistics—Provides document statistics and allows you to update the information.

3   Click the OK button to accept changes; Cancel to return to the document; Help to find out more information; Reset to remove any changes you just made.

Getting Help

There are a couple of different ways you can get help while using StarOffice, though books like this one may prove to be your best resource.

TO USE HELP CONTENTS

1   Choose Help, Contents to open the Help window (see Figure 1.9).

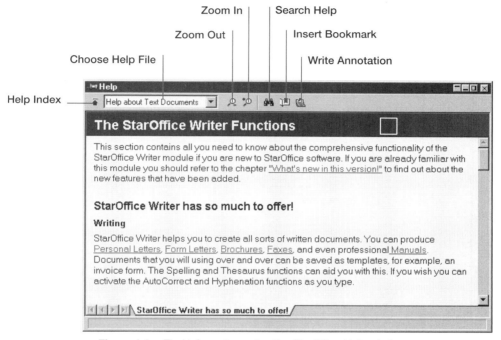

Figure 1.9   Find information using the StarOffice Help window.

2   Click through the links and read the corresponding information.

You can also click the tabs along the bottom of the Help window to quickly move to the different sections within each topic. To return to the main help index, click the Help Index button.

NOTE   The contents of Help correspond to the StarOffice application you are currently in. Click the Choose Help File drop-down list to select the particular StarOffice application about which you have a question.

3   Click the Search Help button to open a Find window, which gives you a couple of options:

•Index tab—Allows you to type in the feature you need help with, click on the applicable index entry, click the appropriate topic, and click the Display button.

•Text tab—Allows you to type in a feature, select the appropriate radio button that corresponds to the type of search you wish to perform, click the Find button (StarOffice will create an index if you leave the Create Index checkbox selected), and click the Display button to view the search results.

4   Click the Insert Bookmark button to create a bookmark for a help topic that you commonly use.

You can access the bookmark by double-clicking on it in Explorer under the Help, Bookmark folder.

5   Click the Write Comments button to add a comment directly into the help system.

Bookmarks and Write Comments are convenient when you want to refer back to an answer to a problem that you had in the past.

6   Type your comment and click the OK button.

You can access your comments in the Help Contents by clicking on the Comment icon to the left of the corresponding help topic selected when you wrote the annotation.

To Use the Help Agent

1   Choose Help, Help Agent to open the Help Agent window (see Figure 1.10).

StarOffice will automatically display help according to the task you are trying to perform (known as context-sensitive help).

If the help you need doesn't appear immediately, click the Find button.

NOTE   You can also click the Help Agent button on the Function bar to launch the help application. It looks like a cartoon speaking bubble with a question mark inside.

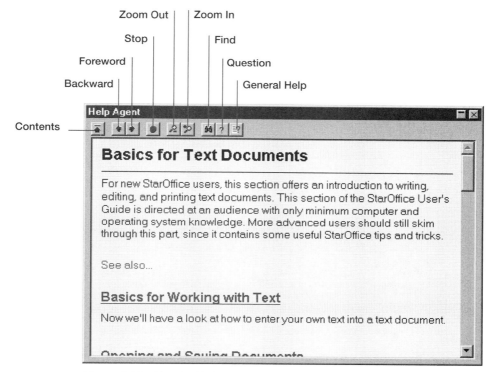

Figure 1.10   Use the Help Agent to receive context-sensitive help.

NOTE   When working in Help, to keep the help topic on the topic that you want to review (instead of jumping to the next logical, context-sensitive topic), click the Stop button.

2   Click the Question button to type in a question and click the Search button.

You can then click on the links available to help you with your task.

3   Click the General Help button to open the Help Contents window (refer to Figure 1.9).

TO USE EXTENDED TIPS AND TIPS

1   Choose Help, Extended Tips.

This feature is very convenient when you want to know the purpose of a button or menu command.

2   Move the mouse pointer over the item you want information about and a
Help tip will appear, with a brief description of its function.

If you have the Help, Tips command selected, only the name of the button or command will appear in a Help tip. If neither Tips nor Extended
Tips are selected, no Help tips will appear.

To Use Online Help

1   Type www.sun.com/staroffice/knowledgedatabase into the URL field on
the Hyperlink bar. If the Hyperlink bar isn't displayed, choose View, Toolbars, Hyperlink Bar to add it to your desktop.

This is the troubleshooting area on the Sun Knowledge Database Web
site, for registered StarOffice users.

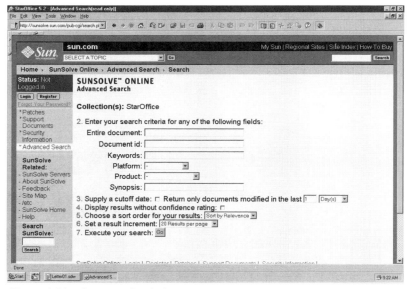

Figure 1.11   Access online help according to the search criteria you enter.

> **NOTE**   Be aware that sometimes open documents will close
> automatically when you use Online Help, and you might loose
> changes that you made before you last saved; so save often.

2   Press the <Enter> key to access the Web site.

If you need to get online, do so now. StarOffice will activate your default
online service so you can sign on. Once you are online, the StarOffice Web
site will ask you to register.

3   Type in your user ID and password.

In order to download the software, you needed to register, and create a user ID and password.

4   Type in your search criteria and review the information available (see Figure 1.11).

Closing a Document

When you have finished working in a document, and perhaps saved it, you can close the document.

TO CLOSE A DOCUMENT

1   Choose File, Close to close the active document. You can also click the X close button in the upper right corner of the document window.

If you recently saved the document and haven't made any other changes to it, it should close automatically.

If you have made changes to a document or haven't saved it yet, you will be asked whether you want to save, discard, or cancel closing the document. Click the Save button to save changes; Discard button to close the file without saving the document; Cancel button to return to working in the document.

2   Repeat step 1 for each text document you have open in Writer, or refer to the next section on closing all documents.

TO CLOSE ALL DOCUMENTS

1   Choose Window, Close All to quickly close all the documents open in StarOffice.

This will close all documents within StarOffice (spreadsheets, presentations, and so on), not just text documents.

If any of the documents need to be saved, you will be prompted to save. Once all the documents are closed, you will be returned to the StarOffice Desktop.

Exiting StarOffice Writer

When you have closed the last open text document, Writer is technically closed, although the StarOffice desktop and menus are still visible.

Choose File, Exit to exit StarOffice completely. You can press <Ctrl+Q> to exit as well.

Make sure you exit StarOffice before you turn off your computer; otherwise you might lose data from the open files. If you forget to exit StarOffice and try to shut the computer down, you will be asked if you want to save your files. Refer to the sections, "Opening a Document" and "Closing a Document" if this happens.

Working with Documents

Opening a Document

In the previous chapter, you learned how to enter text into a document, save the file (for example, as <u>Letter01</u>), and close the file. In order to make any changes to the document, you must open the file. If you already know how to open files, you can quickly skim this section or skip to the section "Moving Around in a Document."

TO OPEN A DOCUMENT

1   Choose File, Open or click the Open File button on the Function toolbar.

    The Open dialog box displays.

2   Click (for example, <u>Letter01</u> from Chapter 1) a document that you want to open in the file list (see Figure 2.1).

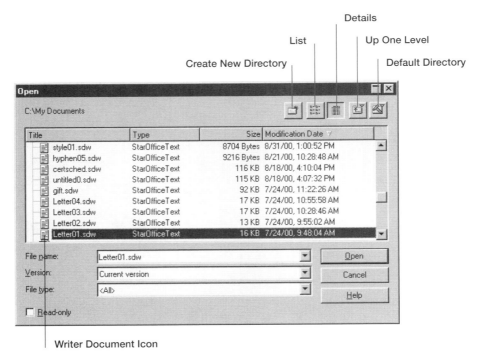

Figure 2.1   Choosing a document in the Open dialog box.

StarOffice displays <All> file types in the Open dialog box by default. You can tell if a document is a Writer document because a document icon will appear to the left of the document name (versus a different application).

The list of files in Figure 2.1 displays all the files and folders located in the current folder. The current folder and drive name are listed below the Open dialog box name (for example, C:\My Documents). The following list details the options available with the Open dialog box:

- Create new directory button—Creates a new folder in the current directory.
- List button—Views the list of filenames.
- Details button—Views the file type, size, and date created (or the last date a file was modified). Click the detail header to sort the files ascending or descending according to the header.
- Up One Level button—Moves up one folder. You can click and hold this button (as with any StarOffice button containing a green arrow) and select from your default directory and available drives.
- Default directory button—Opens the folder last selected in this dialog box, or the default folder for Writer. You can click and hold this button (notice the green arrow) and select from your Workplace drives, the Explorer, your Desktop, or other default directories.
- Double-Click the folder name in the file list—Moves down one level to a different folder.
- Version drop-down list—Views and selects from the available document versions (according to the file comments and date). Refer to the section "To Save Document Versions" in Chapter 1 for more information on versions.
- File type drop-down list—Views and selects files other than Writer documents. To see all documents in a folder (the default option), select <All> from the list.
- Read-only checkbox—Prevents a file from being edited and resaved. The file will be opened only to read; (read-only) will be displayed next to the document name in the Title bar.

NOTE If you don't find the Letter01 file, scroll through the list; it is possibly on another drive or in another folder. Be sure that you are looking at the correct drive and folder. The file should appear in the same drive and folder you saved it to in Chapter 1.

3   Click the Open button.

The file will open in the document window (see Figure 2.2). To see the document name in the Writer window Title bar, you cannot be in the integrated desktop environment (choose the View menu and select Integrated Desktop to make sure it doesn't have a checkmark). The document name, however, will be listed with the drive and folder location in the Load URL list box on the Function bar.

Open File | Edit File |

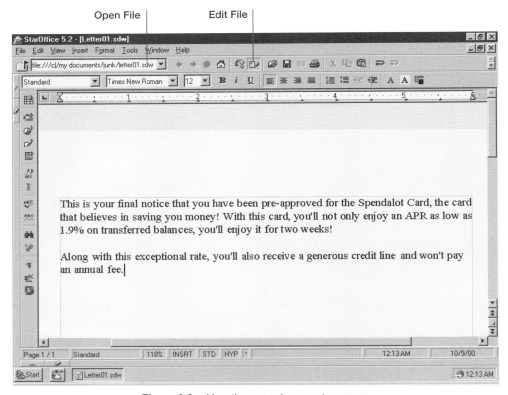

Figure 2.2   How the open document appears.

> **NOTE**   Once you open a document, you can switch between edit
> mode to read-only mode by clicking the Edit File button on the
> Function bar. The document name in the Title bar will display (read-
> only) if you are in read-only mode.

If you see the file you wish to open in the Open dialog box, you can double-click directly on the file instead of selecting the filename and clicking the Open button.

If you recently used the file you want to open, choose the File menu to see the last four saved files listed at the bottom of the menu. If it is listed, you can click on the filename and the document will open.

Files can also be opened before you start StarOffice by double-clicking on the filename if you know exactly where you saved the document (for example, on the Desktop). In addition, files can be opened by locating them in Explorer and double-clicking on the filename.

Moving Around in a Document

Table 2.1 lists some of the common keyboard shortcuts for moving around in a document.

Table 2.1   Keyboard Shortcut Moves

KEY(S)	ACTION
Left Arrow	One character to the left.
Right Arrow	One character to the right.
Up Arrow	Up one line.
Down Arrow	Down one line.
Ctrl+Left Arrow	One word to the left.
Ctrl+Right Arrow	One word to the right.
Ctrl+Up Arrow	Moves the entire paragraph, up one paragraph.
Ctrl+Down Arrow	Moves the entire paragraph, down one paragraph.
Home	To the beginning of the line.
End	To the end of the line.
Ctrl+Home	To the beginning of the document.
Ctrl+End	To the end of the document.
Page Up	Up one window or page.
Page Down	Down one window or page.
Ctrl+Page Up	To the top of the previous page.
Ctrl+Page Down	To the top of the next page.

If you wish to find specific text, see section "Finding and Replacing Text" in Chapter 10, "Reviewing, Collaborating, and Merging." If you would like to learn to navigate quickly through your longer documents, refer to Chapter 11, "Working with Long Document Features."

To Open a New Window

1   Open a document that you wish to review or edit.

Don't let the term "new window" make you think you are going to create a new text document—this isn't the case. Creating a new window allows you to view two parts of the same document at the same time. You can create a new window when you are working with a lengthy document (though sometimes this is convenient even with a two-page document, for example, if you are copying and pasting multiple passages) and you need to compare or review information from one place in the document to another. For example, instead of constantly moving from page 5 to page 55 in the same document, simply create a new window and simultaneously view both page locations.

2   Choose Window, New Window.

The document displays side by side in two windows. If you click in the main window (on the left), the Title bar lists the document file name; if you click in the new window (on the right), the Title bar lists the document file name plus a number 2. Both document windows will also be listed at the bottom of the Window menu.

3   Click the mouse pointer into the window on the right.

This will make this window the active window. Notice the cursor (see Figure 2.3).

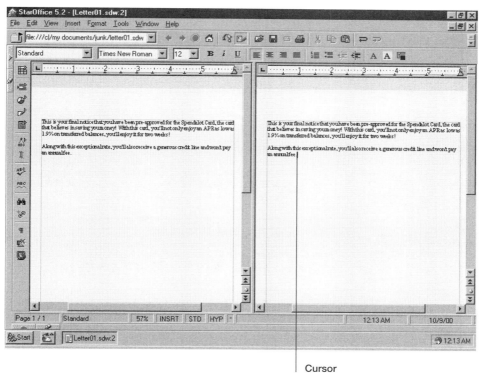

Cursor

Figure 2.3 You can see the same document from two different locations.

> **NOTE** To open more than one new window, simply choose Window, New Window for each one you want to create. In addition, if you make edits to any of the document windows, they are made to each document window and are entered into the original file.

4 Choose File, Close.

You can save or discard your changes, but you cannot go back to viewing only one window. You must close and reopen the document to view it without multiple windows.

TO WORK WITH MULTIPLE DOCUMENT WINDOWS

You can open several documents that you wish to review or edit in Writer. If you prefer to work in one document or another, you can switch between them using a few different options:

- Click the document icon on the StarOffice Task bar of the open document you want to view.

- Switch back and forth between open documents by choosing the document name from the Window menu.
- Choose Cascade, Tile, Horizontal, or Vertical from the Window menu to display each of the multiple documents in a different display. If you close one of the files while in one of these views, you must select the command from the Window menu again to redisplay the files.

Inserting New Text

A very convenient feature of a word processor is the ability to insert new text into a previously created document.

TO INSERT NEW TEXT

1   Open a document (for example, the Letter01 document you saved in Chapter 1).

2   Press <Ctrl+Home> to move the insertion point to the beginning of the document (if it isn't already there).

> **NOTE**   An interesting default Writer feature is that when you open a document, the document will open to the exact location your cursor was at when you last saved the file. So, if you are on page 12 of a 37-page document, you don't need to remember where your edits ended.

3   Press the <Enter> key twice to enter two hard returns (blank lines).

4   Press the <Up Arrow> key twice to move to the beginning of the document again.

5   Choose Insert, Fields, Date (see Figure 2.4).

This will enter the current date in the default format of MM/DD/YY with gray highlighting to indicate it is a field. If the field displays "Date (fixed)", it means that you have the Fields option activated on the View menu (refer to the section "To Use the View Menu" in Chapter 1). If there is no gray highlighting, it means the Field Shadings option is *not* activated.

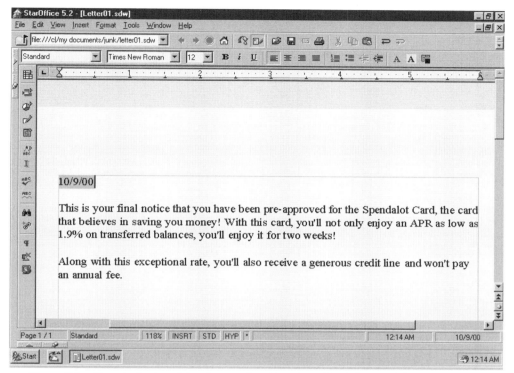

Figure 2.4   Move to the top of the document and insert two blank lines and the current date.

6   Press the <Enter> key two times and type the following text. Make sure
    you press <Ctrl+Enter> at the end of each line to create a soft return:

```
Ms. Julie Price
3620 Winter Street
Scottsdale, AZ 85999
```

7   Press the <Enter> key and type the following text:

```
Dear Ms. Price:
```

Your inserted text will appear as in Figure 2.5.

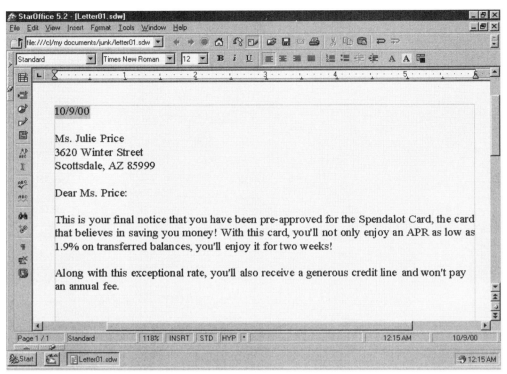

Figure 2.5   The opening information for a letter has been added.

8   Click the Save Document button on the Function bar if you wish to save the file as the original filename (for example, the <u>Letter01</u> document); Writer will not ask you to save the file with a new name.

TO INSERT TEXT WITH THE DIRECT CURSOR

1   Click the DirectCursor on/off button on the Main Toolbar.

The I beam insertion point now has a triangle icon accompanying it, which indicates exactly where you wish to begin inserting text and whether the text should be left, center, or right justified.

2   Move the mouse pointer to where you wish to insert text and click the mouse button once (see Figure 2.6).

3   Type `Sincerely,`

Reload

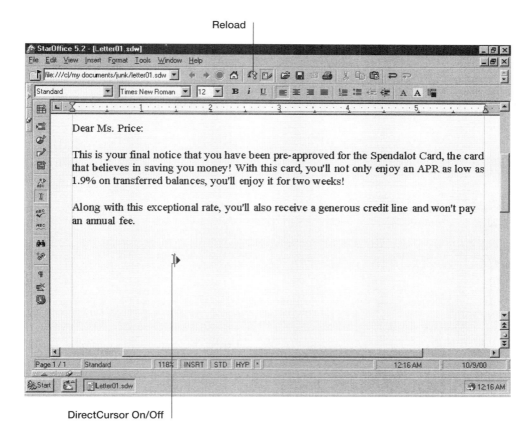

DirectCursor On/Off

Figure 2.6   Insert the text directly using the cursor.

4   Move the mouse pointer to where you wish to insert text again, click the mouse button, and type your name.

You have now inserted text into your document using the direct cursor. If you prefer to stop using the direct cursor, click the DirectCursor on/off button again.

5   Choose File, Save As to save the file with a different name (for example, Letter02).

Writer will then display the Save As dialog box (refer to the section "Saving a Document" in Chapter 1 for more information). Change the filename to a different name (for example, <u>Letter01</u> to <u>Letter02)</u> and click the Save button.

> **NOTE**   If you have recently entered some new edits to your document, but decide you wish to go back to the last saved version of the document, choose File, Reload (or click the Reload button on the Function bar; two buttons to the left of the Open File button).

Correcting Text

Instead of creating and typing in a new document each time you wish to make a change to a letter, you can make corrections to a current document.

TO CORRECT TEXT WITH THE BACKSPACE

1   Click the insertion point in your document at the end of the text you want to correct.

Place it after the exclamation mark in the second sentence of the first paragraph of your document (for example, the <u>Letter02</u> document you saved in the previous section).

2   Press the <Backspace> key as many times as necessary to delete the text you wish to correct (14 times, to the space after the word "it" if you are in the <u>Letter02</u> document).

If you need to delete a lot of text, you can also select the text you wish to delete with the mouse pointer (refer to the section "Selecting Text" in Chapter 3 for more information).

> **NOTE**   You can also place the insertion point at the beginning of the text you wish to correct and press the <Delete> key the number of characters you want to remove. Pressing the <Backspace+Control> keys will delete the word and preceding punctuation.

3   Type the following text instead (see Figure 2.7):

    as long as you do not default under any Spendalot Card Agreement.*

4   Save the document again (for example, as <u>Letter02</u>). (The continuous save references are to make this a good habit.)

Save Document

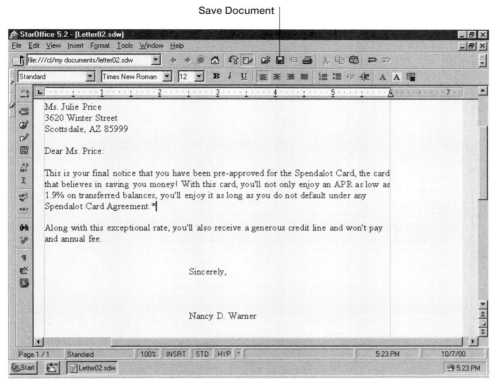

Figure 2.7   Text corrected with the Backspace key.

To Use Overtype and Insert Mode

1   Click the insertion point in your document at the beginning of the text
    you wish to correct.

    Place it before the word "final" in the first paragraph.

2   Click the INSRT field on the Status bar (see Figure 2.8).

    This will switch you from Insert mode to Overtype mode (the field now
    displays "OVER"). Writer will overwrite (or erase) existing text as you
    type new text when you make a correction in this mode.

3   Type the word `first` so that it replaces "final".

    No text actually moves because it is typed over the current text.

4   Click the OVER field on the Status bar to return back to Insert mode (the
    default mode).

5   Click the insertion point after the word "it" in the first paragraph, and
    type the following:

    until January 1, 2002,

    Note that in Insert mode, the inserted text moves the other text to the
    right (see Figure 2.8). Save the document.

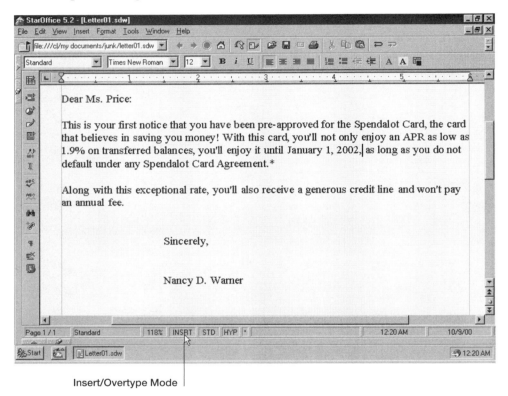

Insert/Overtype Mode

Figure 2.8   Text corrected using Overtype mode and Insert mode.

Printing a Document

Check your printer to make sure it is turned on, has paper, and displays the little
light telling you that it is online and ready to go. Writer gives you the option to
print a hard copy to mail or perhaps file a copy for your records. If you have been
saving the document as you work through this chapter, keep it open, otherwise,
open a document you wish to print.

TO PREVIEW A DOCUMENT

1   Choose File, Page Preview (see Figure 2.9).

It is a good habit to preview your documents before you print them. You can find errors before they are printed, and thus save paper and other resources.

Your document will display as it would if you printed it. Notice the new Page Preview bar available when in page preview (see Table 2.2). Some of the buttons are active only if they apply to the current document. For example, this document is only one page, so the Previous Page and Next Page buttons are inactive.

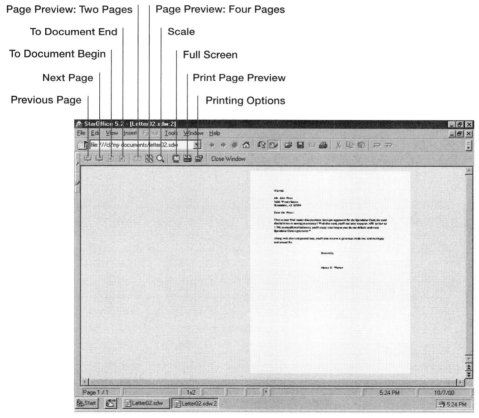

Figure 2.9   Preview your document before you print.

Table 2.2   Page Preview Bar

BUTTON	ACTION
Previous Page	Click to move to the previous document page.
Next Page	Click to move to the next document page.
To Document Begin	Click to quickly move to the first page of the previewed document.
To Document End	Click to quickly move to the last page of the previewed document.
Page Preview: Two Pages	Click to preview two pages at a time.
Page Preview: Four Pages	Click to preview up to four pages at a time.
Zoom	Click to display the Zoom dialog box. Rows displays the number of pages in a row; Columns displays the number of pages in columns. Enter them in the View and click the OK button. You can also double-click the row and column display coordinates in the status bar (1X2, for example) and alter the view.
Full Screen	Click to view a document full screen with only the Page Preview bar. Click again to return to Page View/Print Preview.
Print page view	Click to open the Print dialog box and print the document.
Print options page view	Click to view the Print Options dialog box and define the number of pages printed on a single sheet.
Close Window	Click to close the page preview.

NOTE   You can also use the Page Up and Page Down keys (and the Arrow keys) on the keyboard to move through your document in page preview.

2   Click the Close window button to return to the normal document view.

You can also double-click directly on the page to make any edits to your document, which will exit page preview and return to the normal document view.

TO PRINT A DOCUMENT

1   Choose File, Print.

The Print dialog box will display with the default printing options, which prints one copy of all the pages in your document.

If you wish to print the default print settings, click the Print File Directly button on the Function bar and your document will print immediately.

2   Choose the desired printing options available on the Print dialog box (see Figure 2.10) as described in Table 2.3, if necessary.

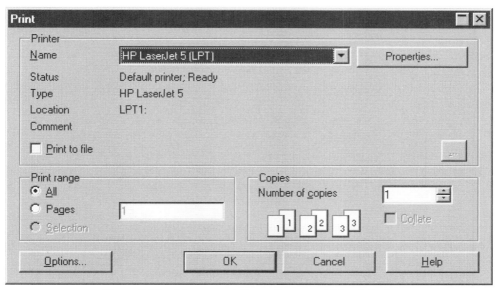

Figure 2.10   Alter your printing options or print the defaults.

Table 2.3   Printing options

OPTION	ACTION
Print to file	Click this option if you wish to print to a file instead of hard copy. For example, in you need to prepare your document for printing on a high-resolution printer that isn't currently attached to your computer or network. The Save As dialog box will appear in order to assign a Filename. If you need to change the file location, click the ellipsis (...) button and reselect the Print to file location.
All	Prints all pages in your document.
Pages	Click this option and only the pages specified in the text box will print. For example, 3, 7–11, 15.
Selection	This option will be available if you selected text before choosing File, Print. Then, only the text you selected in the document will print.
Number of copies	Alter the number of copies to print by clicking the up or down spin box buttons. If you choose more than 1 copy, you can click the Collate checkbox to automatically print and sort each document copy in full.
Options button	Click this button and edit the Printer Options dialog box. The Contents area allows you to exclude certain objects from printing. The Pages area allows particular printing format (only left or right pages, in reverse order, or in brochure format). The Notes area allows you to not print the Notes you have added; print the Notes only; or print the Notes at the end of the document or the end of each page. The Fax drop-down list box lets you select the fax printer to fax directly from your document. The Paper tray checkbox allows you to use the defined paper source defined in the printer setup (when your printer uses multiple trays).

NOTE   If you would like to fax your document from StarOffice Writer and already have fax software installed on your computer, choose File, Print to open the Print dialog box. Then click the Options button, select the fax printer, and click the OK button.

3   Click the OK button and your document will begin printing.

To Change the Printer and Print Properties

1 Choose File, Printer Setup.

   The Printer Setup dialog box will appear listing the current printer Name, Status, Type, and Location.

2 Click the Name drop-down list box and choose an available printer.

   NOTE   If the printer you wish to print to isn't available in the Name list, you must first add a new printer through your operating system. If you are on a network, contact your network administrator to find out which printers you may print to.

3 Click the Properties button to open the properties dialog box for your current printer (see Figure 2.11). The options available to you will depend on your operating system and printers.

   On the Paper tab, you can select Paper size, Orientation, Paper source, Media Choice, or the More Options button to alter your Paper properties. If you alter these options and wish to return to your original defaults (before you click the OK or Apply buttons), click the Restore Defaults button. You can also alter the Graphics (resolution, intensity, and graphics mode), Fonts (how to handle TrueType fonts), and Device Options (print quality and printer memory usage) by clicking the particular tab and modifying the defaults.

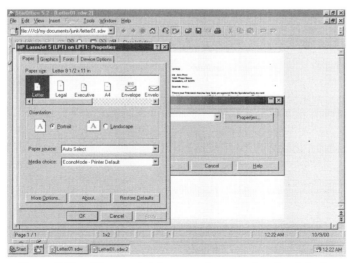

Figure 2.11   Alter your printer properties or restore the defaults.

4 Click the OK button in all dialog boxes to accept your changes; click the Cancel button if you don't wish to accept your changes.

Preparing and Printing Envelopes

When you create envelopes using StarOffice Writer, you have a few choices:

- Create a new document for the envelope. Use this option if you simply need to create and print an envelope without printing a corresponding document to be inserted in it. (You might not even want to save the envelope document that gets created.)

- Insert the envelope as the first page in your document. Use this option if you wish to keep the envelope saved with the accompanying letter or document.

Regardless of how or whether you save the envelope information, you prepare and print envelopes the same way.

> **NOTE**   Keep in mind, though, that if you perform a form letter mail merge (refer to Chapter 10), you will most likely want to create matching labels instead of envelopes. Envelopes in Writer are more suited to printing a few at a time (perhaps along with the document), and labels are more suited to mail merges. This only makes sense because it can be difficult feeding multiple envelopes into your printer.

TO PREPARE AND PRINT ENVELOPES

1   Choose Insert, Envelope to open the Envelope dialog box.

    You must already be in a text document.

2   Click the Envelope tab.

    Enter the Recipient and Sender information. If the Sender checkbox is selected, the Sender information will be the address that was entered when the StarOffice software was installed. You can also access Database and Table data (for example, information from your Address Book), which will be covered in Chapter 10, "Reviewing, Collaborating, and Merging Documents."

3   Click the Format tab.

    Alter the Positions of the Recipient and Sender addresses along with the Size of the envelope. You can also click the Edit button to format the character and paragraph style (for example, to use a different font).

4   Click the Printer tab.

    Alter the way the envelopes will be fed into your printer, depending on your individual print feeder. Click the Setup button if you need to send the envelope to a different printer.

5   Click the button according to how you want to save the envelope information:

- •New Document button—Creates a new document and insert the envelope as the first page. Choose File, Print and click the OK button once you have the envelope correctly placed in the printer tray feed.
- •Insert button—Inserts the envelope as a new page at the beginning of the active document. Choose File, Print to open the Print dialog box. You can print the entire document using the printer tray feed, or choose the specific page (page 1) and insert the envelope into the printer tray feed.

The previous step will also automatically close the Envelope dialog box. You must choose Insert, Envelope, to modify the envelope specifications (see Figure 2.12), and click the Modify button to accept the changes.

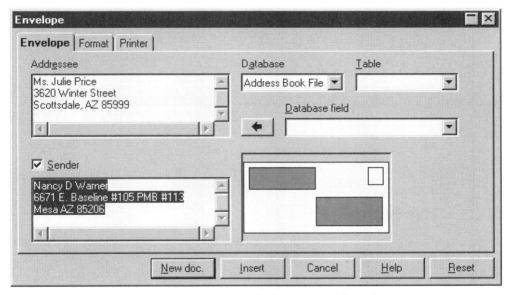

Figure 2.12   You can modify the envelope information.

Preparing and Printing Labels

Perhaps you have a large envelope that cannot be fed into your printer, want to create your own return address labels, or want to print labels to accompany a mass mailing; in either of these situations you can create one label, multiples of the same label, or multiple different labels to accompany a mail merge.

To Prepare and Print Labels

1   Choose File, New, Labels to open the Labels dialog box.

2   Click the Labels tab (see Figure 2.13).

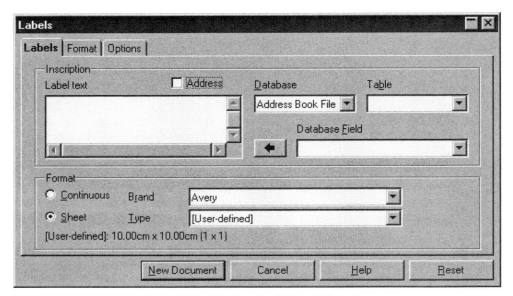

Figure 2.13   Create and print label information.

If the Address checkbox is selected, the Label text will be the address that was entered when the StarOffice software was installed.

3   Type in the specific Inscription Label text information if you want all the labels to be exactly the same and move directly to step 4. If you want all the labels to have different label text, either type each one (and repeat steps 4 through 9 every time) or designate the Label text data from a database table where the information resides. To do so, complete the following steps:

Deselect the Address checkbox, if selected. Select the Database you want to pull the label data from the drop-down list box (for example, the Address Book or a Contacts database you have access to). Select the Table from the database that contains the label data (for example, a Clients table).

NOTE   If you want to create a set of mail merged letters for these labels, refer to the section "Performing a Form Letter Mail Merge" in Chapter 10.

The fields in the database table you have selected, will display in the Database Field drop-down list box (for example, Last Name, First Name, Address, and so on). Select the first field in the label from the Database Field drop-down list box (for example, First Name). Then, click the left arrow button to move the field to the Label text area. Repeat this for each of the fields that you would like to display on each label. Press the <Spacebar>, <Enter>, and punctuation keys within the Label text area to present the label information as you like, for example:

```
<Contacts.Clients.First Name> <Contacts.Clients.Last Name>
<Contacts.Clients.Address>
<Contacts.Clients.City>, <Contacts.Clients.State>
Contacts.Clients.Zip>
```

This will display the following example label text in the actual label:

```
Julie Price
3620 Winter Street
Scottsdale, AZ
85999-9999
```

4   Select the Continuous option Format if you use a label-specific printer, otherwise the Sheet default will apply.

5   Select the Brand and Type of labels you are printing on from the drop-down list boxes. This will automatically update the label formatting style on the Format tab. If you select the [User-defined] Type, you can alter the formatting for the labels as you like on the Format tab.

6   Click the Format tab.

Alter the following options:

- Horizontal pitch—The distance between the left edge of one label and the left edge of the label immediately to the right.
- Vertical pitch—The distance between the top edge of one label and the top edge of the label immediately below.
- Width—The exact width of the label.
- Height—The exact height of the label.
- Left margin—The distance from the left edge of the page to the left edge of the labels.
- Top margin—The distance from the top edge of the page to the top edge of the labels.
- Columns—The number of label columns on a page.
- Rows—The number of label rows on a page.

7   Click the Options tab.

If you wish to print the same label on an entire sheet of labels, click the Entire page radio button. After doing so, if you wish to update all your labels to match the one you altered, click the Synchronize contents button. You must select this option before you create a New Document of labels; otherwise, you will have to edit each one individually or create a new label document.

If you wish to specify where on a page you want a single label printed, click the Single label radio button and indicate the specific Column number and Row number.

If you need to send the label to a different printer, click the Setup button and refer to the section "To Change the Printer and Print Properties."

8   Click the New Document button to create a new document with the label specifications and text inserted automatically.

9   Choose File, Print and click the OK button once you have the label sheet correctly placed in the printer tray feed.

If you have multiple label sheets, alter the Copies field on the Print dialog box before you click the OK button and include more sheets in the printer tray feed.

Preparing and Printing Business Cards

It can get expensive creating new business cards each time you change your address, job title, or phone number. StarOffice lets you prepare and print your own business cards and use card stock that you can buy from office supply stores.

TO PREPARE AND PRINT BUSINESS CARDS

1   Choose File, New, Business Cards to open the Business cards dialog box.

2   Click the Medium tab.

Your business card Format will most likely be a Sheet, but if not, select the Continuous option. If you choose the Sheet option, click the Type drop-down list and select the brand of business cards you will be using with your printer.

3   Click the Business cards tab (see Figure 2.14).

Make sure the correct AutoText section is selected from the drop-down list. By choosing an AutoText section, you can quickly specify which types of text elements are included on your business card. If you choose Business Card, Home: the Private tab information will be used. If you choose Business Card, Work: the Business tab information will be used. Then, select from the applicable Content options. The Preview area will display what the business card will look like.

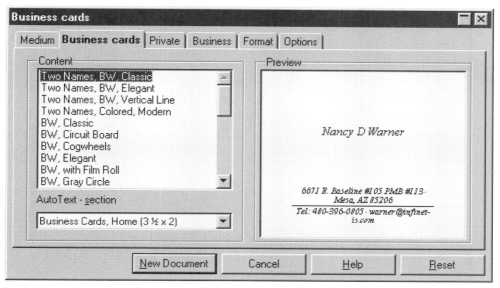

Figure 2.14   Create and print business card information.

4   Click the Private tab if you wish to create a Home business card; click the Business tab if you want to create a Work business card.

Enter in any missing information you wish to display on your business card. Any current information has been pulled from the information you entered when StarOffice was installed.

5   Click the Format tab if you need to adjust the size of your business card (even after choosing a standard format in the Medium tab).

Alter the following options:

- •Horizontal pitch—The distance between the left edge of one business card and the left edge of the business card immediately to the right.
- •Vertical pitch—The distance between the top edge of one business card and the top edge of the business card immediately below.
- •Width—The exact width of the business card.
- •Height—The exact height of the business card.
- •Left margin—The distance from the left edge of the page to the left edge of the business cards.
- •Top margin—The distance from the top edge of the page to the top edge of the business cards.
- •Columns—The number of business card columns on a page.
- •Rows—The number of business card rows on a page.

6   Click the Options tab.

If you wish to print the same business card on an entire sheet of business cards, click the Entire page radio button. Select the Synchronize contents checkbox if you prefer to make changes to a single business card. After doing so, if you wish to update all your business cards to match the one you altered, click the Synchronize contents button. You must select this option before you create a New Document of business cards, otherwise you will need to edit each one individually or create a new business card document.

If you wish to specify where on a page you want a single business card printed, click the Single label radio button and indicate the specific Column number and Row number.

Click the Setup button if you need to send the business cards to a different printer.

7   Click the New Document button to create a new document with the business card specifications and text inserted automatically.

8   Choose File, Print and click the OK button once you have the business card sheet correctly placed in the printer tray feed.

If you have multiple business card sheets, alter the Copies field on the Print dialog box before you click the OK button and include more sheets in the printer tray feed.

chapter 3

Editing Documents

IN THIS CHAPTER:

Selecting Text

You can make numerous changes to individual elements of a document—paragraphs, sentences, lines, words, single characters, or any combination. In order to make these changes, you almost always need to first select the elements you want to change. Often, the fastest way is with keyboard shortcuts (see Table 3.1).

Table 3.1   Keyboard and Mouse Selection Shortcuts

SHORTCUT	SELECTION FUNCTION
Shift+Arrow Key	A character in the direction of the arrow key you choose, from the insertion point.
Shift+Ctrl+Left Arrow	A word to the left of the insertion point.
Shift+Ctrl+Right Arrow	A word to the right of the insertion point.
Shift+Up Arrow	All text up one line, before the insertion point.
Shift+Down Arrow	All text down one line, after the insertion point.
Shift+Home	All text to the beginning of the line, before the insertion point.
Shift+End	All text to the end of the line, after the insertion point.
Shift+Ctrl+Home	All text to the top of the document, before the insertion point.
Shift+Ctrl+End	All text to the bottom of the document, after the insertion point.
Ctrl+A	All text in the entire document.
Double-click the mouse	The word that is clicked on.
Triple-click the mouse	All text on the line that is clicked.
Click+Shift(hold)+Click	All text between the two click locations.

TO SELECT TEXT

1   Open a file you saved previously (for example, <u>Letter02</u> from Chapter 2).

2   Choose File, Save as and assign the document the File name (for example, <u>Letter03</u>).

3   Move the I-beam mouse pointer before a word or group of words you would like to select (for example, the words "Spendalot Card").

4   Click the left mouse button and drag the mouse pointer to the end of the word or group of words.

The words "Spendalot Card" now appear to be highlighted in black and the text is white. This means the text is selected (see Figure 3.1).

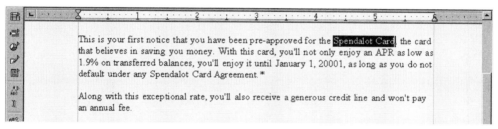

Figure 3.1   This is how selected text appears in Standard (STD) Selection Mode.

5   Click the selection mode field on the Status bar to toggle between selection options:

   • STD (Standard Selection Mode)—Selects a new block of text and the old selection is deselected. For example, you can select the word "Spendalot" and then select "Card." (STD is the default Selection mode.) Note that you can select multiple noncontiguous blocks of text even in STD mode if you press <Ctrl> before selecting the next block.

   • EXT (Extend Selection Mode)—Selects from the old to the new selection. For example, you can select the word "Spendalot", click once for the EXT selection mode, then click after the word "money" and all the text between "Spendalot… money" will be selected.

   • ADD (Additional Selection Mode)—Adds the new text selection to the old selection. This allows you to make select nonconsecutive blocks of text. For example, click twice for the ADD selection mode, and then select each word you wish to include (see Figure 3.2).

NOTE   To cancel the selected text in any of the selection modes, press the <Esc> key and all text will be deselected. When in Standard selection mode (STD), you can also click anywhere in or around the document window to cancel the selection.

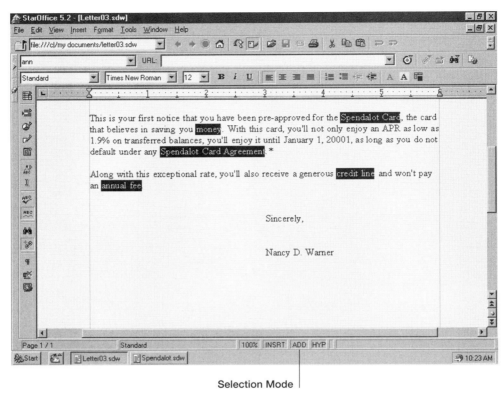

Figure 3.2   This is how selected text appears in Additional (ADD) selection mode.

Copying and Moving Text

You will find the ability to copy and move text to be very convenient. Many times you will type a document and then decide that information needs to be moved around or copied from a different document.

The actions of copy, cut, and paste can behave differently depending on the operating system you are using. For example, if you are using Windows, copied and cut elements are placed on the *clipboard* until you paste them. Table 3.2 lists some shortcut keys that StarOffice utilizes.

Table 3.2   Keyboard Shortcuts to Cut, Copy, and Paste Text

SHORTCUT	FUNCTION
Shift+Delete or Ctrl+X	Cut text
Ctrl+Insert or Ctrl+C	Copy text
Shift+Insert or Ctrl+V	Paste text

NOTE   Keep in mind that copying and moving objects is similar to copying and moving text, refer to Chapter 8, "Working with Frames, Graphics, and Objects" for more information.

TO COPY TEXT

1   Open a file that contains information you wish to insert into your document (this example, shows a <u>Spendalot</u> document open).

You should still have the document open from the previous section.

2   Select the text you would like to copy to your document (see Figure 3.3).

You can tell that <u>Letter03</u> is *not* the current document because the other document button looks like it is pressed on the Taskbar, making <u>Spendalot</u> the current document.

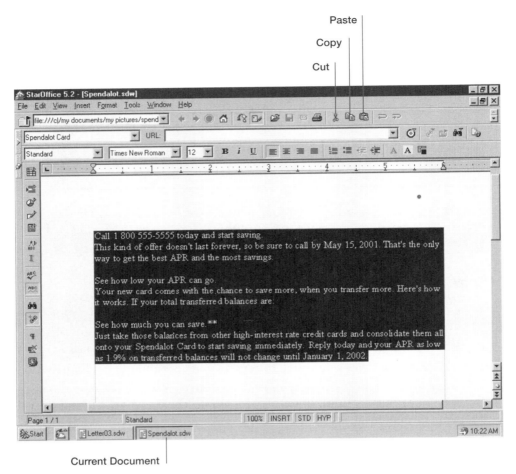

Figure 3.3   Text selected to copy.

3   Click the Copy button on the Function bar.

   You can also choose Copy from the Edit menu, or use one of the keyboard shortcuts from Table 3.2.

4   Click the Letter03 document button on the Taskbar to switch the current document.

5   Move the insertion point to the location in the current document where you wish to paste the copied information (a couple lines below the last text paragraph).

6   Click the Paste button on the Function bar.

You can also choose Paste from the Edit menu, or use one of the keyboard shortcuts from Table 3.2.

The copied text will appear in the current document.

NOTE   The Paste Special command on the Edit menu allows you to define the content of the clipboard. You can paste content as: formatted text, items in HTML format, unformatted text, a GDIMetaFile (if the selection for pasting is already a graphic), or a Microsoft Word Document. Use Paste Special if you want the copied content to retain its original format within the StarOffice Writer document.

TO MOVE TEXT

1   Select the text you would like to move within your document.

2   Click the Cut button on the Function bar.

Notice that the Cut and Copy buttons are no longer available on the Function bar when the clipboard is *full*. This means that there has been information copied or moved to the clipboard that needs to be pasted.

If you don't want to paste the current clipboard information, but want to select another block of text for pasting, select the new information and the Cut and Copy buttons will again become available.

3   Move the insertion point to the location where you wish to insert the cut information.

4   Click the Paste button on the Function bar.

You can also choose Paste from the Edit menu, or use one of the keyboard shortcuts from Table 3.2.

NOTE   When you use the cut (or copy) command, you are placing the selected information on the Windows clipboard (depending on your operating system), where the information will remain until you replace it with another item. This means that you can use the paste command multiple times with the same-copied element.

To Drag & Drop Text

1   Select another block of text that you would like to move using the Drag & Drop method.

> **NOTE**   Dragging and dropping text and objects can be useful when moving information from nearby locations in the same document. It can also be useful between multiple documents, though you might want to tile your windows (refer to the section "Moving Around in a Document" in Chapter 2).

2   Move the mouse pointer over the selected block of text, then press and hold the left mouse button.

The pointer will first appear as a circle with a slash through it while it is over the selected block, and then it will change to an arrow with a gray box below it when you move it outside the selected block.

3   Drag the pointer to the new location (see Figure 3.4) and release the mouse button to drop the text.

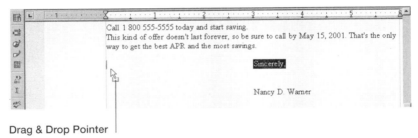

Drag & Drop Pointer

Figure 3.4   Drag & Drop text with the mouse pointer.

4   Save any changes to your document (for example, <u>Letter03</u>).

Using the Undo Feature

You can reverse the actions performed on a document (for example, moving, correcting, copying, and so on) by using the Undo feature.

TO UNDO AND REDO CHANGES

1   Click the Undo button on the Formatting toolbar and the previous action will be reversed.

The button looks like a U-turn sign on its side. If it is inactive (grayed out), there hasn't been any action performed on the document that can be reversed.

You can also choose Undo from the Edit menu. The previously performed action will most likely accompany the word Undo. For example, Undo: Move. In addition, you can press the <Ctrl+Z> key combination to undo changes.

2   Click the Redo button on the Formatting toolbar.

This button will only appear active if you have recently clicked the Undo button. Undo and Redo together allow you to view the document before the change and after the change.

You can also Redo the last change by choosing Repeat from the Edit menu.

> **NOTE**   You can click the Undo and Redo buttons back to the first edit you made when you opened the document—even if you resaved the document during that time. The number of undos and redos allowed is 20 by default, and can be raised to 100 by choosing Options, General, Save and altering the Undo Number of steps field (refer to the section "To Alter Document Save Options" in Chapter 14 for more information).

Checking a Document for Spelling Errors

In Chapter 1, you briefly learned how to use the AutoSpelling button to immediately locate misspelled words or words that weren't in the StarOffice dictionary (indicated by the wavy red underline). In this section, you will learn how to use the options available in the Spelling dialog box.

TO CHECK A DOCUMENT FOR SPELLING ERRORS

1   Open a document in which you wish to check spelling (or you can use the Letter03 document).

2   Press <Ctrl+Home> to move to the top of the document, if you wish to check the document from the beginning.

You can also first select a particular block of text, which will check only the spelling within the selection.

NOTE   You can check the spelling from any location, but if you are not at the beginning of the document, when you get to the end of the document, you will be asked if you want to continue searching from the beginning of the document. StarOffice Writer does this to make sure that the entire document has been checked from the insertion point to the end, and from the beginning back to the insertion point.

3   Click the Spelling button on the Main toolbar.

The Spelling button appears as a checkmark with the letters ABC over it. You can also choose Tools, Spelling, Check. The AutoSpellcheck command on the submenu corresponds to the AutoSpelling button on the Main toolbar. If the button is activated, there will be a checkmark next to the AutoSpellcheck command.

The first word that is not in the StarOffice dictionary will be flagged and the Spelling dialog box will appear (see Figure 3.5).

NOTE   Just because a word isn't in the StarOffice dictionary doesn't mean it is misspelled—it might be a proper name, a foreign word, or a word that is simply too obscure or specialized to be included in the dictionary.

Check Word

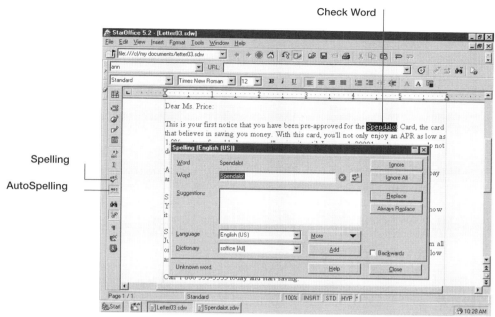

Spelling

AutoSpelling

Figure 3.5   This shows a word not in the StarOffice dictionary.

4   Choose from the following list of options available on the Spelling dialog
box:

- •Word—You can type a correction directly into the Word box.
- •Check word—If you type a correction into the Word box, click this
button to re-check the spelling of the word.
- •Suggestions—Lists possible replacements for the word not in the
dictionary.
- •Language—Allows you change the language of the spelling dictionary.
This is convenient if you have reason to use a foreign word in your
document and wish to verify the spelling. You must switch back to
English (U.S.) when you're ready to continue, otherwise the new
language will become the default dictionary. In addition, if you choose a
language that hasn't been installed, return to the Setup program (refer
to Chapter 14, "Customizing the Writer Environment").
- •Dictionary—The location where a new word is saved when added to the
dictionary.
- •More—Choose either AutoCorrect (adds the correct and incorrect word
spellings to the AutoCorrect replacement list after you've selected or
typed the correct text you want to use); refer to Chapter 12, "Using
Document Automation"); Thesaurus (activates the Thesaurus dialog
box; see the next section "Using the Thesaurus"); or Other (activates

the Language dialog box to choose from alternate language spell checking options).

- Add—Click to add a word to the selected dictionary (for example, StarOffice provides you with a few different built-in dictionaries: soffice, standard, Sun).
- Ignore—Skips the unknown word and continues checking the rest of the document.
- Ignore All—Skips the unknown word each time it is encountered while checking the rest of the document.
- Replace—Replaces the incorrect word with either the word you typed into the Word box or selected from the Suggestions list.
- Always Replace—Replaces all occurrences of the incorrect word (in the current document) with either the word you typed into the Word box or selected from the Suggestions list.
- Backwards—Reverses the search direction toward the beginning of the document, instead of toward the end.
- Close—Click if you prefer to stop checking the document spelling before Spelling finishes checking the document.

If the beginning of your document hasn't been checked, you will be asked if you wish to continue checking from the beginning; click Yes to continue checking or No to stop checking.

If the document has been completely checked, a message box will appear telling you it is finished.

5   Click the OK button to return to the document.

Using the Thesaurus

The Thesaurus provides various meanings of a word and lists synonyms (words with similar meanings) to help you replace the appropriate word.

To Use the Thesaurus

1   Move the insertion point so that it is within the word you wish to look up in the thesaurus.

You can also have the insertion point before or after a word or a word selected, and that will be the defined word.

2   Choose Tools, Thesaurus or press <Ctrl+F7> to open the Thesaurus dialog box (see Figure 3.6).

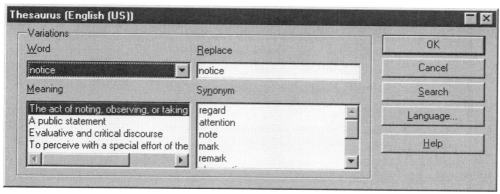

Figure 3.6   A word looked up in the Thesaurus.

3   Choose from the following list of options available on the Thesaurus dialog box:

- •Word—Displays the word you are looking up in the thesaurus.
- •Meaning—Selects the correct word meaning according to the context described in the list box.
- •Synonym—Click on the word in the list box to replace the current word.
- •Replace—Lists the synonym to replace the current word.
- •Search—Click to define the word in the Replace box, as the next synonym search. This is convenient if none of the synonyms are the word you are looking for and you wish to continue searching.
- •Language—Click to define the language that StarOffice will use to search for meanings and synonyms.

4   Click the OK button to replace the word with the synonym; click the Cancel button to return to the document without changing the word.

Checking a Document for Hyphenation

When you check for possible hyphenation in a document, you are checking to see if any words at the end of a line (on the right margin) can be hyphenated instead of wrapped as a whole word to the next line.

TO CHECK A DOCUMENT FOR HYPHENATION

1 Press <Ctrl+Home> to move the insertion point to the beginning of your document.

2 Choose Tools, Hyphenation to open the Hyphenation dialog box (see Figure 3.7).

StarOffice Writer will automatically move to the first word (if any) in which hyphenation might be applied. If the hyphenation is acceptable, you will receive a message informing you that the hyphenation check has been completed.

NOTE   If hyphenated text is edited and words at the end of the line move, you can still see the hyphenation, but it is grayed out. However, the hyphen no longer prints.

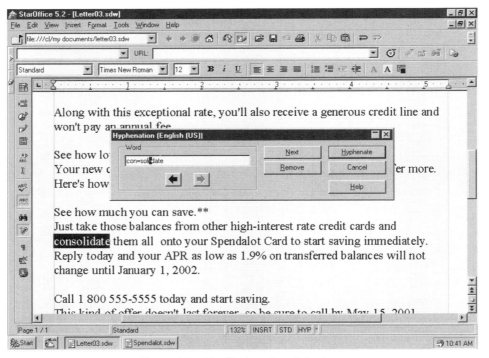

Figure 3.7   The Hyphenation dialog box.

NOTE   Applying hyphenation can give your document a fuller look, especially if your paragraphs are justified. Refer to the section "Changing Text Alignment" in Chapter 5, "Formatting Paragraphs," for more information.

3   Select from the various buttons available on the Hyphenation dialog box:

•Next—Skips to the next word to review possible hyphenation.
•Remove—Clears the hyphen position for the current word.
•Hyphenate—Applies the indicated hyphenation and moves to review the next word.

The Arrow Keys (right and left) allow you to set the hyphen at the desired position, if the word has multiple hyphenation possibilities.

4   Click the OK button when you are notified that the hyphenation check is complete.

You can click the Cancel button to stop checking the document hyphenation at any time.

NOTE   For more information on maintaining consistency in your documents with regards to how the text flows (for example keeping paragraphs together and eliminating widows and orphans), refer to the section "Altering Paragraph Text Flow," in Chapter 5.

Formatting Text

Applying Bold, Italics, or Underlining

One of the fastest and most effective ways to enhance your text is to select the text and apply bold, italics, or underlining. You can also set these effects and type new text that will then display the enhancement automatically.

TO APPLY BOLD, ITALICS, OR UNDERLINING

1   Open a document that you want to work with (for example, the Letter03 document you edited in Chapter 3).

2   Select the text you would like to enhance.

    For example, select "See how low your APR can go".

3   Click the Bold button on the Object bar.

    The selected text will be enhanced with bolding.

    Repeat this for other text selections, such as, "See how much you can save**" and "Call 1 800 555-5555 today and start saving" by applying bold.

4   Place the insertion point on a new line (for example, on the line before "Dear Ms. Price:").

5   Click the Bold button on the Object bar.

    This will set the Bold type style as the default for new text you type.

6   Type the following:

    ```
    With the Spendalot Card the more you transfer, the lower your
    APR on transferred balances, the more you save
    ```
    The text will be enhanced with bold as you type.

> **NOTE**   If you apply bold, italics, or underlining before you type in new text, the settings become the defaults for new text; you must remove the settings to return to typing regular text.

7   Click the Bold button on the Object bar.

    This will return the default type style back to Normal.

8   Select the text you would like to italicize (for example, the words "Spendalot Card Agreement").

9   Click the Italic button on the Object bar.

    Italics can emphasize the meaning of a word or group of words, or draw attention to a specific term. The italics in this situation help to emphasize the group of words because there will be a footnote explaining the asterisk next to it.

10   Select the text you would like to underline (for example, words "January 1, 2002" in the first paragraph).

11   Click the Underline button on the Object bar.

Underlining a word or group of words can draw your visual attention to specific information on a document. The future date is important to this letter because the recipient of the letter is to take special notice.

Now your document will have bold, italic, and underline enhancements (see Figure 4.1).

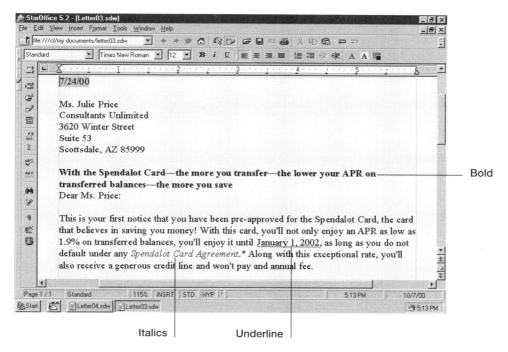

Figure 4.1   Examples of using bold, italics, and underlining.

12   Save the changes to your document (for example, as Letter04).

Keep in mind that you can apply multiple enhancements to a block of text. For example, you could bold, italicize, and underline a word. It is rare that text looks good with all the enhancements applied, so make sure it is appropriate for the document. If you are trying to draw special attention to a word, consider using the formatting options described in the sections throughout the rest of this chapter.

Inserting Special Characters

There are special characters available in StarOffice that aren't on your keyboard. For example, you won't find a "checkmark": key, a "copyright symbol" © key, or an "accent over the letter A" Á key. These and other kinds of special characters are organized by font, and can be inserted directly into your document.

TO INSERT SPECIAL CHARACTERS

1   Move the insertion point to the location in the document where you wish to insert a special character.

    For example, after "Spendalot Card" on the line after the address (you added this bold text in the previous section).

2   Choose Insert, Special Character.

    The Special Character dialog box will open with your current font in the Font drop-down list box. You can also click the Insert button (the topmost button) on the Main toolbar and select the Insert Special Character button from the submenu.

3   Click the symbol you want to insert (for example, the em dash symbol "—") with the mouse pointer or by pressing the <Up Arrow> and <Down Arrow> keys and the <Spacebar> key (see Figure 4.2).

> **NOTE**   If there is more than one special character that you need to insert into your document, click each character before you click the OK button. They will all be displayed along the bottom of the Special Character dialog box, and then all inserted next to each other when you click OK. Once the characters are in your document, if necessary, you can cut and paste them to the locations you need them, without revisiting the Special Character dialog box. If you decide not to use the multiple characters, click the Delete button within the Special Character dialog box and start over again.

    You can click any symbol you wish or even click the Font drop-down list box and choose from the symbols available with different fonts.

    It is more visually appealing to insert a special character using the same font as your text, although sometimes a particular character is available in only one font (for example, an hourglass from the Wingdings font).

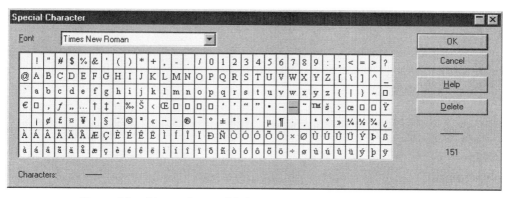

Figure 4.2 Choose the special character to insert into your document.

4   Click the OK button to insert the chosen character(s).

You can also double-click the character to insert it into your document and close the Special Character dialog box simultaneously. If you decide not to insert the chosen character(s), click the Cancel button.

5   Press the <Delete> key on the keyboard to remove the extra space in the text (you might have to press the <Right Arrow> key to move to the extra space location).

6   Press <Ctrl+Right Arrow> four times and the Backspace key once, in order to move the insertion point after the word "transfer" as well as remove an extra space.

7   Insert the same special character with the Special Character dialog box (refer to steps 2 through 4).

8   Press <Shift+Left Arrow> to select the special character; press <Ctrl+C> to copy the special character; press <Ctrl+Right Arrow> seven times and the Backspace key once, to delete the space and move the insertion point after the word "balances"; press <Ctrl+V> to paste the special character.

All of this was to illustrate that you can copy and paste special characters once they are inserted into your document, as with regular text. The shortcut commands were to get you used to using them, though you could have also used the mouse and the buttons on the Formatting bar.

Working with Bulleted and Numbered Lists

StarOffice Writer treats all listed items as *numbered lists*. This includes bulleted lists, which are also considered a type of numbered list.

TO INSERT A BULLETED LIST

1   Move the insertion point to the beginning of the line where you wish to add a bulleted list.

For example, add a line after the line that reads "If your total transferred balances are:" by pressing the <Enter> key.

2   Click the Bullets on/off button on the Object bar.

This activates the bulleted list field and any text you type will automatically be part of the bulleted list. Notice that the bullet appears as a Field (highlighted in gray if you have the View, Field Shadings option activated).

3   Type the following list item:

```
Greater than or equal to $3,500, your APR will be 1.9%
```

4   Press the <Enter> key to end the line and begin the next bulleted list line.

5   Type the following list item:

```
Less than $3,500, your APR will be 2.9%
```

NOTE   When your cursor is on a line that contains a bulleted list (or a numbered list, for that matter), a small left-pointing triangle button appears on the right-most side of the Object bar. This is called the Object Bar button. Click this button to switch from the Text Object bar to the Numbering Object bar. This is because the Object bar is context-sensitive to what you are trying to perform in your document. The Numbering Object bar will be covered in the section "To Combine Numbering and Bullets."

6   Press the <Enter> key to move to the next line (see Figure 4.3).

Type in another list item or do one of the following if you are finished with the list:

• Press the <Enter> key again. Writer will stop adding bullets on lines that follow.
• Click the Bullets on/off button on the Text Object bar to deactivate the bulleted list field.

Your list will consist of only the lines where text was typed.

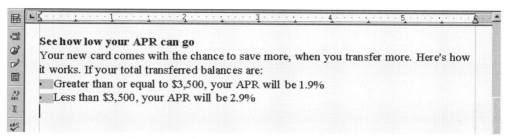

Figure 4.3   Insert bulleted list points one at a time.

TO ALTER THE BULLETS IN A LIST

1   Move the insertion point so that it is somewhere in a bulleted list line.

   You can be at the beginning of the list line or anywhere in the bulleted list; all bullets in the list will be altered.

   If you *select* a particular line, only that line's bullet will be altered.

2   Choose Format, Numbering/Bullets to open the Numbering/Bullets dialog box.

   The following tabs provide various options to alter your bullets:

   • Bullets—Allows you to choose from the most common bullet styles.
   • Graphics—Allows you to choose a graphic as your bullet style. Click the desired picture from the Selection area; select the Link graphics option if you wish to be able to make a change to the graphic later and automatically update via the link. This is also useful if you are using the graphical bullet in an HTML document.

   NOTE   If you have a particular graphic that you would like to serve as a bullet, place it in the StarOffice share\gallery\bullets directory. It will appear as an option in the Selection area of the Graphics tab on the Numbering/Bullets dialog box. You can also see it by clicking the Gallery, Bullets option in the Explorer and viewing the bullets in the Beamer.

   • Customize—Allows you to choose a special character for your bullet style. Click the Character button to open the Special Character dialog box with the StarBats font in the Font drop-down list box. Click the special character you would like to appear as the bullet in your bulleted list (for example, the box with a checkmark in it) and click the OK button.

3   Select the bullet style you desire (see Figure 4.4) and click the OK button on the Numbering/Bullets dialog box to accept your changes.

The bullet style will automatically update in the document.

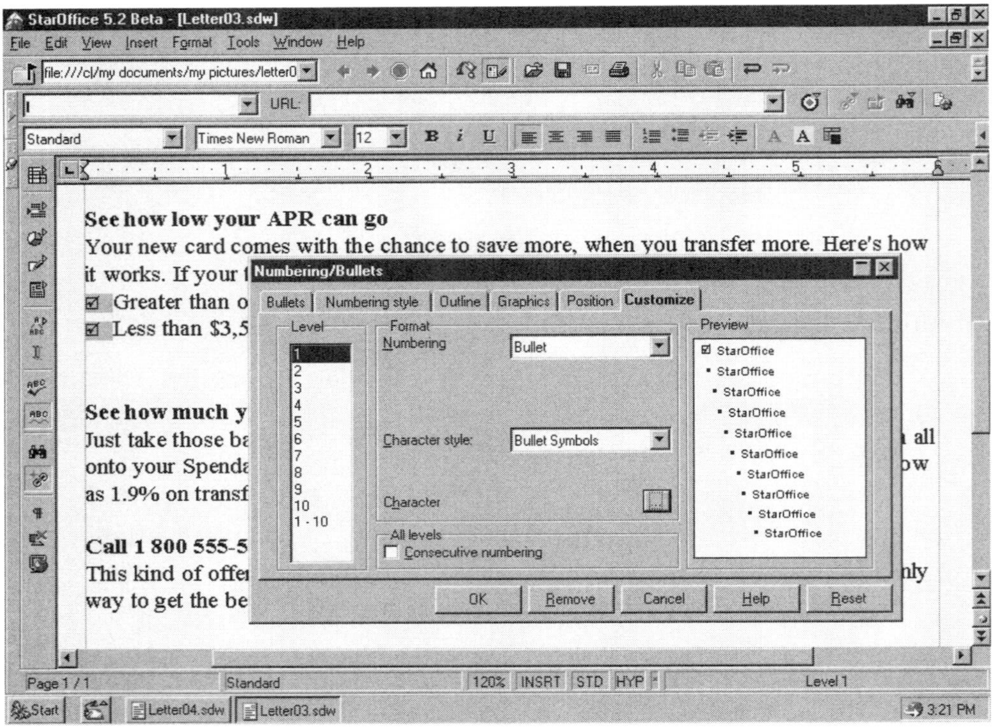

Figure 4.4   You can use a common bullet, graphic, or customize your own.

TO INSERT A NUMBERED LIST

1   Move the insertion point at the beginning of the line where you wish to add a numbered list.

For example, press <Ctrl+End> to move to the end of the document and press <Ctrl+Enter> to insert a page break and move to the next page.

2   Type `Spendalot Card Agreement` and press the <Enter> key to move to the next line.

Click the Numbering on/off button on the Object bar.

This activates the numbered list field and any text you type will automatically be part of the numbered list. Notice that the number appears as a Field (highlighted in gray if the View, Field Shadings option is activated).

3   Type the following list item:

This offer is only valid for new accounts. Terms and conditions subject to change.

4   Press the <Enter> key to end the line and begin the next numbered list line.

5   Type the following list item:

You must be at least 18 years of age and have an annual income of at least $8,000.

6   Press the <Enter> key to move to the next line (see Figure 4.5).

Hard Page Return

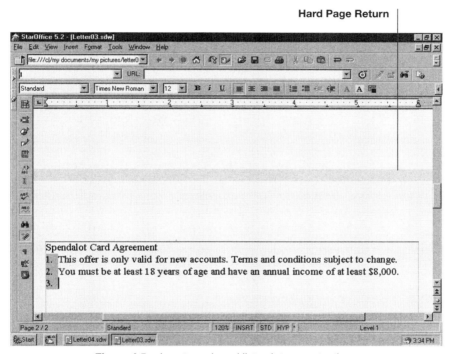

Figure 4.5   Insert numbered list points one at a time.

Type in another list item or perform one of the following if you are finished with the list:

• Press the <Enter> key again; the numbered list field will disappear.
• Click the Numbering on/off button on the Text Object bar to deactivate the numbered list field.

Your list will consist of only the lines where text is typed.

To Alter the Numbers in a List

1   Move the insertion point so that it is somewhere in a numbered list line.

    This can be at the beginning of the list line or anywhere in the numbered list; all numbers in the list will be altered.

    If you *select* a particular line, only that line's number will be altered.

2   Choose Format, Numbering/Bullets to open the Numbering/Bullets dialog box.

3   Click the Numbering style tab.

    You can choose from the most common number styles.

4   Click the Customize tab.

    You can alter the type of number and what comes before and after the number:

    • Numbering—Click the drop-down list box and select the format you would like. For example, you can choose different types of numbers (1,2,3), alphabetic order (A,B,C), or Roman numerals (i,ii,iii).
    • Before—Type a character or symbol to appear before the number (this is blank by default). For example, if you wish the number to be surrounded by brackets, you would enter the left bracket "[" here.
    • After—Type a character or symbol to appear after the number (a period "." appears by default). For example, if you wanted the number to be surrounded by brackets, you would enter the right bracket "]" here.

5   Select the number style you desire (see Figure 4.6) and click the OK button on the Numbering/Bullets dialog box to accept your changes. You can see your changes in the Preview area.

    The number style will automatically update in the document.

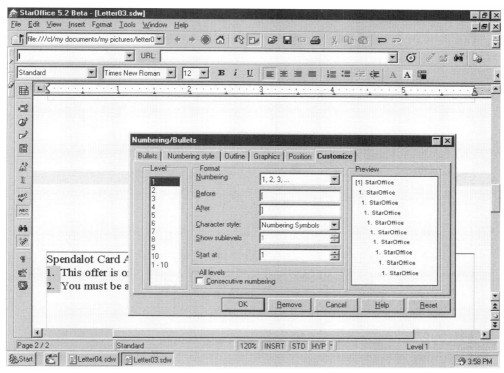

Figure 4.6   You can use numbers, letters, or customize your own.

TO COMBINE NUMBERING AND BULLETS

1   Move the insertion point to the beginning of the line where you want to add a numbered list.

For our example, we prefer to continue the numbered list we created in the previous section, so place the insertion point at the end of line number 2. However, if you place the insertion point on the line below line number 2, there is no way to continue the consecutive numbering.

> **NOTE**   To discontinue consecutive list numbering, click the Restart Numbering button on the Numbering Object bar. Refer to Figure 4.7 if you need help locating this button.

2   Press the <Enter> key to begin a new line number.

3   Click the Object bar button to toggle between the regular Text Object bar and Numbering Object bar (see Figure 4.7).

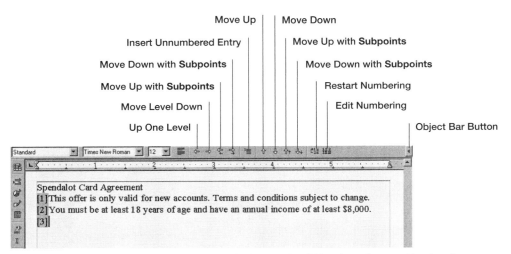

Figure 4.7   The buttons available on the Numbering Object bar when working in a list.

The buttons available on the Object bar are context-sensitive to what you are trying to perform in your document. When working in text, the Text Object bar is the default; when working in a numbered list, the Numbering Object bar becomes the default. If you need to access some of the Text Object bar features while working in a numbered list (for example, to bold a term in a list), click the triangular button on the right side of the Object bar to switch from the Numbering Object bar back to the Text Object bar.

NOTE   The Numbering Object bar can also be used when working with bulleted lists.

4   Type the following text on line list number 3:

    To process the Pre-Approved Acceptance Form for a new Spendalot account, the Form must be:

5   Press the <Enter> key to move to the next line.

    Instead of entering text on the fourth line number, let's make a bulleted list within the numbered list.

6   Click the Move Level Down button on the Numbering Object bar.

    This will move the insertion point to the right and from Level 1 to Level 2. The Level number of the active line (the line which contains the insertion point) is displayed in the Status bar. This also indents the text; refer to Chapter 5, "Formatting Paragraphs," for more information.

7   Click the Edit Numbering button on the Numbering Object bar.

8   Click the Customize tab (see Figure 4.8).

Notice that the Level on the left side of the dialog box indicates Level 2, reflecting the level of numbering that is currently selected.

9   Click the Numbering drop-down list and select Bullet.

The default bullet is sufficient; if you wish to alter the bullet style, see the previous section, "To Alter the Bullets in a List."

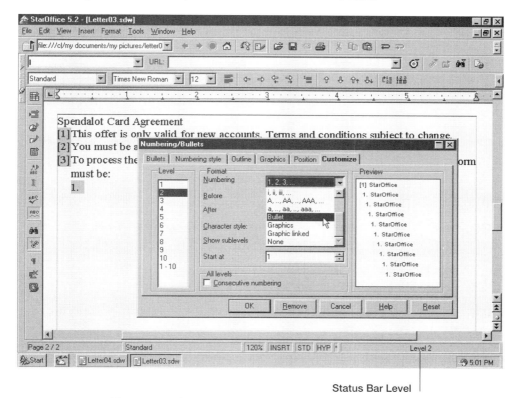

Status Bar Level

Figure 4.8   Customize your numbered list to include bullets.

10   Click the OK button to return to the document.

11   Type the following text and press the <Enter> key between each line (to create a hard return):

```
Accurately completed

Signed; verifiably correct

Returned by the expiration date
```

You should be on the fourth bulleted list line.

12   Click the Up One Level button on the Numbering Object bar.

This will move the insertion point to the left and back to Level 1.

13   Type the following text:

     ```
     Please send the Pre-Approved Acceptance Form in the enclosed
     postage-paid envelope to:
     ```

14   Click the Insert Unnumbered Entry button on the Numbering Object
     bar.

15   Type the following text, but this time press the <Shift+Enter> keys
     between each line (to create a soft return), and then press Enter to create
     a hard return *after* the last line:

     ```
     Spendalot Card Offer
     One Dollar Way
     Nowhere, Indiana 49999
     ```

16   Click the Numbering Off button on the Numbering Object bar.

     Notice that the Object bar returned to Text by default.

17   Save the changes to your document (see Figure 4.9).

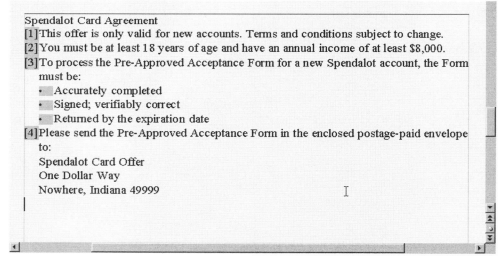

Figure 4.9   Use the different Numbering Object bar buttons to create different parts of a list.

Default Options

You can choose the default effect options, covered in the following sections, before
you type text into your document. These will become the default options for new
text entered while working in the document—for example, font and font size;
font color and highlighting; outline and shadow; strikethrough and underline.

Text already in the document will not change unless you select text and apply each specific effect.

Changing the Font and Font Size

A *font* describes the letters, numbers, and symbols that make up a given electronic typeface. There are some common categories when working with fonts:

- Serif—The letterforms have little strokes, referred to as serifs (or sometimes tails). For example, Times.
- Sans Serif—Usually more rounded, with clean lines and no strokes (tails). For example, Helvetica.
- Script—Type that resembles a person's handwriting. For example, *Brush Script*.
- Monospaced—Like a typewriter, letters and spaces take up the same amount of width on a line. For example, `Courier`.
- Decorative—Any type that has been made interesting with the use of shapes or designs to the individual letters. For example, RUSTICANA.
- Dingbat—Type that is filled with pictographic faces and can be useful in creating borders, edges, and interesting visuals. For example, ✺✂■ℽ♋♌✂■ℽ♋✦ (Wingdings).

To Change the Font and Font Size

1   Select the text in which you wish to change the font.

    You can press <Ctrl+A> to select the entire document.

2   Click the Font Name drop-down list box on the Object bar (see Figure 4.10).

    You will see an alphabetical listing of all the available fonts in StarOffice Writer.

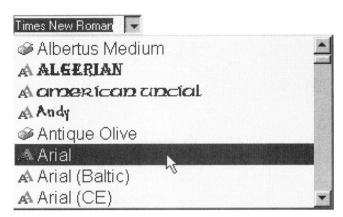

Figure 4.10   Each available font name is displayed in the actual font.

3   Click the name of the font from the list.

For example, Arial.

The font automatically applies to the selected text.

NOTE   If you know the name of the font you are looking for, click the Font Name drop-down list and press the first letter of the name of the font on the keyboard. This will move you directly to the place in the font list that begins with that letter in the alphabet. In addition, once you are in the Font Name list, you can use the Page Up, Page Down, and arrow keys to move through the list. You can also type the name of the font directly into the Font Name list and press the <Enter> key.

4   Select the text in which you wish to change the font size.

You can press the <Ctrl+Home> keys to move to the beginning of the document; then press <Shift+Down Arrow> to select the first line, which is the current date.

5   Click the Font Size drop-down list box on the Object bar.

You will see a numerical listing of the most common font sizes. Notice how some numbers are missing, for example, 15.

6   Choose the font size from the list.

Or, to set a font size that isn't listed, click the mouse pointer in the Font Size box, type the number, and press the <Enter> key.

The font size automatically applies to the selected text.

Changing the Font Color and Highlighting

You can alter the color of your text or the background of the text if you wish to bring emphasis to a particular word or block of text.

To Change the Font Color and Highlighting

1   Select the text in which you wish to change the font color.

    For example, select "Spendalot Card" in the first paragraph.

2   Click and briefly hold the Font Color button on the Object bar until a color palette appears; then you can release the mouse button and freely move the mouse pointer (see Figure 4.11).

    If you don't click on the Font Color button long enough, you will apply the currently selected font color to the selected text. Simply try clicking and holding the Font Color button again until the palette displays.

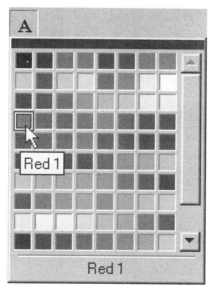

Figure 4.11   Choose any Font Color from the palette.

3   Click the color from the palette.

    For example, Red 1. Notice that the name of the color displays along the bottom of the color palette, and may appear as a Tip immediately below the cursor, if you have set StarOffice to display Tips.

    The font color automatically applies to the selected text.

4   Click the mouse pointer somewhere in the document so that no text is selected.

5   Click the Highlighting button on the Object bar.

    Notice that the Highlighting button is still selected and the mouse pointer has changed to a paint can with paint pouring out. This indicates that you can apply the color to any text you like. If text was still selected, the highlight color would have applied to the selection and no paint can would appear.

    NOTE   The default highlighting color is Yellow; if you wish to change the highlight color first, follow the previous steps 2 and 3 (except using the Highlighting button) to select a color. You can also select the text to be highlighted first, as in steps 1 through 3.

6   Click & Drag the insertion point to select the text in which you wish to apply Highlighting.

    For example, select "1 800 555-5555" in the last paragraph.

    When you release the mouse button from the Click & Drag, the highlighting color is applied. Notice that the mouse pointer is still a paint can, which means you can continue to apply the highlighting.

7   Click the Highlighting button again to turn this feature off.

Applying Outline and Shadow Effects

You may apply outline and shadow effects to your text to bring emphasis to a particular word or block of text.

TO APPLY OUTLINE AND SHADOW EFFECTS

1   Select the text in which you wish to apply a font effect.

    For example, select "Spendalot Card" in the first paragraph.

2   Choose Format, Character to open the Character dialog box.

3   Click the Font tab if it does not already appear (see Figure 4.12).

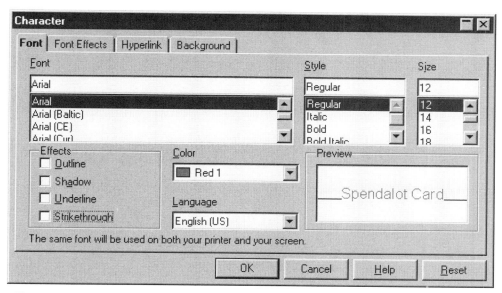

Figure 4.12   The Character dialog box contains many of the settings available on the Object bar.

NOTE   Notice the settings in the Character dialog box. If you have text selected, the most recent settings display. If no text is selected, the default settings you selected will display. These options can all be changed on this dialog box at the same time instead of using the individual fields on the Object bar.

4   Locate the Effects area of the dialog box and note the following effects:

•Outline—Click this checkbox option to make only the contour of the font visible (similar to the outline of a box not filled in).

•Shadow—Click this checkbox option to cast a dark silhouette behind the text.

You can see each effect in the Preview area of the dialog box. Click the Reset button at any time if you wish to see how the selected text originally appeared and begin applying effects over again; click the Cancel button to return to the document without applying any changes.

5   Click the specific effect checkbox and click the OK button to apply the changes to the text.

Because the effects are checkboxes, you can apply more than one effect to the text (for example, Outline and Shadow); if the effects were radio buttons, you could only apply one effect.

Applying Strikethrough and Underline Effects

You can apply different types of lines to mark through (strikethrough) or underline your text.

TO APPLY STRIKETHROUGH AND UNDERLINE EFFECTS

1   Select the text in which you wish to apply a font effect.

    For example, select "Spendalot Card" in the first paragraph.

2   Choose Format, Character to open the Character dialog box.

3   Click the Font tab and locate the Effects area.

4   Click the Underline and Strikethrough checkbox options.

5   Click the Font Effects tab (see Figure 4.13).

    In order for the Underlining and Strikethrough options to be available on the Font Effects tab, you must perform the previous steps 3 and 4.

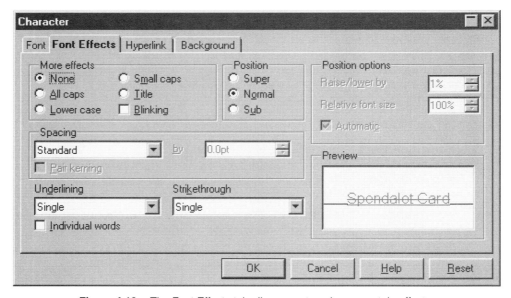

Figure 4.13   The Font Effects tab allows you to enhance certain effects.

6   Click the Strikethrough drop-down list box and choose from the various types of lines (for example, Single, Double, Bold, With /, With X, and so on).

7   Click the Underlining drop-down list box and choose from the various types of lines (for example, Single, Double, Dotted, Dash, Dot Dash, Wavy, and so on).

You can see each effect in the Preview area of the dialog box. Click the Reset button at any time if you want to restore the text to its original appearance and start applying effects over again; click the Cancel button to return to the document without applying any changes.

NOTE   You can go directly to the Font Effects tab on the Character dialog box if your selected text has already been underlined using the Underline button on the Object bar (refer to the section "Applying Bold, Italics, or Underlining"). You can then choose the type of underline from the Underlining drop-down list box.

8   Click the OK button to apply the changes to the text.

Changing the Font Capitalization and Character Positioning

You can alter the capitalization of your text (for example, you typed a paragraph and realized it must be in UPPER CASE, you don't need to retype it again). You can also modify the character positioning to slightly raise or lower your text baseline (for example, superscript and subscript mathematical terms).

TO CHANGE THE FONT CAPITALIZATION

1   Select the text in which you wish to apply a font capitalization effect.

For example, select "Spendalot Card Agreement".

2   Choose Format, Character to open the Character dialog box (see Figure 4.14).

3   Click the Font Effects tab and locate the More effects area. Choose from the following:

•Click the All caps radio button to make all the characters capitalized. For example, ALL CAPS.
•Click the Lower case radio button to make all the characters lower case. For example, lower case.
•Click the Small caps radio button to capitalize the first letter of each word in a larger font size and the remaining letters in each word with capitalized letters in a smaller font size. For example, SMALL CAPS.
•Click the Title radio button to capitalize the first letter of each selected word. For example, The Title Of A Story.

You can see each effect in the Preview area of the dialog box. Click the Reset button at any time if you want to restore the text to its original appearance and start applying effects over again; click the Cancel button to return to the document without applying any changes.

4   Click the OK button to apply the changes to the text.

To Change the Character Positioning

1   Select the text in which you wish to apply character positioning.

For example, if you want to elevate the "st" part of "1st".

2   Choose Format, Character to open the Character dialog box.

3   Click the Font Effects tab and locate the Position area of the dialog box (see Figure 4.14).

Text positioning affects a character's baseline; that is, where the bottom of the character sits in relation to Normal text.

Descriptive numbers like "first" and "second" can be displayed as "1st" and "2nd"; you will often see the "st" and "nd" portions as Super script (raised slightly). For example, 1st and 2nd.

Base numbers like 10 base 2 will often be displayed with the "2" portion as Subscript (lowered slightly). For example, 10_2.

4   Click the Super radio button to raise the "st" slightly (see Figure 4.14).

You can see each effect in the Preview area of the dialog box. Click the Reset button at any time if you want to restore the text to its original appearance and start applying effects over again; click the Cancel button to return to the document without applying any changes.

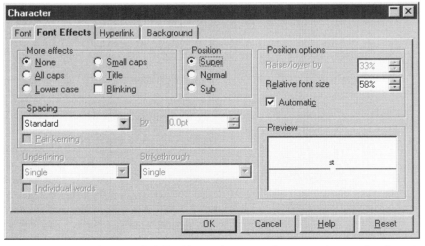

Figure 4.14   Use the Super or Sub Position options to apply superscript or subscript to text.

5   Click the OK button to apply the changes to the text.

Formatting Paragraphs

Changing Text Alignment

Alignment describes how text is placed between the left and right margins. Table 5.1 explains the four options available in Writer.

Table 5.1   Alignment Options

OPTION	EFFECT
Align Left	Aligns text along the left margin only; the left side appears flush. This is the default setting for all new documents.
Centered	Centers text between the left and right margins.
Align Right	Aligns text along the right margin only; the right side appears flush.
Justify	Aligns text along the left and right margins so that both sides appear smooth.

TO CHANGE TEXT ALIGNMENT

1   Move the insertion point to the location in the document where you want to alter the text alignment.

For example, press <Ctrl+Home> to move to the line with the date field of the document from the previous chapter.

2   Click the Align Right button on the Object bar.

Notice that the text is now aligned on the document's right margin.

3   Place the insertion point on a line in which you want to alter the alignment (for example, to the "With the Spendalot Card…" tagline statement).

4   Click the Centered button on the Object bar.

Notice that the text is now centered between the margins.

5   Place the insertion point on another line in which you want to adjust the alignment (for example, to the first main paragraph).

6   Click the Justify button on the Object bar (see Figure 5.1).

Notice that the line extends flush with the left and right margins.

You can also change the alignment of objects in your documents like graphics and tables, or even text and objects within tables. In addition, if you change the alignment and want to change it again, simply click the appropriate alignment button.

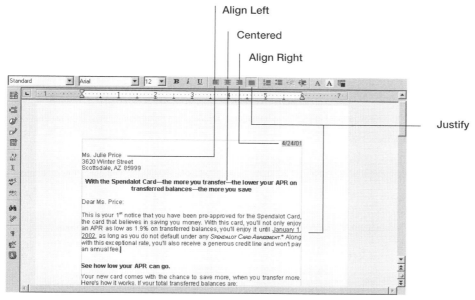

Figure 5.1   Various text alignment options.

NOTE   There may be some situations where no matter the amount of text on the line, all lines must be justified; this is referred to as a *force justify*. The first and last characters on the line will be flush with the left and right margins, even if there is only one word on the last line. To force justify a paragraph, choose Format, Paragraph, and click the Alignment tab. Then click the Justify option, click the Expand single word option, select Justify from the Last line dropdown list, and click the OK button.

Changing Line Spacing

Writer uses single-spacing on all new documents by default. You can alter the line spacing to change the amount of spacing between lines. For example, if you need to double-space a document to make a report more readable, you change the line spacing to double.

If you alter the line spacing at the beginning of the document, it will apply to all paragraphs within the entire document; you can also set line spacing for a single paragraph (for example, to draw attention to a quoted passage) so you can have special settings for different types of paragraphs.

TO CHANGE LINE SPACING

1   Select the paragraphs or place the insertion point within a particular paragraph where you want to alter the line spacing.

2   Choose Format, Paragraphs to open the Paragraph dialog box.

    You can also right-click and select Paragraph from the shortcut menu. Or, double-click on the gray, numbered portion of the ruler.

3   Click the Indents & Spacing tab if it is not already open and locate the Line spacing area (see Figure 5.2).

4   Click the Line spacing drop-down list and choose from the available options in Figure 5.2 (see Table 5.1).

NOTE   Keep in mind that the amount of space on a line also depends on the type and size of the font. Occasionally you may need fixed line spacing that doesn't change when you change the size of the font. To do so, choose Fixed from the Line spacing drop-down list box, and enter the exact line size in the of text box.

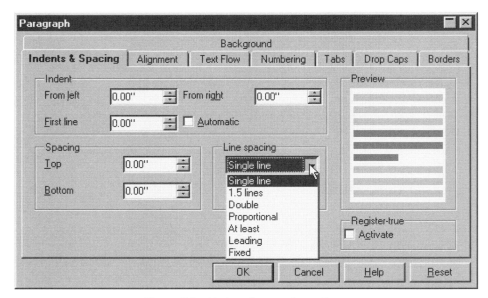

Figure 5.2   Various line spacing options.

Table 5.2 Line Spacing Options

SPACING OPTION	DESCRIPTION
Single line	A small amount of space is added between each line of text so the lines do not run together.
1.5 lines	The line spacing is set to one and a half times that of single line spacing.
Double	The line spacing is set to two times that of single line spacing.
Proportional	Specifies the line spacing between the lines as a percentage of the regular single spacing, which is 100% (for example, double spacing is 200% and 1.5 spacing is 150%).
At Least	Specifies the space between the lines to be at least the value you enter in the of text box; Writer increases the spacing automatically if you are using a larger font and have not supplied a bigger number.
Leading	Adds additional space above each line within the paragraph (specify the amount in the of text box).
Fixed	Sets an exact amount of space (that you specify in the text box) for each line of the paragraph.

Writer also provides keyboard shortcuts for changing the line spacing to the most common single line, 1.5 lines, or double. Press <Ctrl+1> for single-spacing, <Ctrl+2> for double-spacing, and <Ctrl+5> for 1.5 spacing. You can also right-click the text in a paragraph to open the shortcut menu, and then select Single Line, 1.5 Lines, or Double spacing from the Line Spacing submenu.

Changing Paragraph Spacing

Writer allows you to set the amount of vertical space above and below paragraphs. You might want to do this if you need text to fit in a particular way on a page. For example, if your 1-page resume looks a little sparse and you have 1/4 of the page empty at the bottom, perhaps try increasing the line space between the paragraphs on your resume.

To Change Paragraph Spacing

1   Select the paragraphs or place the insertion point within a particular paragraph where you want to alter the spacing.

2   Choose Format, Paragraph to open the Paragraph dialog box.

    You can also right-click and select Paragraph from the shortcut menu. Or, double-click on the gray, numbered portion of the ruler.

3   Click the Indents & Spacing tab and locate the Spacing area.

4   Click the Top and Bottom spin boxes and select the point size you wish to use. For example, to add 0.10" above and below each paragraph, set each spin box to 0.10" and click the OK button.

    Figure 5.3 shows a comparison of three similar paragraphs with 0" Top and 0" Bottom spacing each paragraph and .10" Top and .10" Bottom spacing.

You can also alter the paragraph spacing before you begin typing into a document, which will make it the default spacing.

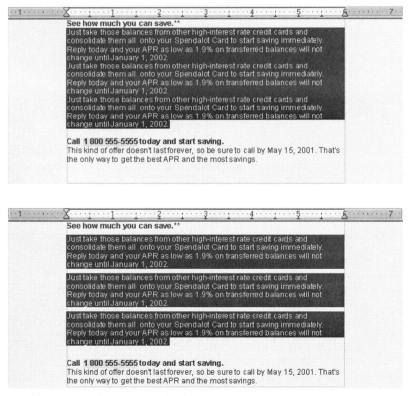

Figure 5.3   Comparison of before and after adding paragraph spacing.

Indenting Text

Simply press the <Tab> key if you need to indent the first line of a paragraph (this moves the cursor 5 spaces to the right, which is Writer's default number of spaces in a tab). If you need to indent all the lines in a paragraph, you should use the Indent feature. Do not simply add a tab at the beginning of each line of your paragraph instead of using the Indent feature; you may have problems later with blank areas in your text when you add more text or rearrange the document.

TO INDENT TEXT WITH THE PARAGRAPH DIALOG BOX

1 Select the paragraphs or place the insertion point within a particular paragraph where you want to indent the text.

2 Choose Format, Paragraph to open the Paragraph dialog box.

You can also right-click and select Paragraph from the shortcut menu. Or, double-click on the gray, numbered portion of the ruler.

3 Click the Indents & Spacing tab and locate the Indent area.

4 Enter the desired indent depending on where you want the indent:

- From left—Enter the distance between the left page margin and the paragraph.
- From right—Enter the distance between the right page margin and the paragraph.
- First line—Enter the distance between the left page margin and the first line of the paragraph. This is sometimes referred to as a *hanging indent* or a *single line indent*. Note that you can also enter negative values if you prefer the first line to start to the left of the paragraph.
- Automatic—If this is selected, whatever you indicate in the From left or From right box will automatically apply to newly created paragraphs (when you press the <Enter> key).

You can enter a From left and From right indent if you want to indent both sides of a paragraph. Perhaps you would like to make a paragraph stand out; for example, if you are quoting a passage.

Figure 5.4 displays the selected indent options in the Preview area.

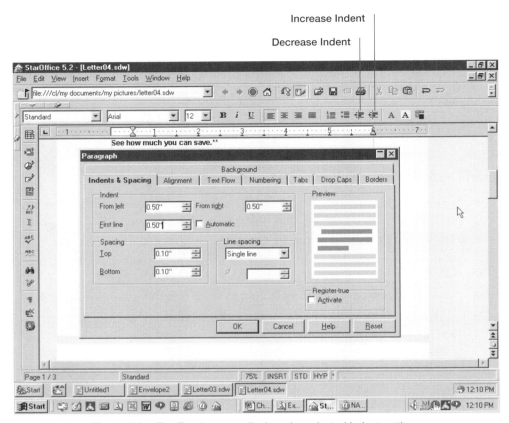

Figure 5.4   The Preview area displays the selected Indent settings.

5   Click the OK button to accept your changes.

NOTE   The Object bar has two Indent buttons (refer to Figure 5.4). The Increase Indent button indents the text (from the left side only) to the next tab setting. Each time you click this button, the text moves one tab setting to the right. The Decrease Indent button moves the text to the left by one tab setting.

To Indent Text with the Ruler

1   Select the paragraphs or place the insertion point within a particular paragraph where you want to indent the text.

2   Click the First line indent marker (refer to Figure 5.5) and drag it to the 2" mark on the ruler. This will indent the first line of the paragraph.

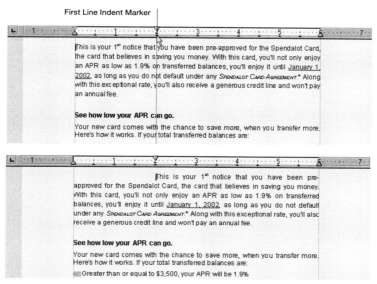

Figure 5.5 Move the First line indent along the ruler (before and after).

3 Click the From left indent marker (refer to Figure 5.6) and drag it to the 1" mark on the ruler. This will indent the entire paragraph.

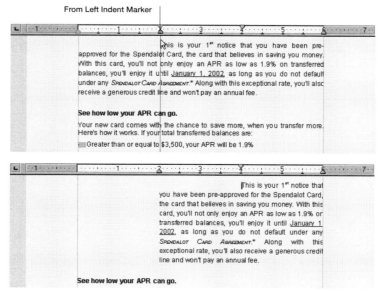

Figure 5.6 Move the From left indent along the ruler (before and after).

Notice that the First line indent marker moved over an additional 2" to the 4" mark because you set it first. To remove the first line indent, simply click the First line indent marker and drag it back to the left, flush with the From left indent marker. Or, you could drag it past the From left indent marker to make the first line begin *before* the rest of the paragraph.

NOTE   If you adjust the First line indent setting without having selected a paragraph first, it will affect any *new* lines (when you press the <Enter> key) that you create immediately after the paragraph where the cursor resides. This is because when you alter the formatting of a paragraph without having specific text selected, the formatting (whether fonts, bolding, line spacing, and so on) becomes the default and will apply to any new paragraphs added directly below the paragraph. If you already have blank lines after the paragraph you are altering (from pressing <Enter>), move the cursor to one of those lines, and the original defaults will still apply to those lines.

Inserting a Line Break

When you have typed enough text to fill a current line, Writer automatically creates a new line for you, and continues the text you enter onto the next line. This is called a *soft line break* (or sometimes a "soft return") because it happens automatically. If you want to control where a line break occurs and force text to the next line, you can manually enter a line break. This is called a *hard line break* (or a "hard return").

A good example of when you would want to do this is to maintain formatting within a paragraph (on a new line), without creating a new paragraph. For example, you would use a soft return when you want two specific sections of text to fall under the same bullet point, instead of two separate bullets.

TO INSERT A LINE BREAK

1   Place the insertion point where you want the line break to occur.

2   Choose Insert, Manual Break.

      The Insert Break dialog box is displayed.

3   Select the Line break option (see Figure 5.7) and click OK.

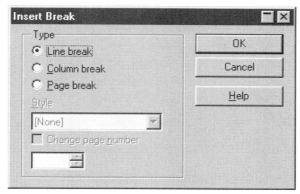

Figure 5.7   Insert a line break.

As an alternative, you can simply press <Shift+Enter> to insert a line break at the point you indicated.

NOTE   If you want to insert a page break, refer to the section "Inserting a Page Break" in Chapter 6, "Formatting Pages."   •

Inserting Tabs

When you are using tabs, you are simply setting a specific place for the paragraph text to align. This is similar to changing the text alignment, except that it is aligned with the tab stop, instead of the margins. Tabs might sound confusing or like too much work, but they can be a real time saver when it comes to changing documents, altering information, and formatting text.

Perhaps you have opened up a document that you worked on in a different word processing application (or perhaps a previous version with different fonts) only to have the text jumbled. This is most likely because they inserted spaces with the <Spacebar> and depending on the font and font size, the actual width that the blank spaces take up will vary.

For example, if you are updating your resume and a portion of it looked like this:

```
May 1992-December 1992          Chicago, IL
End User Consultant - The NutraSweet Company

     · Proposed and implemented an inventory procedure and database for all
computers.

     · Provided training to sales representatives on remote access network
capabilities.

     · Designed transaction forms, training manuals, and customer informa-
tion brochures.
```

But when you opened it in a different application or pasted it into a new document, it might look like this (all jumbled):

```
May 1992–December 1992                          Chicago, IL
    End User Consultant - The NutraSweet Company
                          · Proposed and implemented an inventory
procedure and database for all computers.
                          · Provided training to sales represen-
tatives on remote access network capabilities.
· Designed transaction forms, training manuals, and customer informa-
tion        brochures.
```

Due to the tabs, spaces, and different font sizes, the text appears all jumbled. One way to keep this from happening is to insert specific tab stops instead of pressing the <Tab> key to insert regular tabs or pressing the <Spacebar> numerous times to add blank spaces. Another way to keep text spaced correctly is to use a table, which will be covered in Chapter 9, "Working with Tables." Specifically, refer to the section "Converting Tables and Text."

Instead of trying to detail all the intricacies of resume arrangement, this section works with all the different tab types and how you apply them to text.

To Set Tabs Manually with the Ruler

1   Open a document in which you want to apply tabs.

For our example, add the following text to Letter05 (see Figure 5.8). Make sure you actually press the <Tab> key instead of typing <Tab>:

Your current APR<Tab>12.9%<Tab>15.9%<Tab>21.9%
Transferred<Tab>Your Citibank APR<Tab>Your Savings
$2,000<Tab>2.9%<Tab>$138.00<Tab>$180.00<Tab>$269
$4,000<Tab>1.9%<Tab>$302.00<Tab>$388.00<Tab>$564
$20,000<Tab>1.9%<Tab>$1,050.00<Tab>$1,200.00<Tab>$2,023.00

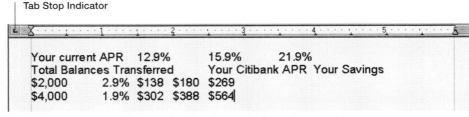

Figure 5.8   Regular text before tabs are added.

2   Place the insertion point somewhere on the first line (perhaps at the beginning, but it doesn't matter).

You can also select multiple lines (paragraphs) to align them simultaneously.

3   Make sure the tab stop indicator is in the right-facing "L" position.

If you click directly on the tab stop indicator, it toggles through the indent options:

- Left—Aligns text and numbers to the left.
- Right—Aligns text and numbers to the right.
- Centered—Centers text and numbers horizontally on the line.
- Decimal—Aligns text to the left; places numbers in line with the decimal point (the decimal point is exactly on the tab stop).

NOTE   The Decimal setting also allows you to specify a different Character in place of the decimal point. For example, if you want to align on an asterisk instead, simply select the Decimal option and type the character in the text box. See the next section, "To Set Tabs with the Paragraph Dialog Box" for more information.

4   Click the mouse pointer on the 3" mark, then click it on the 4" mark, and then on the 5" mark of the white, numbered ruler (see Figure 5.9). Notice that where you originally pressed the <Tab> key in the text is where the tab stop automatically moves the text. If you didn't press the <Tab> key in the text, the text will not move over until you do.

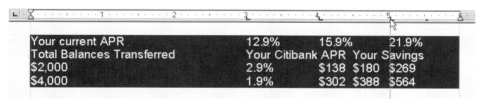

Figure 5.9   The text automatically moves the tabbed text to the tab stop.

You can place the <Tab> directly into the text first, then insert the tab stop; or, insert the tab stop and then press the <Tab> key in the text.

You may have also noticed that the tab stops actually pushed the text on the second line onto another line. To correct this, place the cursor at the beginning of that line and follow the steps in the next section.

To Set Tabs with the Paragraph Dialog Box

The Paragraph dialog box allows you to set tabs with more precision and more control than using the Ruler. But, sometimes using them both in conjunction will make your job a lot easier.

1   Place the cursor at the beginning of the line you want to insert a tab stop.

2   Choose Format, Paragraph, and click the Tabs tab.

    You may notice that any tabs you added manually are displayed in the Position area. Notice also that the tab stops added using the ruler are often not exact (5.02" instead of 5").

3   Select a tab stop on the Paragraph dialog box (for example, Figure 5.10, the 3.99" tab from the previous section).

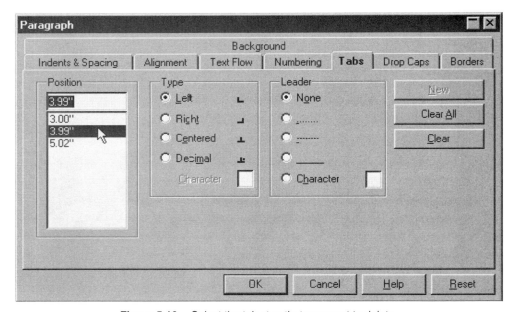

Figure 5.10   Select the tab stop that you want to delete.

4   Click the Clear button.

    This deletes the tab position and leaves the rest of the tabs. If you want to delete them all, you can click the Clear All button instead.

5   Select the Centered type tab option to insert a centered tab.

6   Select the text in the top Position text box and type in the new tab stop location (for example, 3.2)

7   Click the New button to add the new tab stop.

If you want to add a tab stop Leader, choose from the available Leader options:

- None—No leaders (the default).
- Dots—Adds periods leading to the text at the tab stop.
- Dashes—Adds dashes leading to the text at the tab stop.
- Lines—Adds underline leading to the text at the tab stop.
- Character—Adds the specific character you type in the text box, leading to the text at the tab stop.

NOTE   If you didn't delete the 3" Left tab stop, the Centered tab stop wouldn't have affected the text until you added another tab (or it would have defaulted to the very next tab). Of course, Writer only uses as many tabs as you've specified on any given line by pressing the <Tab> key. It disregards others you may have set but not utilized.

8   Select the 5.02" tab stop Position and click the Centered Type option (see Figure 5.11).

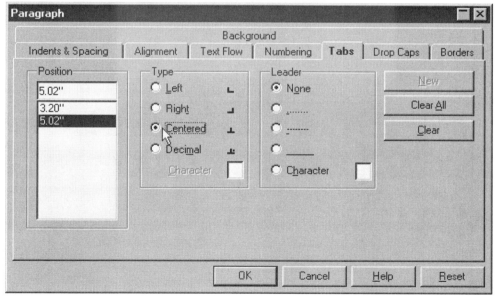

Figure 5.11   Select the tab stop that you want to change.

9   Click the OK button to accept the changes. You will have changed the Left tab to a Centered tab.

TO MODIFY TAB STOPS WITH THE RULER

1   Select the lines of text where you want to insert tabs (see Figure 5.12). This time use the Control key to select multiple, non-continuous lines. This is a really handy feature in StarOffice Writer because you will often find that you need to add tabs to multiple lines that are separated by lines in which you don't want to add tabs.

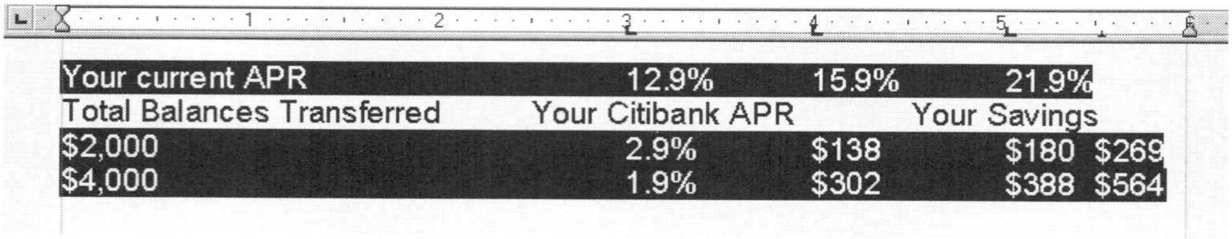

Your current APR		12.9%	15.9%	21.9%
Total Balances Transferred	Your Citibank APR		Your Savings	
$2,000		2.9%	$138	$180 $269
$4,000		1.9%	$302	$388 $564

Figure 5.12   Select the non-continuous lines text in which you want to change tab stops.

2   Click and hold the tab stop indicator at the 4" position, drag it to the right and release the mouse button at the 4.3" mark.

3   Click and hold the tab stop indicator at the 5" position, drag it to the left and release the mouse button at the 4.9" mark.

4   Click at the 5.5" position to add a tab stop.

Your text appears to almost be arranged symmetrically (see Figure 5.13). The only problem is the first line.

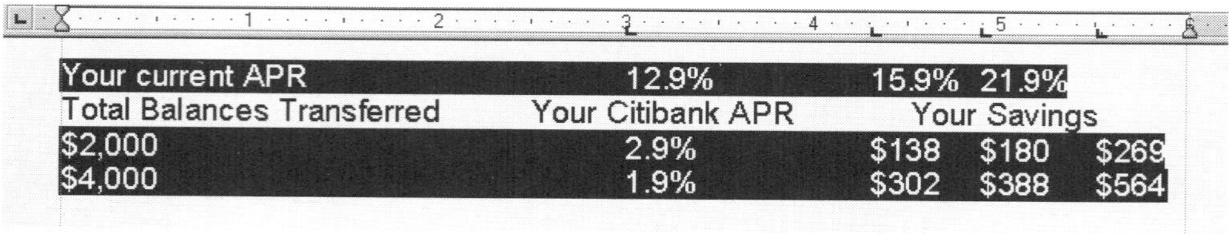

Your current APR		12.9%	15.9% 21.9%	
Total Balances Transferred	Your Citibank APR		Your Savings	
$2,000		2.9%	$138 $180	$269
$4,000		1.9%	$302 $388	$564

Figure 5.13   Modify the tab stops along the ruler.

5   Place the cursor in the first line, then click and drag the 3" tab stop down to delete it from the Ruler.

NOTE   If you select the four lines in which you altered the tab stops, no tab stops will be indicated in the Ruler. This is because they are not all the same. To see the specific tab stops for each of the four lines, you must place the cursor in each line separately.

Adding Paragraph Borders

Borders can be added to many other elements in addition to paragraphs; for example, pages, frames, graphics, tables, and embedded objects (even headers and footers). You will learn about those objects later, but the options when adding borders to regular paragraphs apply to the other types of elements as well.

To Add Paragraph Borders

1   Select the paragraph in which you want to add a border. You can also place the cursor in the specific paragraph or select multiple paragraphs.

2   Choose Format, Paragraph, and click the Borders tab. The available option areas are as follows:

   • Presets—Select from defaults that allow you to choose which edges of the paragraph you wish to border. The selection will display in the Frame area.

   • Frame—You can click directly on the sides of the frame to apply a paragraph border. In addition, you can click the Spacing button to enter the distance you wish the border to be from the text on the Left, Right, Top, and Bottom of the paragraph. With the Synchronize check box checked, whatever number you enter for one side of your border will automatically be used for all other sides. If you want to set separate values for each side, clear the Synchronize check box. Click OK to return to the Borders tab.

   • Line—Choose the Style from the different line weights and types of double lines. You can click the Color drop-down list to select the line color.

   • Shadow style—Select where (or whether) you want a shadow to fall outside your border, how large the shadow should be, and what Color it should be.

3   Click the OK button when finished to see how the paragraph border appears in your document (see Figure 5.14).

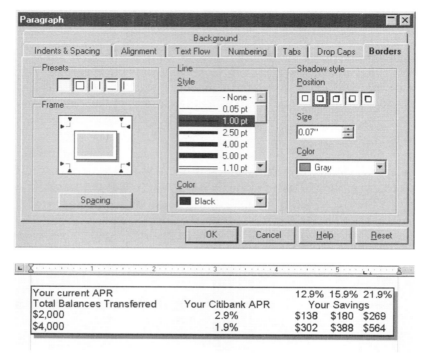

Figure 5.14   Adding borders to paragraphs.

NOTE   To prevent splitting a paragraph's formatting between two pages, you can tell Writer to keep the paragraph lines together (refer to the next section "Altering Paragraph Text Flow").

Adding Paragraph Backgrounds

Backgrounds can be added to paragraphs and many other elements, including pages, frames, graphics, tables, and embedded objects (even headers and footers). You will learn about those objects later, but the options to add backgrounds to regular paragraphs apply to the other types of elements as well.

TO ADD A PARAGRAPH BACKGROUND COLOR

1   Select the paragraph in which you want to add a background color.

2   Choose Format, Paragraph and click the Background tab.

You can also click the Background Color button on the Object bar and select a color from the drop-down list.

3   Choose Color from the As drop-down list and select a Background color (for example, Blue gray).

4   Click OK to accept the changes (see Figure 5.15).

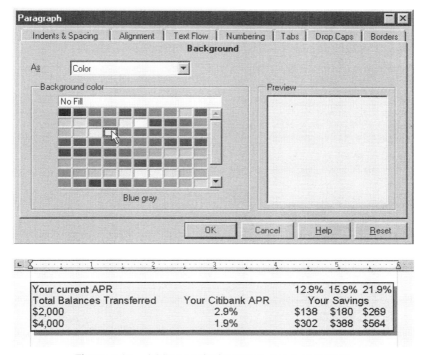

Figure 5.15   Adding a color background to a paragraph.

The entire area of the paragraph as a block will have shading behind it, not only the text. Note that if the text has any highlighting, it will appear in front of the background.

TO ADD A PARAGRAPH BACKGROUND GRAPHIC

1   Select the paragraph in which you want to add a background color.

2   Choose Format, Paragraph and click the Background tab.

3   Choose Graphic from the As drop-down list and click the Browse button to locate the graphic you prefer for the background.

   • Preview—Used to review the background graphic (should be selected by default).

• Type—Choose Position to place the graphic in the paragraph according to the location options; choose Area to place the graphic so that it fills the entire paragraph; choose Tile to fill the paragraph with multiples of the graphic.

4   Click the Browse button to locate the graphic you want to apply as the paragraph background. Select the file and click the Open button.

5   Click the Link option if you want future changes to the graphic to automatically update in your document.

6   Click the OK button to accept the changes (see Figure 5.16).

Notice how you need to be careful about the graphics you choose, as any text in the paragraph may become difficult to read.

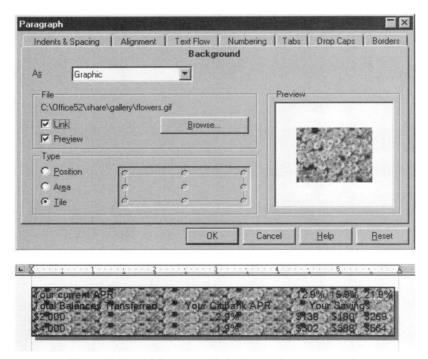

Figure 5.16   Adding a graphic background to a paragraph.

The entire area of the paragraph as a block will have shading behind it, not just the text. In addition, if the text has any highlighting, it will appear in front of the background.

Altering Paragraph Text Flow

Whenever you apply formatting effects to a paragraph, you must think about what will happen if a page break falls in the middle of that paragraph; for example, you may sometimes add enough text to a document to force an automatic page break. If the page break happens in the middle of a paragraph with a border, then each half of the paragraph will be surrounded by a border (on separate pages). This can look awkward and work against the effect you were trying for.

TO ELIMINATE ORPHANS AND WIDOWS

1   Select the paragraph you want to eliminate orphans and/or widows. These terms are defined as follows:

- Orphans are where a single line at the beginning of a paragraph is printed (or displayed) along the bottom of a page.
- Widows are where a single line at the end of a paragraph is printed (or displayed) along the top of a page.

2   Choose Format, Paragraph and click the Text Flow tab (see Figure 5.17).

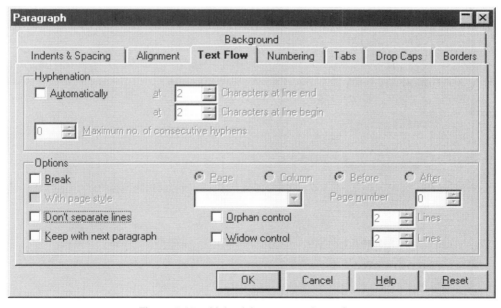

Figure 5.17   Maintaining paragraph text flow.

3   Select the Orphan control checkbox and select the minimum number of lines allowed to eliminate orphans. Select the Widow control checkbox and select the minimum number of lines allowed to eliminate orphans.

4   Click the OK button to accept the changes.

To Keep Multiple Paragraphs Together

1   Select the paragraphs that you want to keep together.

2   Choose Format, Paragraph and click the Text Flow tab.

3   Select the check box Keep with next paragraph and click OK.

Now all the paragraphs (and any included formatting) will stay on the same side of any page break that might occur later when you add lines, text, or other elements.

NOTE   Select the Don't separate lines option if you insert a break and want to shift the entire paragraph to the next page or column.

Setting Paragraph Hyphenation

You can hyphenate words or phrases automatically or manually. In addition, you can use optional hyphens to control a break at the end of a line and nonbreaking hyphens to prevent a hyphen breaking at the end of a line. Refer also to the section "Checking a Document for Hyphenation" in Chapter 3.

To Set Paragraph Hyphenation

1   Select the entire paragraph or place the cursor in the paragraph in which you want to set hyphenation options.

You can also apply hyphenation effects to the entire document if you set the options before you begin entering text into the document.

2   Choose Format, Paragraph and click the Text Flow tab.

3   Select the Automatically option in the Hyphenation area.

This will allow you to establish the following options:

• Characters at line end—The number of characters to remain at the end of the line after hyphenating. Figure 5.18 shows an example of hyphenation with Characters at line end set to 4.

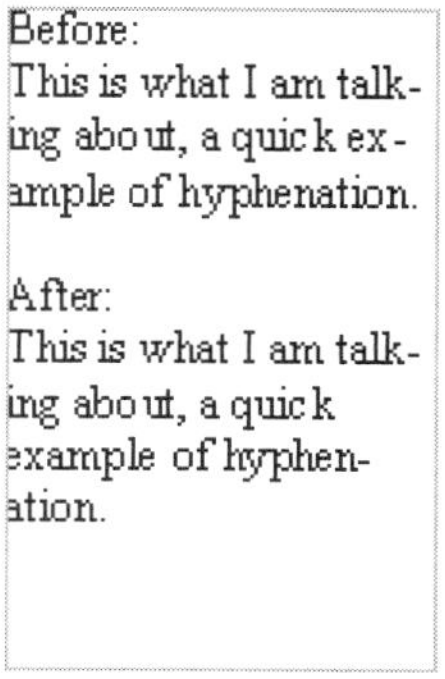

Before:
This is what I am talk-
ing about, a quick ex-
ample of hyphenation.

After:
This is what I am talk-
ing about, a quick
example of hyphen-
ation.

Figure 5.18   Characters at line end set to 4.

• Characters at line begin—The number of characters to remain at the beginning of the line that follows the hyphenation. Figure 5.19 shows an example of hyphenation with Characters at line begin set to 4 and Characters at line end set to 2.

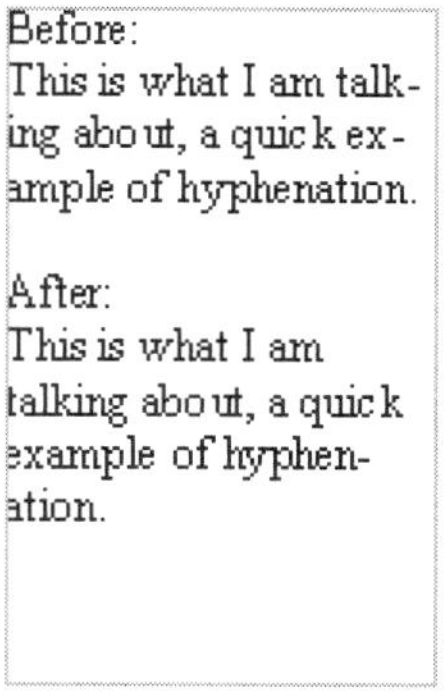

Before:
This is what I am talk-
ing about, a quick ex-
ample of hyphenation.

After:
This is what I am
talking about, a quick
example of hyphen-
ation.

Figure 5.19   Characters at line begin set to 4, then back to 2.

• Maximum number of consecutive hyphens—The number of lines that can be hyphenated consecutively. For example, as shown in Figure 5.20, if you set the maximum number to 1, you cannot have more than one consecutive line with hyphenation applied at the end.

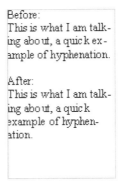

Before:
This is what I am talking about, a quick example of hyphenation.

After:
This is what I am talking about, a quick example of hyphenation.

Figure 5.20   Maximum number of consecutive hyphens set to 1.

4   Click the OK button.

Now the hyphenation setting will apply to the paragraph.

Inserting Line Numbering

Line numbers can be applied to the entire document or only a particular portion. Line numbering is convenient when writing a script or legal document in which you must refer to specific lines in a document.

TO INSERT LINE NUMBERS

1   Choose Tools, Line Numbering to open the Line Numbering dialog box.

2   Click the Show numbering checkbox to activate the View, Separator, and Count options (see Figure 5.21).

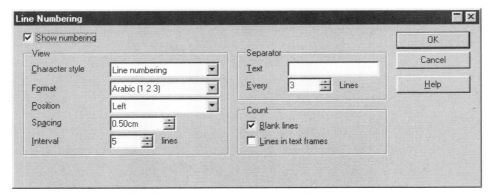

Figure 5.21   The Line Numbering tab on the Paragraph dialog box.

3   Choose from the available options:

- •Character style—You would most likely leave this set to the default Line numbering style, but you can select another style (for example, if you have already created a specific character style in the document).
- •Format—Choose the number format between arabic, roman numerals, or letters.
- •Position—Set where you want the line numbering to appear in relation to the text. Left or right of the text border; or on the inner or outer side of the page, depending on the even or uneven page numbering.
- •Spacing—Set the distance between the text and the line numbering.
- •Interval—Set how often a line number is displayed. The default setting places a line number on every fifth line; if you want a line number on every line, choose 1.
- •Text—Enter a character that will display as a line number character. This can be in conjunction with the line numbering, but will only display if the line numbers Interval is set to greater than 1.
- •Every x Lines—Set how often a text-based line number is displayed.
- •Blank lines—Select if you want blank lines to be counted as individual lines.
- •Lines in text frames—Select this option if you have inserted a text frame into your document and you prefer the textual lines to be numbered in the frame as well.

4   Click the OK button to accept the changes.

Applying Drop Caps

Writer allows you to format text so that it uses a large initial capital letter at the beginning of a paragraph. This design feature is commonly used at the beginning of magazine and newsletter articles.

TO APPLY DROP CAPS

1   Choose Format, Paragraph, and click the Drop Caps tab.
2   Select the Show drop caps setting (see Figure 5.22).

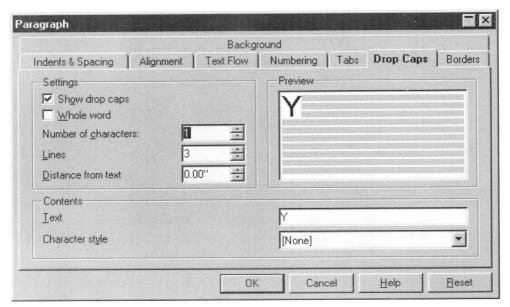

Figure 5.22   The Drop Caps tab on the Paragraph dialog box.

This will increase the size of the first letter at the beginning of the paragraph and activate the following available options:

- •Whole word—Increases the size of the entire first word at the beginning of the paragraph.
- •Number of characters—Increases the size of the specific number of characters that you set.
- •Lines—Sets the size of the drop cap to the height of a specific number of lines.
- •Distance from text—Sets the distance that the drop cap displays to the left of the text.
- •Text—Specifies alternative text for the drop cap.
- •Character style—Sets a predefined text style.

3   Click the OK button to accept the changes.

Formatting Pages

Changing Margins

The margin settings determine how much space there is between the text and the edge of the document. You can specify left, right, top, and bottom margin settings for any document. Writer has default margins of 1" on the top and bottom, and 1.25" on the left and right sides.

NOTE   To change the default margins setting when you create a new text document, you must create and assign a new default template. Refer to the section "Changing the Standard Template," in Chapter 7, "Working with Styles and Templates."

To Change Margins

1   Open a document in which you wish to change the margins.

2   Choose Format, Page, and click the Page tab (if it isn't already displayed).

  This tab features a Preview area (see Figure 6.1) so that you can review your changes before they are applied to the document.

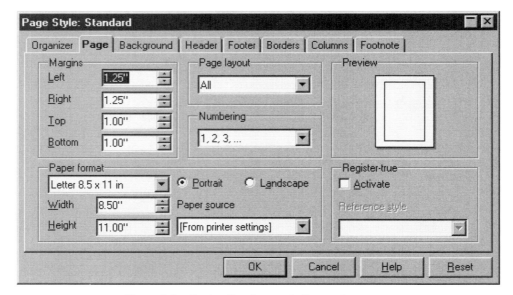

Figure 6.1   Review the changes in the preview area.

3   Type an alternate number into the in the Left text box in the Margins area; for example, 1".

You don't need to type in the (") inch character, simply type in the number or click on the Up/Down spin boxes to move through the numbers by .02.

4 Press the <Tab> key (or click the mouse pointer in the Right text box and select the text) and type "1" in the Right text box.

5 Press the <Tab> key again, which moves you down to the Top text box and selects the contents.

6 Click the OK button.

The new margins are applied to the document, and Writer automatically repaginates the text accordingly.

NOTE If your document requires a special binding (such as spiral, three-ring, or "perfect binding" for professionally printed documents) the left margin may require extra space to allow for the part of the page that is hidden in the binding.

TO CHANGE THE PAGE LAYOUT

1 Open a document in which you want to change the page layout.

2 Choose Format, Page, and click the Page tab (if it isn't already displayed).

3 Click the Page layout drop-down list.

4 Choose from the following available options:
   - All—All pages of the document will utilize the current margin settings.
   - Mirrored—Documents that are to be stapled, bound, or printed on both sides will have the same Inner and Outer Margins on the left page and right page.
   - Right—Margin settings are applied only to the Right pages of a document (for example, if the first page of a book chapter must begin on a right page).
   - Left—Margin settings are applied only to the Left pages of a document (for example, if the last page of a book chapter must end on a left page).

5 Click the OK button to apply your changes.

NOTE You can also change the left and right margin settings using the ruler. Move the mouse pointer over the area on the ruler where the gray becomes white (this might be directly between the Left and First line indent markers). When the pointer changes to a two-headed arrow, click the left mouse button and drag the left margin (or the right margin) to the desired size. This change will affect the entire document, unless you have inserted separate sections into your document. In this case, you will need to either select the entire document or alter the margin settings in each separate section. Refer to the section "Working with Sections Breaks" later in the chapter.

Altering Page Orientation

Page orientation refers to the direction you are printing your document. *Portrait* orientation prints the text with the narrow end of the paper at the top (for example 8.5" X 11"). *Landscape* orientation prints the text with the wide end of the paper at the top (for example 11" X 8.5"). Most documents are printed as portrait, which is the default, but you may prefer to use landscape orientation if you have a wide table or a long amount of text that runs across the page.

To Alter Page Orientation

1   Open a document in which you want to change the page orientation.

2   Choose Format, Page, and click the Page tab (if it isn't already displayed).

3   Click the Landscape option in the Paper format area. The document's Width and Height settings are swapped.

    The Preview area displays your change before it is applied to the document.

4   Click the OK button to apply your changes.

Adding Page Borders

Borders can be added to pages and many other elements (paragraph borders were covered in Chapter 5). Using page borders can help give your documents a clean look and published feel.

To Add Page Borders

1   Place the cursor somewhere on the page in which you want to add a border. You may also select multiple pages.

2   Choose Format, Page, and click the Borders tab. The available option areas on the Page Style dialog box are as follows:

    • Presets—Select from defaults that allow you to choose which edges of the page you wish to border. The selection will display in the Frame area.
    • Frame—Click directly on the sides of the frame to apply a page border. In addition, you can click the Spacing button to enter the distance you prefer the border to be from the text on the Left, Right, Top, and Bottom of the page. With the Synchronize check box checked, whatever number you enter for one side of your border will automatically be used for all other sides. If you want to set separate values for each side, clear the Synchronize check box. Click OK to return to the Borders tab.

- Line—Choose the Style from the different line weights and types of double lines. You can click the Color drop-down list to select the line color.
- Shadow style—Select where (or whether) you want a shadow to fall outside your border, how large the shadow should be, and what Color it should be.

3   Click the OK button when finished, to see what the page border looks like in your document (see Figure 6.2). If you decrease the Zoom area, you can see the entire page's border.

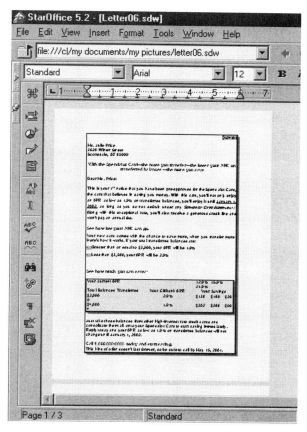

Figure 6.2   Adding borders to pages.

Adding Page Backgrounds

Backgrounds can be added to pages and many other elements in your document (paragraph backgrounds were covered in Chapter 5). This can help give your documents a distinctive look and feel.

TO ADD A PAGE BACKGROUND COLOR

1   Open the document in which you want to add a background color.

2   Choose Format, Page and click the Background tab.

    You can also click the Background Color button on the Object bar and select a color from the drop-down list.

3   Choose Color from the As drop-down list and select a Background color (for example, Light gray).

4   Click OK to accept the changes (see Figure 6.3).

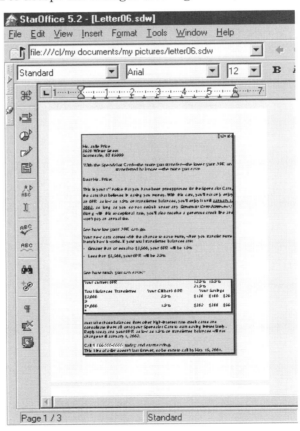

Figure 6.3   Adding a color background to a page.

The entire area of the page as a block will have shading behind it, not just the text. Note that if the text has any highlighting, it will appear in front of the background.

To Add a Page Background Graphic

1 Open the document in which you want to add a background color.

2 Choose Format, Page and click the Background tab.

3 Choose Graphic from the As drop-down list and click the Browse button to locate the graphic you desire for the background.

   • Preview—Used to review the background graphic (should be selected by default).
   • Type—Choose Position to place the graphic on the page according to the location options; choose Area to place the graphic so that it fills the entire page; choose Tile to fill the page with multiples of the graphic.

4 Click the Browse button to locate the graphic you want to apply as the page background. Select the file and click the Open button.

5 Click the Link option if you want future changes to the graphic to automatically update in your document.

6 Click the OK button to accept the changes (see Figure 6.4).

Notice how you need to be careful about the graphics you choose, as any text on the page may become difficult to read.

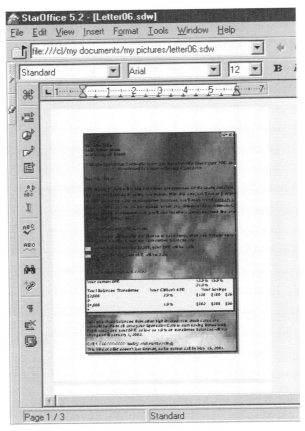

Figure 6.4   Adding a graphic background to a page.

The entire area of the page as a block will have shading behind it, not just the text. In addition, if the text has any highlighting, it will appear in front of the background.

Inserting a Page Break

Writer automatically creates a new page whenever you have typed more text than can fit on your current page with your current settings. Additional text and elements continue onto the next page. This type of break in the page is called a *soft page break* because it happens automatically. If you want to force text to the next page, you can manually enter a page break. This is called a *hard page break*.

TO INSERT A PAGE BREAK

1   Place the insertion point where you want the page break to occur.

2   Choose Insert, Manual Break to open the Insert Break dialog box.

3   Select the Page break option (the default) and click OK.

In addition, you can simply press <Ctrl+Enter> to insert a page break at the location of the cursor.

TO INDICATE A TEXT FLOW BREAK

1   Place the cursor at the location in your document where you want to control the text flow.

You can control the flow of text in a paragraph before or after a page break with text flow options (perhaps where you know you prefer a new page to begin automatically). If you will be adding more text before the break, setting the text flow options can save you from having to reformat your pages.

2   Choose Format, Paragraph, and click on the Text Flow tab.

3   Check the Break option to insert a page or column break before or after the current paragraph.

4   Click the Page option to insert a page break for the paragraph break.

5   Select from the following options:

•Before—To insert a page or column break before the selected paragraph.

•After—To insert a page or column break after the selected paragraph.

6   Click the OK button.

Designating Columns Before Entering Text

To enter text into columns, you must tell Writer how many columns you prefer. By default, Writer separates the columns so that each column is the same width and all columns have the same amount of space separating them. When you enter text, the text fills the first column to the bottom of the page and then moves to the top of the second column.

NOTE   If you want columns of text to stay in the same place on the page and *not* flow as you edit, you might also consider using tables (refer to Chapter 9).

To Designate Columns

1   Open a new text document. Save the blank document.

2   Choose Format, Columns to open the Columns dialog box.

3   Select the number of columns in the Amount box or from the five example defaults.

    The default options are one column, two columns, or three columns spaced evenly, or even two columns with the largest column residing on the left or right of the page. Whatever choice you make, Writer will place the same amount of white space between each column. Choose three columns for now.

4   If you want the default column width options, leave the AutoWidth checkbox selected. If you prefer to alter the widths of your columns, clear it, and make your choices from the following options:

    • Width—Increase or decrease the area of each columns' text individually.
    • Spacing—Increase or decrease the space between each column of text individually.

    Keep your eye on the Preview area to see how your column options will appear on the page.

5   Click the Line drop-down list and select the point size of the line between the columns. Retain the default None if you don't desire column (if so, skip to Step 8).

6   Click the Height spin box arrows (or simply type in the percentage) for the length of the line separating the columns, as measured by percentage of the full size of the page from top to bottom margin.

7   Click the Position drop-down list to choose whether you want the Line at the Top, Bottom, or Centered between the columns (see Figure 6.5).

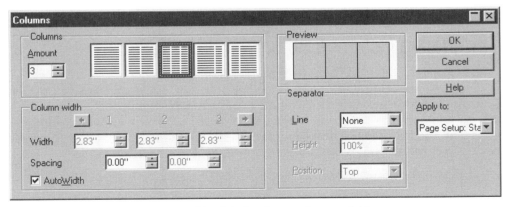

Figure 6.5   The default column options available.

8   Click the OK button to apply the changes and return to your document.

The columns will be surrounded by gray boxes (for visual purposes only—these boxes will not print by default). Any column lines will appear (see Figure 6.6) and *will* print.

Notice that the Ruler is now divided into column areas; between each section is a column marker. The markers show the space between the columns. You can begin typing the text into your columns.

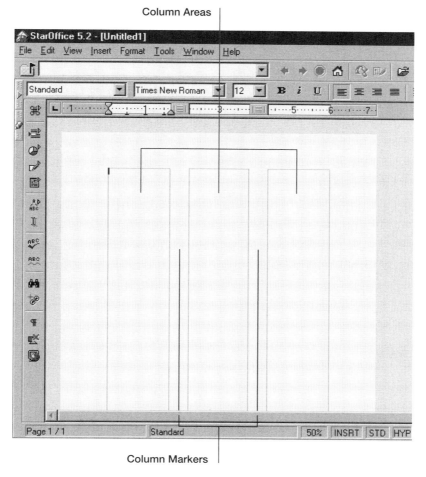

Figure 6.6   Column options applied to the new text document.

Assigning Columns to Previously Typed Text

If you aren't sure how many columns you need in your document until you have typed the text in your document, you can assign columns afterward.

TO ASSIGN COLUMNS TO PREVIOUSLY TYPED TEXT

1   Open a document that doesn't already have columns.

The cursor can be anywhere in the document, unless the document has sections. If it does, you need to place the cursor in the section that you want to have columns. For more information on sections and columns, see the section "Working with Sections."

2   Choose Format, Columns to open the Columns dialog box.

3   Select the number of columns in the Amount box, or choose from the five example defaults.

The default options are one column, two columns, or three columns spaced evenly, or even two columns with the largest column residing on the left or right of the page. Whatever choice you make, Writer will place the same amount of white space between each column. For example, choose two columns with .5" Spacing between the columns.

4   Click the OK button and your text will flow into the columns (see Figure 6.7). You can always go back into the Columns dialog box and increase or decrease the number of columns.

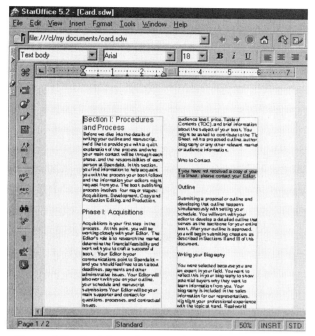

Figure 6.7 Applying columns to the text in a document.

The columns will be surrounded by gray boxes (for visual purposes only—these boxes will not print by default). Any column lines will appear and *will* print.

Notice that the Ruler is now divided into column areas; between each section is a column marker. The markers show the space between the columns.

Resizing Existing Columns

If you are working in two columns and you prefer them to be of unequal width, you can use Writer's preset left and right column options. If you need to change your columns to a specific length, you can resize them with the Columns dialog box or by using the Ruler (each will be described in the following section).

To Resize Columns

1   Choose Format, Columns to open the Columns dialog box.

2   Click the AutoWidth option to allow you to alter the column text width manually.

3   Click the Width boxes for each column (indicated by the numbers above each box) or simply type in the new width size in inches.

    If you have more than three columns, you will need to click the right and left arrow keys to move between the column width settings (see Figure 6.8).

Figure 6.8   Resizing columns in the document.

4   Click the OK button and your columns will update automatically and the text will adjust.

    Notice that the Ruler is now divided into column areas; between each section is a column marker. The markers show the space between the columns.

5   Move the mouse pointer over a column marker.

    • When the pointer changes, as shown in Figure 6.9, you can alter the size of the text area in the columns to the left and right of the marker (the Width box on the Columns dialog box).

Width Pointer

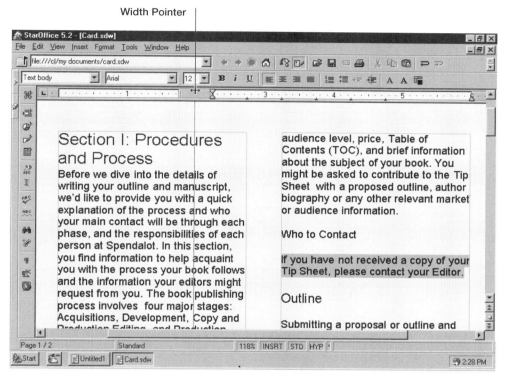

Figure 6.9 Resizing the column text area in the document.

- When the pointer changes, as shown in Figure 6.10, you can alter the amount of space between the columns (the Spacing box on the Columns dialog box).

Spacing Pointer

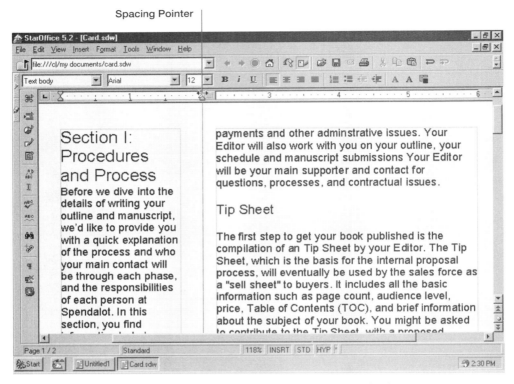

Figure 6.10   Resizing the space between the columns in the document.

NOTE   You cannot use the Undo command or button to undo the resizing, addition, or deletion of a column. You must go in and change the settings back manually. In addition, you can assign tabs to text in columns as in the section "Inserting Tabs" in Chapter 5.

Working with Sections

You can designate sections within a document so that you can maintain different display options. For example, you could have three different sections in your document: one that displayed text in two columns, one that had text in one column with a background graphic, and one that had text-specific endnotes at the end of the section (instead of the end of the page or end of the document). You can assign these section options while you are creating the new section, or apply them after you have created the section.

To Insert a Section

1 Place the cursor at the location you want to insert a section.

2 Choose Insert, Section to open the Insert Section dialog box.

3 Select the Section tab (see Figure 6.11).

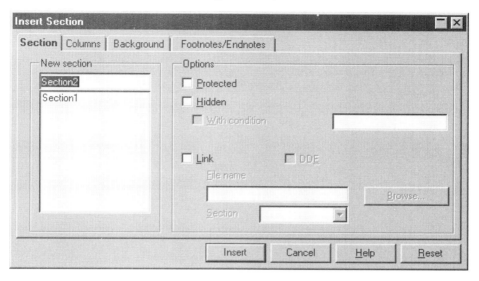

Figure 6.11   The Insert Section dialog box.

4 Type in a name for the New section; otherwise the sections will be assigned a Section number according to the order of insertion into the document (not necessarily where the sections fall in the document).

5 Choose from the Options that you can apply to the specific section:

•Protected—Select this option to keep the section from being modified or edited.

NOTE   If someone wanted to make modifications to a section in which the Protected option was enabled, they could essentially open the Edit Sections dialog box and deselect the Protected option. To make sure a section modification won't happen, you can select the Password protection checkbox, which will require a correct password to edit a particular section.

•Hidden—Select this option to hide specific sections within a document.
•Link—Select this option to link your section to a section in another document.

You can also choose the Column, Background, and Footnote/Endnote tabs to assign these options to only that section. The Column tab was described in the section "Inserting a Column Section." Backgrounds for sections behave the same as backgrounds for pages (except they apply only to the section); backgrounds were covered in the section "Adding Page Backgrounds." Footnotes and Endnotes are covered in the section "Inserting Footnotes and Endnotes" in Chapter 11, "Working with Long Document Features."

6   Click the Insert button to insert the section in the document.

Notice that the section has a line above and below it to let you know there is a section (see Figure 6.12). Also, when you place the cursor in the section, the name of the section appears in the right-most area of the Writer status bar.

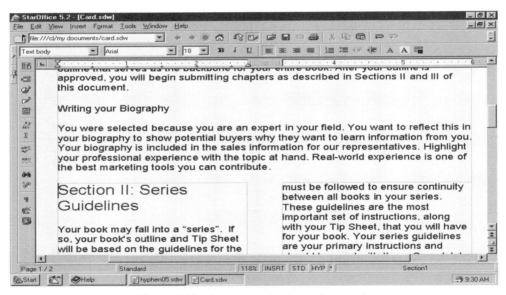

Figure 6.12   Insert a section into a document.

To Apply Columns to a Section

If you already have the section created, place the cursor within the section, choose Format, Sections, and click the Options button on the Edit Sections dialog box. If you want to create a new section and apply columns, follow steps 1–5 in the section "To Insert a Section" and then continue with these steps:

1   Click the Columns tab.

2   Select the number of columns in the Amount box, or choose from the five example defaults. Refer to the earlier sections dealing with columns if you need help with these options.

3   Click the OK button and your text will flow into the columns (see Figure 6.13).

NOTE   You can always go back into the Columns dialog box (choose Format, Columns or choose Format, Sections, Columns tab) and increase or decrease the number of columns, but the section will remain until you delete it (refer to the section "To Edit a Section").

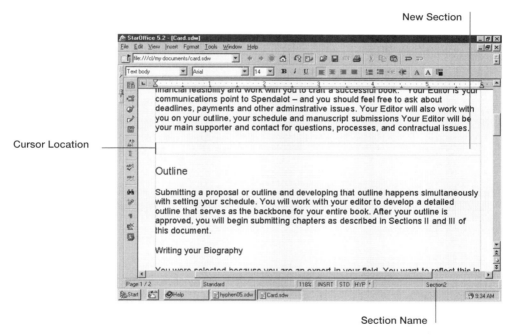

Figure 6.13   Insert a column into a specific section of a document.

TO APPLY A BACKGROUND TO A SECTION

If you already have the section created, place the cursor within the section, choose Format, Sections, and click the Options button on the Edit Sections dialog box. If you want to create a new section and apply a background, follow steps 1–5 in the section, "To Insert a Section" and then continue with these steps:

1   Click the Background tab.

2   Choose whether you want a Color or Graphic from the As drop-down list. Refer to the earlier section "Adding Page Backgrounds" if you need help with these options.

3   Click OK to accept the changes. The entire area of the section as a block will have the color or graphic behind it, not just the text. Note that if the text has any highlighting, it will appear in front of the background.

TO APPLY FOOTNOTES OR ENDNOTES TO A SECTION

If you already have the section created, place the cursor within the section, choose Format, Sections, and click the Options button on the Edit Sections dialog box. If you want to create a new section and apply footnotes and endnotes, follow steps 1–5 in the section, "To Insert a Section" and then continue with these steps:

1   Click the Footnotes/Endnotes tab.

2   Choose whether you want any Footnotes to Collect at end of text or any Endnotes to Collect at end of section. Perhaps you want your endnotes to stay with the particular section instead of at the bottom of the page (the default for footnotes) or end of the document (the default for endnotes).

3   Select whether you want to Restart numbering for the footnotes or endnotes, or you can always choose your Own format from the drop-down list boxes.

4   Click OK to accept the changes.

TO EDIT A SECTION

1   Place the cursor within the section you want to edit.

2   Choose Format, Sections to open the Edit Sections dialog box (see Figure 6.14).

     This menu option will be available only if you have manually added one or more sections to your document; otherwise, you will need to insert a section and apply your options there.

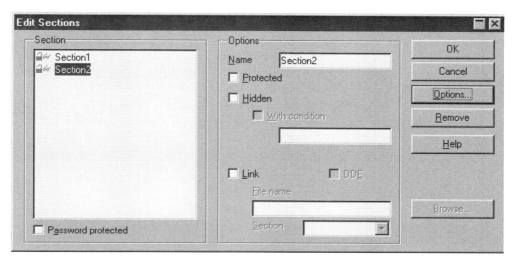

Figure 6.14   Change section options in a document.

3   Click the name of the section in the Section area or type the name directly into the Options Name field. You can rename the section here as well, if you choose.

4   Click the Options button to open the Options dialog box with the Columns, Background, and Footnotes/Endnotes tabs. Make the edits in this dialog box and click the OK button when finished.

5   Choose another section to edit, if necessary, and then click the OK button on the Edit Sections dialog box. This will apply the changes and return to your document.

To Delete a Section

1   Place the cursor within the section you want to delete.

     You don't need to do this, but it will highlight the specific section name when you open the Edit Sections dialog box.

2   Choose Format, Sections to open the Edit Sections dialog box.

3   Click on the name of the section if it is not already selected, and click the Remove button (see Figure 6.14).

This is the best way to delete a section.

> **NOTE**   You can also delete the break directly in the document. I would not advise doing it this way because the formatting can get very convoluted. Place the cursor at the last character space on the line above the section line, then press the <Delete> key; the first paragraph in the below section will become a part of the section above. Place the cursor at the first character space on the line below the section line, then press the <Backspace> key; the last paragraph in the above section will become a part of the section below.

Working with Styles and Templates

Applying Styles

Whenever you create a new text document, the Standard style document (for example, 1" and 1.25" margins for Page styles), text (for example, Times New Roman 12 for Character styles), and paragraphs (for example, single space for Paragraph styles) appear by default in Writer. You can apply all kinds of formatting to your documents; refer to Chapters 4, 5, and 6. Another option to apply formatting is to use Writer styles or apply styles that you create.

Hard formatting is when you apply formats like font, colors, backgrounds, and others directly to the text in your document. Soft formatting is when you apply formats to the text using styles. One of the advantages of applying *soft formatting* styles to your text is that you can alter the style, which will alter the text throughout a document. For example, if you create a document where all the main headings were in italics, but later print the document and don't like the appearance of the italic formatting, instead of going through each heading in the document and selecting the text and removing the italics, you can alter the main heading style once, which will alter all the main headings throughout the document.

TO APPLY STYLES (SOFT FORMATTING)

1   Select the text you wish to style.

2   Choose Format, Stylist to open the Stylist (if it isn't already visible). You can also press <F11> to make the Stylist appear.

    The available styles are listed automatically according to the Style button that is selected (see Figure 7.1).

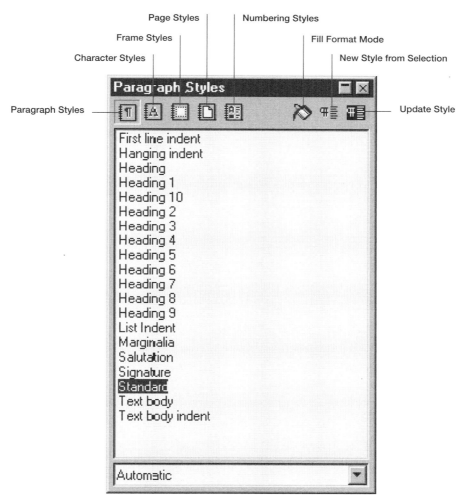

Figure 7.1   The Stylist lists the available styles you may apply.

3   Click the appropriate Style button on the Stylist to choose from the following types of styles:

- Paragraph Styles—To format entire paragraphs; for example, the spacing between lines in a paragraph.
- Character Styles—To format individual characters, words, or sentences; for example, applying different fonts.
- Frame Styles—To format graphic and text frames; for example, frame size and wrapping.
- Page Styles—To format the structure of a page; for example, headers and footers.

• Numbering Styles—To define special settings for bulleted or numbered text.

For now, simply use the default Paragraph Styles.

4   Double-click on the paragraph style from the list (for example, Heading 1).

This will apply the style to the text you have selected.

NOTE   Each time you apply a style to text in your document, that style will be available for further use in the Apply Style drop-down list box to the left of the Font list box on the Object bar. Simply place the cursor in the paragraph for which you want to apply a style, and select the style from the Apply Style drop-down list on the Object bar.

TO APPLY A STYLE MULTIPLE TIMES

1   Choose Format, Stylist to open the Stylist (if it isn't already visible). You can also press <F11> to make the Stylist appear.

2   Click on the Style button and the style name from the list.

3   Click the Fill Format Mode button on the Stylist.

The mouse pointer will change into a pouring paint can.

4   Click on each paragraph in which you want that style applied.

When finished applying the style, click the Fill Format Mode button again to deactivate it.

NOTE   If you have made hard formatting changes to a paragraph (or other style option) without the help of the Stylist, and prefer the paragraph to quickly return to the default style, choose Format, Default.

Creating Your Own Styles

Instead of limiting yourself to default Writer styles, you can create your own; later you can copy them to the Standard styles template or copy them to other documents (refer to the section "Copying Styles").

TO CREATE YOUR OWN STYLES

1   Select some text and apply the text and paragraph formats you would like your style to contain, by using the Object toolbar.

For example, Arial, 20, Bold, and Centered.

2   Choose Format, Stylist to open the Stylist (if it isn't already visible). You can also press <F11> to make the Stylist appear.

3   Click the appropriate style button on the Stylist to view the current styles; you can create any of the following:

•Paragraph Styles—To format entire paragraphs.
•Character Styles—To format individual characters, words, or sentences.
•Frame Styles—To format graphic and text frames.
•Page Styles—To format the structure of a page.
•Numbering Styles—To define special settings for bulleted or numbered text.

In this example, click the Paragraph Styles button (if it isn't already selected by default). If you want to create one of the other types of styles, format the character, frame, page, or numbering as you like and click the appropriate Style button.

4   Click the New Style from Selection button on the Stylist, which will open the Create Style dialog box.

5   Type the name you would like to give the style and click the OK button (see Figure 7.2).

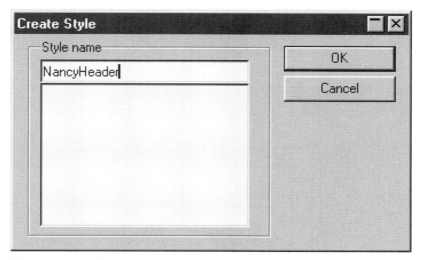

Figure 7.2   The Create Style dialog box allows you to name the styles you create.

Now, any time you wish to apply this style to your current document, it will be available on the Stylist within this document.

> **NOTE**   If you have already named a style and want to give the same style different attributes, repeat steps 1 through 3 and in Step 4, select the same Style name listed and click the OK button. You will be asked if you indeed intend to overwrite the previous style; click Yes if you want to overwrite the style or No if you decide you want to keep the previous style. Keep in mind that you cannot rename a default Writer style (for example, Standard) in this dialog box; to do so, you must modify the default Writer style (refer to the next section).

Modifying Styles

After you have created a style of your own, you can always modify the style. In addition, you can also modify the default Writer styles so that you may work more efficiently with them.

Use the Style Catalog to organize and edit all existing styles and templates. You can also create new styles or modify existing ones, and organize the styles used in the *active* document. But, you must open and close the Style Catalog each time you want to use it. The Stylist, by comparison, can remain open while you work in your document.

TO MODIFY STYLES WITH THE STYLIST

1   Choose Format, Stylist to open the Stylist (if it isn't already visible). You can also press <F11> to make the Stylist appear.

2   Click on the Style button and the style name from the list.

3   Right-click the style and select Modify from the shortcut menu.

    Notice that you can also choose the Delete command to delete a style; but you can only delete a style you have created, not a default StarOffice Writer style.

4   Select your changes from the various style tabs (see Figure 7.3) and click the OK button when finished.

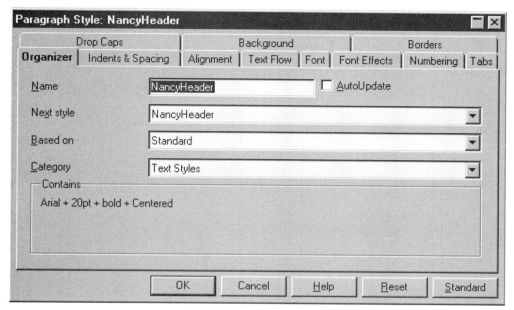

Figure 7.3   Modify the style using the various paragraph style tabs.

NOTE   You can also right-click on a style name in the Stylist and select an option from the shortcut list. You can click New to create a new style (based on the style you right-clicked upon), click Modify to alter the selected style, or Delete to remove the selected style from the Stylist.

TO MODIFY STYLES WITH THE STYLE CATALOG

1   Choose Format, Styles, Catalog to open the Style Catalog dialog box (see Figure 7.4). You can also press <Ctrl+Y>.

Notice that you can also delete new styles or create new styles from this dialog box as well (you cannot, however, delete default Writer styles).

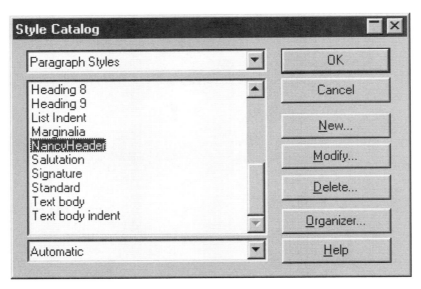

Figure 7.4   The Style Catalog dialog box allows you to modify the styles.

2   Click the Style group from the drop-down list to view the current styles and click on the style name. In this example, choose Paragraph Styles (if it isn't already selected by default).

3   Click the Modify button to open the specific Style dialog box.

    If you apply a setting you don't want, click the Reset button to start over again.

4   Select your changes from the various style tabs and click the OK button when finished.

5   Click the OK button on the Style Catalog dialog box to accept the changes.

    All the text in your document that contains the modified style will automatically update.

TO MODIFY STYLES DIRECTLY IN YOUR DOCUMENT

1   Select the paragraph (or characters, numbering, page, or frame) that contains the style you want to modify. For example, a Standard style paragraph.

2   Make the style changes to the paragraph using the Object bar or Paragraph dialog box (by choosing Format, Paragraph).

If you are modifying a different style—such as character, numbering, page, or frame—make the changes appropriately.

3   Choose Format, Stylist to open the Stylist (if it isn't already visible). You can also press <F11> to make the Stylist appear.

4   Click the Update Style button on the Stylist and all the text in your document that contains the modified style will automatically update.

TO RETURN WRITER STYLES TO THEIR DEFAULT

1   Choose Format, Styles, Catalog to open the Style Catalog dialog box. You can also press <Ctrl+Y>.

2   Click the Style group from the drop-down list to view the current styles and click on the style name. In this example, choose Paragraph Styles (if it isn't already selected by default).

3   Click the Modify button to open the specific Style dialog box.

4   Select the various style tabs that have the formatting you want to set back to the default style settings and click the Standard button on each to return to the default settings.

> **NOTE**   It is unfortunate that you must choose the Standard button on each and every tab that you want to return to the default setting. Another way to get around this would be to copy the default style from another new text document based on the Standard settings. Refer to the next section on, "Copying Styles" if you would rather do this.

5   Click the OK button on the Style Catalog dialog box to accept the changes.

All the text in your document that contains the modified style will automatically update.

Copying Styles

Some styles that you create are useful in only one document, while other styles you may prefer to use in many documents. Suppose that you want to create a specially formatted text heading in other documents that you create. Instead of re-creating this Paragraph style for each new document, you can copy the style to the default Standard template (Standard.vor), where it is available in other documents that you create. Or, you can copy the styles from the Standard template into another document. If you want to copy styles from one document to another, refer to the section "Transferring Styles to the Current Document." For more information on working with the Standard template, see the section "Changing the Standard Template."

TO COPY STYLES TO OTHER DOCUMENTS

1   Open the document into which you want to copy specific styles (choose File, Open and locate the document).

2   Choose Format, Styles, Catalog to open the Style Catalog dialog box (or press <Ctrl+Y>).

3   Click the Organizer button to open the Document Templates dialog box.

     You may also choose File, Templates, Organize to automatically open the Document Templates dialog box.

4   Select Document Templates from the lower left drop-down list box to display the document template folders and select Documents from the lower right drop-down list box to display the current documents you have open in StarOffice Writer (these should be visible by default).

NOTE   If you want to copy styles to a template, simply select Document Templates from the lower right drop-down list box to display the document template folders.

5   Double-click on a folder icon (Standard, for example) to display the document templates it contains.

     You could have also double-clicked on a different folder (if you wanted to copy a style to a different set of templates that StarOffice Writer provides).

6   Double-click on a document template and the Styles and Configurations will display.

7   Double-click on Styles to display all the styles used in the document (see Figure 7.5).

     If you double-click on Configuration as shown in Figure 7.5, it will display the configuration settings; you have defined a custom configuration (for example, assigned keyboard shortcut keys). Refer to Chapter 14 for more information on custom configurations. You can copy the configuration settings the same way you copy styles in this section's set of steps.

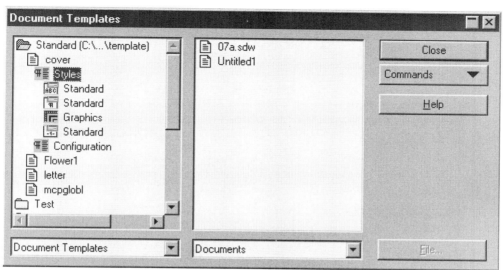

Figure 7.5 The Document Templates dialog box displays the styles contained in a document template.

8   Double-click on the document on the right side of the dialog box, into which you want to copy a style.

9   Double-click on Styles to display all the styles used in the document.

10 Click on and drag each specific style from the left side and drop it on the Styles list of the document on the right side (see Figure 7.6).

If the same style type (and named the same) already exists in the document, you will get a message box asking whether you want to replace the existing style. Click OK if you want to, or Cancel if you do not. The style will not be applied to the document automatically (though the style will be available in the document). To apply the style, you must select the item (in this example, a Graphic) and apply the style directly using the Stylist (refer to "Applying Styles" for how to do this).

NOTE   Just to stress the importance of understanding when you copy styles to other documents: if you update a style within a document, it's updated everywhere in the document; but if you update the same style by importing settings from another document, it's not. Unfortunately this can introduce inconsistencies in your document. To update styles in your document quickly and consistently, refer to the section "Finding and Replacing Styles" in Chapter 10.

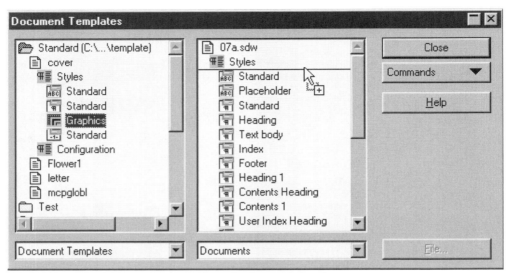

Figure 7.6   Copy the styles to other documents.

> **NOTE**   Styles and other items that you add to Standard.vor are available for all new documents that you create based upon the Standard.vor template. Documents that have already been created, or documents created that were based on other templates, will not contain these styles unless you copy the styles to each specific document.

Transferring Styles to the Current Document

If the styles you want to transfer to your current document reside in another document (instead of the Standard template or another template in your Office52/user/template folder), you can import the styles easily with Writer.

TO TRANSFER STYLES TO THE CURRENT DOCUMENT

1   Open the document into which you want to import specific styles (choose File, Open and locate the document).

2   Choose Format, Styles, Load to open the Import Styles dialog box.

3   Locate the StarOffice Writer document that contains the styles you want to import into the active document (see Figure 7.7). This document can even be currently open when you do this.

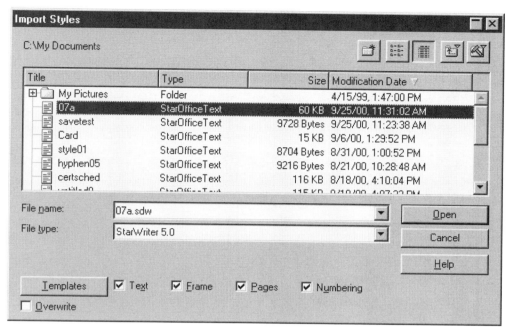

Figure 7.7 Transfer styles to your current documents.

4   Click the Open button to transfer the styles to the current document.

The current document will have all the styles available to it just as the other document had. If you don't see them listed in the Stylist right away, open and close the Stylist and they will automatically display. If you have any styles in the active document with the same name as any styles from the "loading" document, they will not overwrite each other.

Creating a New Document Using Templates

If you have certain documents that you create on a regular basis, consider using a template to create them. A template can include text, formatting, styles, graphics, and other elements, so you don't have to recreate them manually for each new document. Writer comes with templates for a wide variety of documents, and you can add custom templates as well, building them from scratch, or using Writer's built-in templates as a starting point.

To Create a Document from a Default StarOffice Template

1   Choose File, New, From Template to open the New dialog box.

2   Click the particular folder in the Categories list, pertaining to the type of document you want to create (see Figure 7.8).

    For example, click the Education Category and the following templates will be available: Academic Paper, Academic Presentation, Class Schedule, and Master's Thesis.

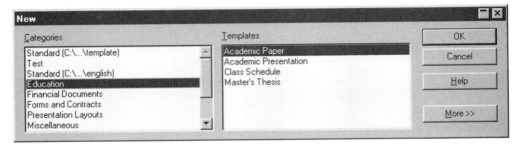

Figure 7.8   Create a new document based on a StarOffice template.

3   Double-click the Template and a new Untitled document will open, with contents and other elements drawn from the template.

To Create a New Document from a New Template

1   Choose File, New, From Template to open the New dialog box.

2   Click the Standard folder in the Categories list (if it isn't already selected).

    This is the default location where newly created templates are saved. If you want to change this location, refer to the section "To Alter the Default Path Options" in Chapter 14.

3   Select the Template from the list, which now displays any new template you created (see Figure 7.9). If you have performed the steps in the section "Creating New Templates," any new templates you have created will be listed as well.

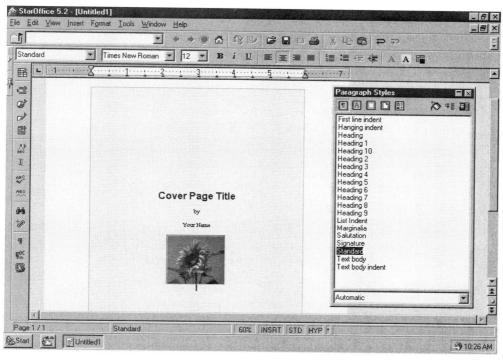

Figure 7.9 Create a new document based on a template you created.

4   Click the OK button to open the template as a new Untitled document.

Creating New Templates

You can build your own boilerplate documents from scratch and save them as templates, or use Writer's AutoPilot to streamline the creation of a Letter, Fax, Agenda, or Memo template. Both approaches are covered in the following sections.

To Create a New Template

1   Create a new document and format it as you would like your template to appear. Or, open a document that you have already saved that you want to save as a template. Our example will be a cover page template.

> **NOTE**   You might want to delete any text that you don't want to appear in every copy of the document. For example, you can replace specific text with instructions such as "Title Goes Here" or "Add Comments Here."

2   Choose File, Templates, Save to open the Document Templates dialog box.

Notice that any other templates you created are listed in the default Standard template Category folder.

3   Type in the name of the New template (see Figure 7.10). In addition, you can choose to place the template in any template folder, for example, place a new Presentation in Presentation Layouts folder.

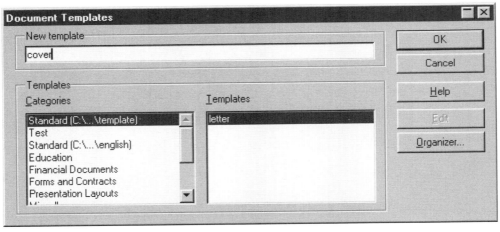

Figure 7.10   Give the new template a name.

4   Click the OK button to save the new template.

The template will now be available to you to use to create a new document from a template (refer to the next section).

NOTE You can also save a document as a template using the Save As dialog box (by choosing File, Save As). Instead of saving the file as a default StarWriter 5.0 File Type, select StarWriter 5.0 Template from the drop-down list and click the Save button. The new document template will get saved to the directory you indicate in the Save As dialog box. If you save the template to the Office52\User\Template folder, you can select it from the list of templates when creating a new document based on a template.

TO CREATE NEW TEMPLATES USING THE AUTOPILOT

1   Choose File, AutoPilot, and select whether you want to create a Letter, Fax, Agenda, or Memo template. This will open the corresponding Auto-Pilot dialog box.

    This section will cover the AutoPilot Letter template option; if you choose a different AutoPilot option, follow along the AutoPilot pages and input and answer the choices available to you.

2   Choose whether you want to create a Business letter or Personal letter; choose the Modern, Classic, or Decorative style you prefer. Then, click the Next button to move to the next page in the AutoPilot.

3   Select whether you want a logo to display as a graphic or as text you enter (or No logo at all—if no logo, move to step 4). Select the Position of the logo on the letter (Left, Center, Right) and how far From left or From top. You can also choose the Size Height and Width of the logo. Click the Next button to move to the next page in the AutoPilot.

4   Make sure the Enter sender address is correct (it will display according to the information you provided StarOffice when you installed the software) and indicate whether you want it to Repeat an addressee field (select or deselect this option and you can see where it displays on the template). Indicate the Position and Size of the sender address information and click the Next button to move to the next page in the AutoPilot.

5   This step is optional, you can leave this page of information blank and skip to Step 6. You would perform this step if you wanted to create a form letter mail merge (see the section "Performing a Form Letter Mail Merge," in Chapter 10 for information) using database table fields. Select the Database name from the drop-down list and then choose the table from the drop-down list to the right. Click on each of the Database fields and click the left arrow button to add them to the Address area according to how you want them to display (you can add spaces and press the

<Enter> key to move fields to the next line). Type in a Salutation for the letter and select the field for the salutation text from the drop-down list. Click the Next button to move to the next page in the AutoPilot.

6   Choose each checkbox field option according to the elements that you want your letter to contain. Each option will display in the preview area on the left to help you determine where the information will be on your letter. Click the Next button to move to the next page in the AutoPilot.

7   Choose from the Footer options and type in any information you want included in the footer. You can also alter the From left and From right Page margins on this page. Click the Next button to move to the next page in the AutoPilot.

8   Choose the continuation page Header and Footer information you want included in case your letter flows over to more than one page. Click the Next button to move to the next page in the AutoPilot.

9   Choose from the Doc Information drop-down Title and Subject list boxes (or leave None as the default). Select the Automatic option in the File name area if you want StarOffice to assign a file name automatically (though you can click the Destination button to indicate where the file should be saved, by default it is saved to your standard StarOffice templates folder). Type the Name and Info you want to be assigned to the Template file name. Click the Next button to move to the next page in the AutoPilot.

10   Select where the Logo and Sender address should be printed; the drop-down list options are Always, First page, Continuation pages, and Don't print. Alter the printer setup and location (if the defaults aren't correct). Click the Create button to create the AutoPilot letter template.

     This template can be accessed again by choosing File, New, From Template, and then choosing the Template name from the Standard section of document template Categories.

NOTE   Type any additional text you want your letter template to contain. You can click the Save button on the Main toolbar to save the letter template as a document. Once you've done so, resave the letter as a template *in the standard StarOffice template folder*, to make it available as a template when you're ready to create new letters based on it.

Importing Document Templates

To be able to use templates that you have created in Writer (which are saved in the Office52/user/template folder), you must first import the template. You might want to do this if you need to use a template from another user's computer across a network to create a specific type of document.

To Import a Document Template

1   Open a document to which you want to import a template.

2   Choose File, Templates, Organize to open the Document Templates dialog box.

3   Click the Commands button and select the Import Template from the submenu.

4   Locate the StarOffice Writer template you want to import (see Figure 7.11).

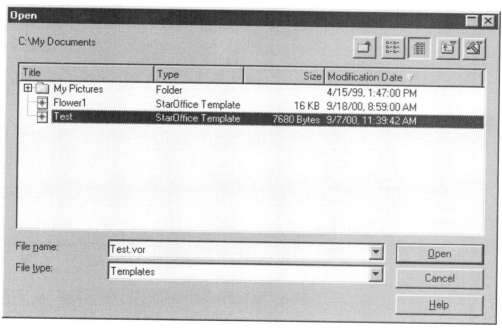

Figure 7.11   Import the template.

5   Click the Open button.

The template you selected will now be included in the default document templates directory (see Figure 7.12).

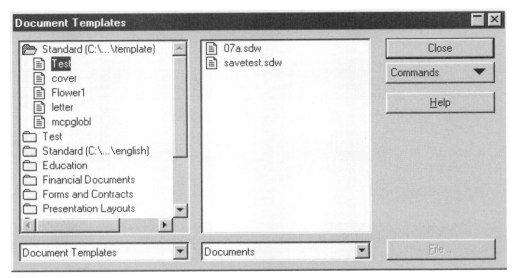

Figure 7.12   The default document templates.

Modifying Document Templates

If you have a particular template that you use, but find that you need to make a modification to it, Writer lets you do this quickly and easily.

TO MODIFY AN EXISTING TEMPLATE

1   Choose File, Templates, Edit to browse your different folders to select the template you want to modify from the Open dialog box.

2   Make the modifications to the template that you want.

3   Choose File, Templates, Save to open the Document Templates dialog box. DO NOT simply click the Save button on the Function bar; this will not save the template modifications.

4   Select the particular template name from the Categories and Templates list and click the OK button (see Figure 7.13).

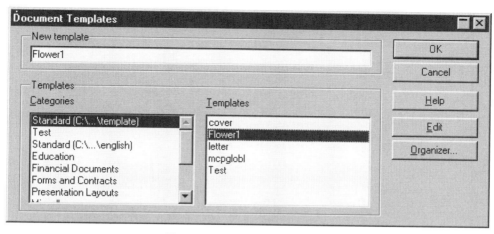

Figure 7.13 Modify a template.

5   You will see a message box indicating that the name is already in use and asking you if you want to overwrite the document template; click Yes to confirm.

The next time you create a document based on this template via File, New, From Template, the document will reflect your modifications to the document template.

Changing the Standard Template

When you create a new document (Choosing File, New, Text Document), Writer automatically assigns the Standard template. Standard is a general-purpose template for any type of document, like Standard is the default style for new paragraphs that you type. Writer also uses the Standard template to store styles, AutoText entries, macros, and custom settings.

If you generally use Writer to create a single type of document, create a template for that document, and set up Writer to open a new document based on that template whenever you open Writer.

A template is a file used to create documents of the same type. The documents that you create based on templates are like form documents (for example, a press release). Instead of retyping the document multiple times, formatting the text, adding headings, paragraph formatting, and page formatting each time, use a template to which you can simply enter your new text and objects and the document is ready. Perhaps you mainly use Writer to create those press releases. If this is the case, why not have Writer open up to your press release template each time you start a new document in Writer.

To Assign a New Default Template

1   Create a new text document or open a document continuing the styles and formatting that you want. If you create a new text document, you need to apply the formatting and styles to this document.

2   Choose File, Save As to open the Save As dialog box.

3   Select the location where you want to save the template.

> **NOTE**   If you save the template to the Office52\Share\Config\New folder, the template will be available as a command on the File, New menu (this will also be available in the Click & Go group in the Explorer). If you save the template to the Office52\User\Template, it will be available as one of the standard templates from the New dialog box (when you choose File, New, From Template).

4   Type a File name in the text box and click the File type drop-down list and select StarWriter 5.0 Template.

5   Click the Save button.

6   Choose Window, Desktop and locate the folder of the template file you just saved. You can also use StarOffice Explorer to locate the folder from your workplace.

7   Select the document that you want to set as the default template (the file you just saved there).

    If you want to select a different file as the default template, locate it in the Explorer Workspace instead.

8   Right-click the file and choose Set Default Template, Text Document from the shortcut menu (see Figure 7.14).

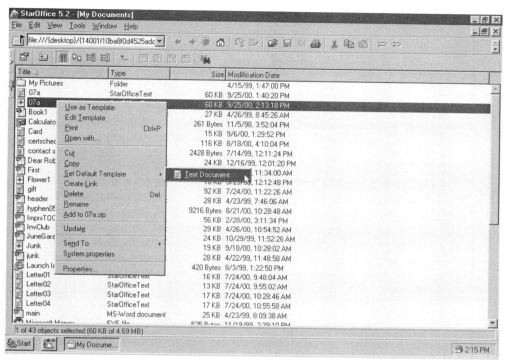

Figure 7.14   Changing the default template.

To Reset the Standard Default Template

1   Choose Window, Desktop and locate the Office52\Share\Config\New folder (see Figure 7.15); or you can always click the Click & Go group in the Explorer.

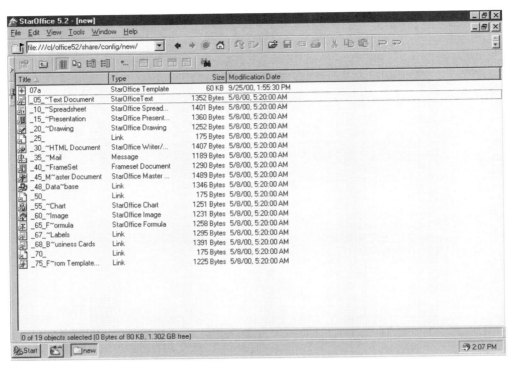

Figure 7.15   Reset the default template.

2   Select the 05 ~Text Document file.

3   Right-click the file and choose Reset Default from the shortcut menu.

Any new documents created will be opened with the StarOffice Writer default Standard template for text documents.

chapter 8

Working with Frames, Graphics, and Objects

Inserting Frames

There are two types of frames that Writer allows you to insert into your documents. A *frame* (also called a text box) is more like a <u>document</u> within a <u>document</u>. You can insert a frame and place text and graphics (even tables and other files) into the frame just as you would in a regular document.

A *floating frame* is more like a <u>file</u> within a <u>document</u>. The file in the floating frame could be another document, but it could also be a Calc file, graphic file, video file, or any other type of file you want inserted. The benefit to using a floating frame is that when updates are made to the file referenced within the floating frame, it will automatically update the file.

TO INSERT A FRAME (TEXT BOX)

1   Choose Insert, Frame to open the Frame dialog box.

> **NOTE**   You can insert a frame (text box) to help you format and position text or graphics in a document. For example, graphics can be added to a text box to create a document logo—and for positioning and anchoring them to text (refer to the section "Formatting Frames, Graphics, and Objects" for more information).

2   Select the Type tab (see Figure 8.1) and choose from the following options to define the size and position of the frame on the page:

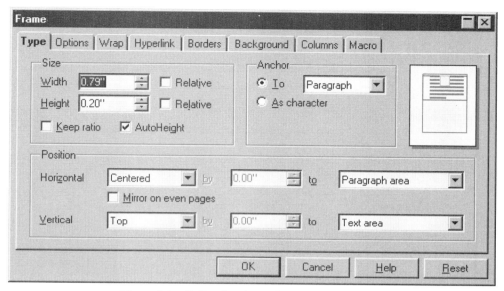

Figure 8.1 Define the size and position of the frame.

- Size—This area designates the width and height of the frame. The Relative options will size the frame according to the frame's contents; the Keep ratio option will keep modifications to the frame proportional; AutoHeight adjusts the height of the frame depending on what the frame contains (if not selected, information larger than the frame will not be visible)
- Anchor—Based on the position of the cursor when you insert the frame, Page aligns the frame with the specific page it is inserted in; Paragraph anchors the frame with the specific paragraph into which it is inserted; Character anchors the frame with a specific character. If you select the As character option, the frame is anchored with the text like a letter (because the letter has a predetermined horizontal position, you can only vary the vertical position).
- Position—You can adjust the Horizontal and Vertical positions based upon the Size of the frame and where the frame Anchor is (page, paragraph, and character).

NOTE Click the Reset button on a particular tab if you want to reset any altered values back to the default.

3   Select the Options tab (see Figure 8.2) and choose from the following options to define and edit the frame properties:

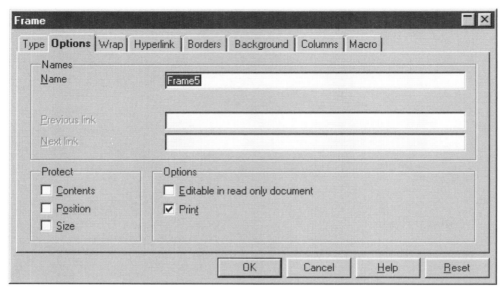

Figure 8.2   Define and edit the frame properties.

- Name—Enter a name for the frame. The Previous link and Next link display if other frames are linked to the current frame.
- Protect—Select whether you want to protect the contents, position, or the frame size from modification once you have created the frame. Also note that this in no way keeps others who have access to your documents from making changes. They can simply choose to unprotect the frames. A better way of enforcing the protection of frames in a document is to assign a password to your entire document (choose Save with password on the Save As dialog box). Refer to the section "To Save a Document the First Time" in Chapter 1 for more information.
- Options—The Editable in read only document option allows you to edit the contents of a frame even if it is a read-only document. If you'd like to have certain text displayed only on your screen, but do not want to have it printed, deselect the Print check box.

4   Select the Wrap tab (see Figure 8.3) and choose from the following options to define the text flow around the frame:

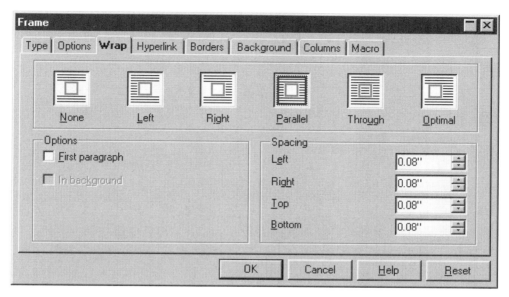

Figure 8.3   Define the text flow around the frame.

- Wrap area—You can choose from the six options for text to wrap around the frame:

  None—The frame will be on a line by itself, no text will wrap on either side.

  Left—Depending on the size of the frame, text will wrap to the left.

  Right—Depending on the size of the frame, text will wrap to the right.

  Parallel (the default)—Wraps text on the left and right side of the frame, centering the object between the margins.

  Through—Text will flow behind the frame and appear to be hidden by the outline of the frame. If you also select the In background option, the text will appear visible *through* the frame.

  Optimal—Writer will automatically wrap the text to the left, right, both left and right, or not at all, depending on the width of the frame.

- Options—The First paragraph option allows you to begin a new paragraph below the object when you press <Enter>. When the Through wrapping option is enabled, text will flow through the frame background.

•Spacing—Allows you to set the distance between the text and any edge (Left, Right, Top, Bottom) of the frame.

5   Select the Hyperlink tab (see Figure 8.4) and choose from the following options to specify the hyperlink properties for the frame:

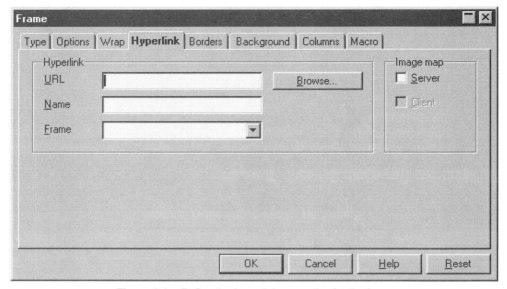

Figure 8.4   Define the hyperlink properties for the frame.

•Hyperlink—You may type in the specific URL you want to link to, Name the URL link for easier reference, and specify the Frame in which to link (click the Browse button if you need to locate the link).
•Image map—You can indicate if the frame is a Server Side ImageMap; Client will be selected automatically if it is a Client Side ImageMap. Note that virtually all image maps these days are client-side, so it would be highly unusual to ever select the Server option.

NOTE   An ImageMap is a reference-sensitive graphic or a text frame. This means that specific places on the graphic or frame will link you to certain URLs. For example, clicking on the name of a logo might take you to a company information URL, whereas clicking on the graphic of a logo might take you to a product information URL.

6   Select the Borders tab (see Figure 8.5) and choose from the following options to set the border options for the frame:

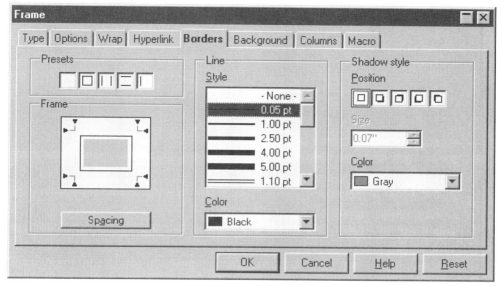

Figure 8.5   Set the border options for the frame.

- Presets—Select from defaults that allow you to choose which edges of the frame you wish to border. The selection will display in the Frame area.
- Frame—You can click directly on the sides of the frame to apply a frame border. In addition, you can click the Spacing button to enter the distance you want the border to be from the text on the Left, Right, Top, and Bottom edge of the frame. With the Synchronize check box checked, whatever number you enter for one side of your border will automatically be used for all other sides. If you want to set separate values for each side, clear the Synchronize check box. Click OK to return to the Borders tab.
- Line—Choose the Style from the different line weights and types of double lines. Click the Color drop-down list to select the line color.
- Shadow style—Select where (or whether) you want a shadow to fall outside your border, how large the shadow should be, and what Color it should be.

7   Select the Background tab (see Figure 8.6) and choose whether you want to define a background color or select a background graphic object. Simply choose the color or locate the graphic file and specify the Type (Position, Area, or Tile).

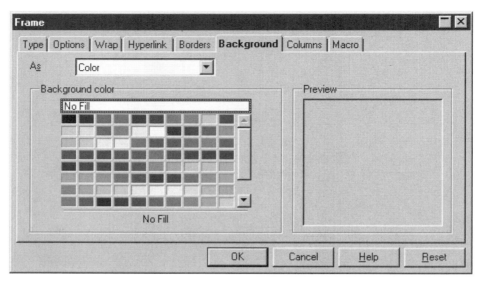

Figure 8.6   Set the background for the frame.

8   Select the Columns tab (see Figure 8.7) and choose from the following options:

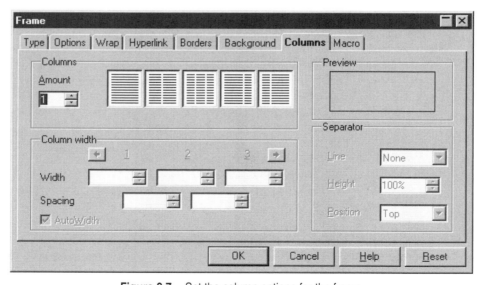

Figure 8.7   Set the column options for the frame.

- Columns—You can define the number of columns to be used in a frame (or in a page or section of a frame).
- Column width—You can indicate the specific widths of the columns and the space between them.
- Preview—You can view what the columns will look like.
- Separator—You can add separators that will fall between the columns.

9　Select the Macro tab (see Figure 8.8) and choose from the following options (for example, you can use this to create a mouseover—when you move the mouse pointer over an area of an object—for a document you're planning to publish on the Web):

- Event—You can choose a macro to be executed when a frame is selected.
- Macros—You can review the macros available in the specified macro libraries.

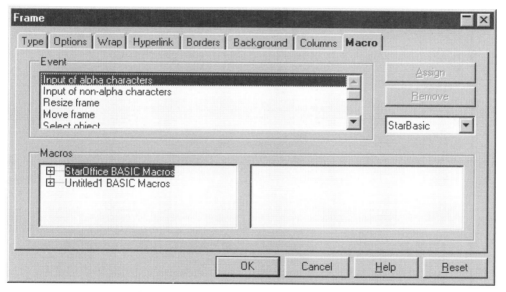

Figure 8.8 Set the macro options for the frame.

10　Click the OK button to accept the frame options and insert the frame into the document.

Keep in mind that you must first click outside the frame and then click inside the frame to be able to enter text into the frame.

NOTE　Keep in mind that when you delete a frame (text box), you also delete the contents of the text box.

To Insert a Floating Frame

You can insert a floating frame referencing a *file* (Calc file, graphic file, video file, or any other type of file) so that when updates are made to the referenced file, it will automatically update in your document.

1   Choose Insert, Floating Frame to open the Floating Frame Properties dialog box (see Figure 8.9).

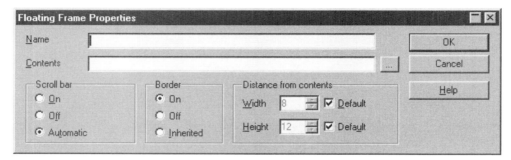

Figure 8.9   Enter the properties for the floating frame.

2   Type a descriptive name for the new floating frame.

3   Type the location of the floating frame Contents. Or, click the Select File (...) button to open the Select File for Frame dialog box, browse to the file, choose it, and click Open.

4   Select from the options available:

- Scroll bar—Select whether you want a scroll bar displayed in the frame (Automatic will only display the scroll bars when the frame contents are larger than the frame).
- Border—Select whether you want the border of the floating frame to be visible (Inherited will apply the same border to the frame if it is within another frame containing a border).
- Distance from contents—Choose the horizontal (width) and vertical (height) distances between the frame border and frame contents.

5   Click the OK button to insert the frame.

To Modify the Floating Frame Properties

1   Click on the border of the frame to activate the sizing handles.

2   Right-click and select Properties from the shortcut menu.

3   Make the modifications to the Floating Frame Properties dialog box and click the OK button.

If you need to make changes to the frame object properties, select the frame, choose Format, Object, and make modifications to the frame using the Object dialog box. Refer to the section "Formatting Frames, Graphics, and Objects" for more information.

Inserting a Horizontal Line

Horizontal lines can be added to your documents to separate text, graphics, or objects. You may also find them useful to add to your headers or footers.

> **NOTE**   Horizontal lines are graphics, and if you don't want to clutter up your document with graphics, you might want to use borderlines instead (refer to the sections discussing borders for pages, paragraphs, as well as headers and footers).

TO INSERT A HORIZONTAL LINE

1   Place the cursor in the location where you want the horizontal line graphic to be inserted in your document.

2   Choose Insert, Horizontal Line to open the Insert Horizontal Ruler dialog box (see Figure 8.10).

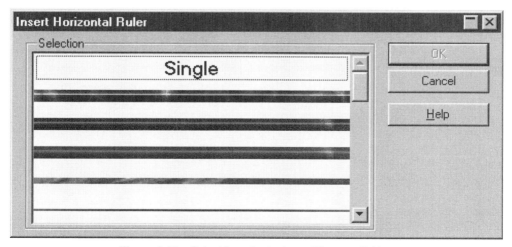

Figure 8.10   Select from the horizontal lines available.

3   Click on the horizontal line in the Selection list box.

4   Click the OK button and the horizontal line is inserted in your document.

To modify the horizontal line graphic, click once on the line and drag the sizing handles to the desired size and location. You can also choose Format, Graphic and make more extensive changes to the horizontal line properties (refer to the section "Formatting Frames, Graphics, and Objects" for more information).

Inserting Graphics

Graphics can enhance your documents by providing visual information that may have taken a lot of text to explain. Graphics, such as images you draw, scan, or import, can also add visual appeal to your documents.

> **NOTE**   Graphics can quickly increase the size of a document. Instead of inserting the graphic into your document, create a link to the graphic file. Refer to the following section "To Insert a Graphic From File" for more information. However, there is a downside of doing this—the graphic has to travel with the document, or remain available from a live Web link.

If you have already inserted graphics into your document and instead want to know how to move, modify, and work with the graphics, refer to the section "Formatting Frames, Graphics, and Objects" later in the chapter.

TO INSERT A GRAPHIC FROM FILE

1   Place the cursor in the location where you want the graphic to be inserted in your document.

2   Choose Insert, Graphics, From File to open the Insert Graphics dialog box (see Figure 8.11). Notice that the Gallery directory is the default graphics file directory.

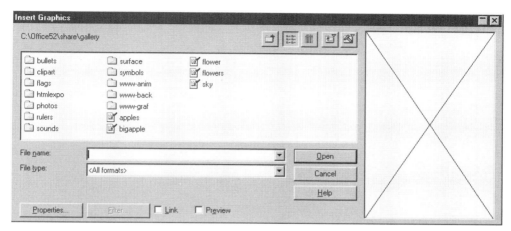

Figure 8.11   Select the graphic file to insert.

3   Locate and click once on the graphic file. (If you double-click on the file, it will be automatically inserted into your document.)

NOTE   If you click once on the graphic file in the Insert Graphics dialog box, you can click the Properties button and manipulate the graphic before it is inserted into your document. But, you can always insert the graphic into your document, make sure the graphic is selected, and then choose Format, Graphic to manipulate the graphic after it is inserted into your document.

4   Click the Open button to place the graphic into the document.

TO INSERT A GRAPHIC FROM IMAGE EDITOR

The Image Editor allows you to create and edit images using image-editing tools while working in your document. Many of the tools found in StarOffice Draw are also available in the Image Editor.

NOTE   Any graphic that you insert into a spreadsheet can actually be edited to some extent using the Image Editor. The file type will dictate what kind of changes you can make to the graphic. OLE objects will have to be edited in the server application that the object was created in.

1   Place the cursor in the location where you would like the graphic to be inserted in your document.

2   Choose Insert, Graphics, From Image Editor to open the New Image dialog box (see Figure 8.12).

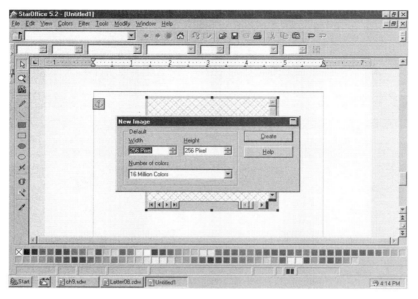

Figure 8.12   You can insert a new graphic that you create.

3   Enter the Default Width, Height, and select the Number of colors.

4   Click the Create button to activate the Image toolbar, which allows you to create the image you want to insert into your document.

5   Click somewhere in the document and the image you created will appear as a separate object in the document.

You can also edit any image that you create with the Image Editor. The image is really inserted as an OLE object, which means that when you double-click on the object the server or parent application is started. When you are working on an Image Editor graphic all of the menu selections and toolbars found in the workspace are for the Image Editor.

You can click once on an image to select it and then drag it to a new location in the document or use the sizing handles to change the height and width of the image. To actually edit the image in the Image Editor, double-click on the image or right-click on the selected image and select Edit from the context menu.

TO INSERT A GRAPHIC FROM SCAN

1   Place the cursor in the location where you want the graphic to be inserted in your document.

2   Choose Insert, Graphics, From Scan, Select Source to open the Select Source dialog box; this is where you select the scanner to use. Select your

attached, installed scanner and click the OK button. If you don't see a scanner in this dialog box, you must first attach and install a scanner.

3   Choose Insert, Graphics, From Scan, Request; this is where you activate your scanner's dialog box. The options you will see depend on the scanner you have attached to your computer or network, as well as the scanning software you have installed.

If you have already scanned in an image, simply refer to the previous section "To Insert a Graphic From File," and select the scanned image file.

Whether or not you can edit a scanned image such as a photo or other graphic will depend on the graphics editing software you have installed on your computer. Since the scan originates from your scanner, the scanner typically also comes with some kind of photo editing software and typically saves the scans in this format.

To edit a scanned image in the document, double-click the scanned image. The photo should open in the software that you use to edit images. If no software is available and (depending on the file format) the Image Editor may open; however the amount of editing that you can actually do to the scanned image will be limited.

Inserting an OLE Object

You can insert OLE (object linking and embedding) objects when you want to link or embed a target object to the document. For example, if you would like to insert a new Calc spreadsheet while working in a document, you could either create a new spreadsheet object (embed it) or link to a file.

In addition to inserting OLE objects from an existing file, you can create one on the fly by selecting a particular application as the parent application for the OLE object.

Keep in mind that when you insert OLE objects in a document you are basically placing the functionality of another application into Writer. For example, you could insert a Microsoft Excel spreadsheet into your document, if you already have access to the OLE-compliant application.

TO INSERT A NEW OLE OBJECT

1   Place the cursor in the location where you want the object to be inserted in your document.

2   Choose Insert, Object, OLE Object to open the Insert OLE Object dialog box (see Figure 8.13).

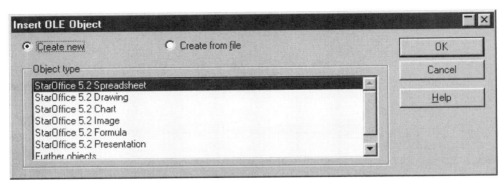

Figure 8.13   You can choose an OLE object to insert.

3   Click the Create new option and scroll down through the Object type list to choose the application you will use to create a new object. For example, you may wish to place a StarOffice 5.2 Spreadsheet into your text document.

4   Select the application for the new object.

If you want to insert an OLE object that is not available in the list, choose the Further objects Object type; when you click the OK button, an Insert Object dialog box will appear. This dialog box essentially lists additional objects that you can insert into your documents. For example, if you want to create a new Microsoft Map and insert it into your document, select the particular OLE-compliant application (as long as it is installed on your computer or network). If you prefer to access the file via an icon, select the Display As Icon option.

5   Click the OK button to insert the OLE object into the document.

The toolbars will automatically change according to the application related to the object type. For example, if you insert a StarOffice 5.2 Spreadsheet, you will see Calc toolbars and you can manipulate the spreadsheet as a separate Calc object (right-clicking on the object will quickly reveal many convenient menu commands); if you insert a Microsoft Map (or other non-StarOffice application), you will see a new window for the application.

To Insert an OLE Object from File

You can also insert an OLE object from an existing file.

1. Place the cursor in the location where you want the object to be inserted in your document.

2. Choose Insert, Object, OLE Object to open the Insert OLE Object dialog box.

3. Click the Create from file option. The list of applications will disappear and the dialog box will supply you with a File box and a Search button.

4. Type the path and file name for the file in the File box. Or if you wish to search for the file, click the Search button. If you use the Search button, the Open dialog box will appear. Use the Open dialog box to locate and select your file and then click the Open button. You will be returned to the Insert OLE Object dialog box.

5. Click OK to place the object in the document.

To Edit an OLE Object

When you edit an OLE object you will actually be starting the parent application. All you have to do is double-click on the OLE object or right-click the object and select Edit from the context menu.

You can also size and move the OLE object using the mouse. Click on the object once to select it and then drag it to a new location or use the sizing handles to change the size of the object.

Inserting a Plug-In

Plug-ins extend the options available to applications. Perhaps you have downloaded a plug-in for a particular application from the Web that allows you to import certain types of files into your applications. For example, you may have found a plug-in that will allow the reader of your document to time how long they have the document open; you can insert this directly into your document.

Plug-ins, for the most part, are used on Web pages, and you can insert plug-ins on a Writer document that has been saved in the HTML format and made part of a Web page (for more about Writer and the Web, see Chapter 13, "Working with StarOffice Tools."

TO INSERT A PLUG-IN

1   Place the cursor in the location where you want the object to be inserted in your document.

2   Choose Insert, Object, Plug-In to open the Insert Plug-In dialog box (see Figure 8.14).

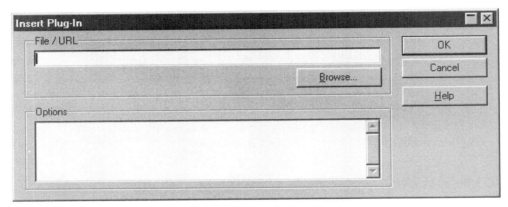

Figure 8.14   You can insert a plug-in.

3   Type in the File name or the specific URL address (click the Browse button if you need to locate the information). The Options field allows you to enter specific parameters to be included in an HTML document export.

4   Click the OK button to insert the plug-in into the document.

NOTE   You can quickly indicate whether you want to activate or deactivate a plug-in contained in your document. Select the plug-in and choose the Edit menu to see the Plug-In toggle command. If there is a checkmark next to the Plug-In command on the Edit menu, it is activated; if there is no checkmark, it means the plug-in is deactivated.

Inserting a Sound

Sounds can enhance a document by drawing attention to information or providing background noise.

To Insert a Sound

1   Place the cursor in the location where you want the object to be inserted in your document.

2   Choose Insert, Object, Sound to open the Insert sound dialog box (see Figure 8.15).

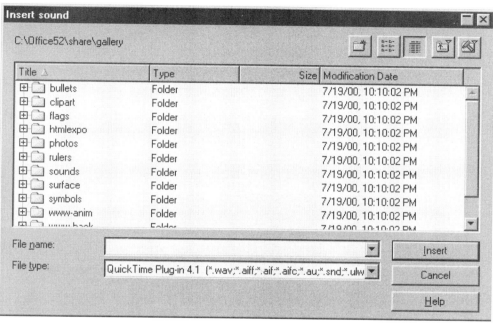

Figure 8.15   You can insert a sound.

3   Type in the File name or select the <All> File type and locate the sound.

4   Click the Insert button and the sound will be inserted into the document. It will appear as a sound control with Volume, Play, Stop, Rewind, Forward, and Options buttons.

Once you insert the sound file into the document you can play it back by right-clicking on the object and then clicking Play on the context menu.

You can also move sound objects (basically their icons) by dragging the icon to a new position. As far as editing the object, that will depend on the type of sound editing software that you have installed on your computer and the type of media file that you have inserted into Writer. To edit the object, right-click the object and choose Edit on the shortcut menu; this will open the parent application.

In most cases, it is probably easiest to insert sounds as already existing files. Running media creation software from inside Writer does require a lot of computer resources and can provide mixed results.

> **NOTE**   If you want to insert a new sound while working in your document, choose Insert, Object, OLE Object, select the Create new option and Further objects from the Object type list, then select the specific Object Type from the list on the Insert Object dialog box (for example, Wave Sound) and click OK. The appropriate application will activate. When finished recording, the icon will display in your document.

Inserting a Video

Video clips can enhance a document by providing additional information or examples that support the text.

TO INSERT A VIDEO

1   Place the cursor in the location where you want the object to be inserted in your document.

2   Choose Insert, Object, Video to open the Insert video dialog box (see Figure 8.16).

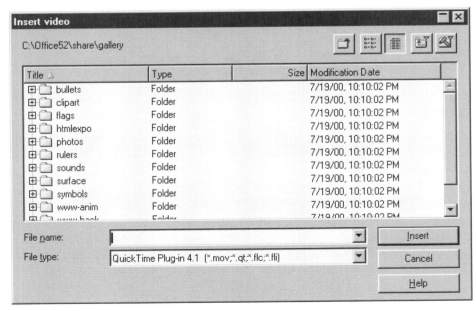

Figure 8.16   You can insert a video clip.

3   Type in the File name or select the <All> File type and locate the video clip.

4   Click the Insert button and the video clip will be inserted into the document. It will appear as a video control with Volume, Play, Stop, Rewind, Forward, and Options buttons.

Once you insert the video file into the document you can play it back by right-clicking on the object and then clicking Play on the context menu.

You can also move video objects (basically their icons) by dragging the icon to a new position. As far as editing the object, that will depend on the type of video editing software that you have installed on your computer and the type of media file that you have inserted into Writer. To edit the object, right-click the object and choose Edit on the shortcut menu; this will open the parent application.

In most cases, it is probably easiest to insert videos as already existing files. Running media creation software from inside Writer does require a lot of computer resources and can provide mixed results.

> **NOTE**   If you want to insert a new video while working in your document, choose Insert, Object, OLE Object, select the Create new option and Further objects from the Object type list, then select the specific Object Type from the list on the Insert Object dialog box (for example, Video Clip) and click OK. The appropriate application will activate. When finished recording, the icon will display in your document.

Inserting an Applet

Applets are typically found associated with Web pages and are contained in files that are in the HTML file format. Java Applets are used widely on the Web to provide interactive items such as animations or games. Since StarOffice is enabled for Java applets, you can actually place an applet in a regular Writer document. This means that you are placing a mini-application right in the document.

For example, you may want to place a Java-based calculator applet in a document. This allows you to actually use the calculator while you are inserting values and other data into the document. It means that you don't have to open the system calculator when you want to do a quick calculation to check a formula result.

To Insert an Applet

1   Place the cursor in the location where you want the object to be inserted in your document.

2   Choose Insert, Object, Applet to open the Insert Applet dialog box (see Figure 8.17).

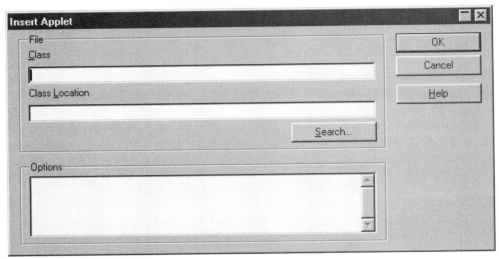

Figure 8.17   You can insert an applet.

3   Type in the applet Class description and Class Location (click Location to find where it is stored). The Options field allows you to enter specific parameters to be included in an HTML document export.

4   Click the OK button and the applet will be inserted into the document.

To Use the Applet

Once the applet is actually inserted in the Writer document, you should be able to use it immediately. In most cases the applet does not have to be selected. It should run in its own window as if it is a separate application. As with any object, you can move the applet to any location on the sheet by first selecting it and then dragging it by its border.

Inserting a Formula

Formulas inserted into documents are actually created in StarOffice Math. The formulas cannot perform calculations; StarOffice Math is only a formula editor in which you can write and edit formulas. If you do want a formula that performs calculations, you can insert a table or Calc spreadsheet into your document (refer to Chapter 9, "Working with Tables," and the section "To Insert a Graphic from File" in this chapter).

TO INSERT A FORMULA

1 Place the cursor in the location where you want the object to be inserted in your document.

2 Choose Insert, Object, Formula to open the Commands window (see Figure 8.18).

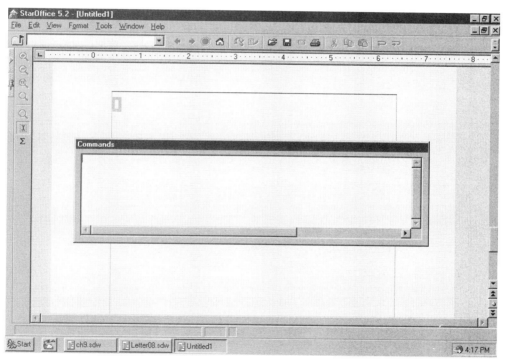

Figure 8.18 You can insert a formula using the Commands window.

3 Type in the formula you would like displayed in your document.

4 Click somewhere in the document and the formula you entered will appear as a separate object in the document.

Right-click on the formula object and choose Edit if you need to edit the formula later. Choose View, Selection to include basic formula formats, and Tools, Symbols, Catalog to utilize Greek characters (essential to the serious formula writer).

Inserting a Chart

Charts can quickly explain data by giving them visual impact. You can create a chart based on a table, or first create the chart and then enter the chart data it should be based upon.

TO INSERT A CHART BASED ON A TABLE

1   Place the cursor in the location where you want the chart to be inserted in your document. If you would like the chart to be based on a particular table, place the cursor in that table and select the cells you want the table to be based upon.

2   Choose Insert, Object, Chart. The AutoFormat Chart dialog box (see Figure 8.19) walks you through four pages to help create a chart. Click the Next or Back buttons to continue adding information or return to information. You can click the Create button at any time if you would rather insert the chart immediately as is, and change your options later. For now, click the Next button as you fill in each page with information.

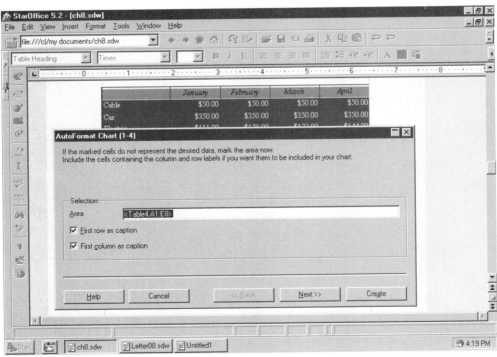

Figure 8.19   Use the AutoFormat Chart dialog box to help create your chart.

3 Type in the Area for the chart you want to create (page 1 of 4). If your cursor was located in a table, the Selection Area should contain the table information. You can also select whether you prefer the First row as caption (if you have a header row) or First column as caption (if you have a header-type column). Click the Next button.

4 Select the Show text elements in preview checkbox to get a better idea of what the chart will look like (page 2 of 4).

5 Select whether you prefer the Data series in Rows or Columns.

6 Choose a chart type (page 3 of 4) and click the Next button.

7 Choose (page 4 of 4) how you would like the Grid lines displayed (Y axis by default; you can select to display the X axis and Z axis (if the chart is 3D). Click the Next button.

8 Select whether you want to include a Chart title; if you do, type it in the text box. Select whether you want to Add legend and whether to include Axis titles (you can change them in the appropriate text box). Click the Create button and the chart is inserted into the document as an object (see Figure 8.20).

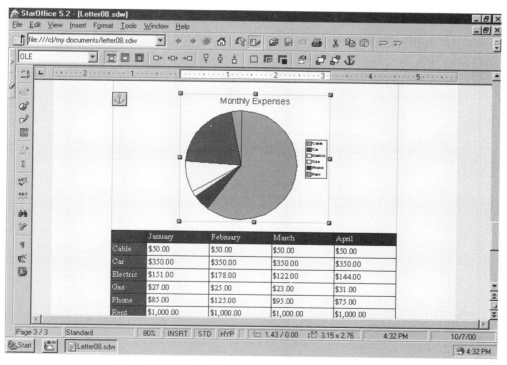

Figure 8.20   Your chart is inserted into your document.

Later, if you make any changes to the data in the table that corresponds to the chart, select the chart by clicking on it once; then choose Tools, Update, Update All to apply the changes automatically to the chart.

To Insert a New Chart Based on Chart Data You Enter Later

You can insert a *new* chart if you know your document needs a chart, but you don't have the data, or if you don't actually want the data to appear in your printed document, but you do want it stored with your document (in the Chart Data window).

1   Place the cursor in the location where you want the object to be inserted in your document.

2   Choose Insert, Object, Chart.

3   Click the Create button to skip the last 3 input pages and immediately create a chart based on sample data provided by StarOffice.

4   Double-click directly on the chart to activate the charting options on the Main toolbar.

5   Click the Chart Data button.

   The Chart Data window appears in which you can input your chart data (see Figure 8.21). Notice that dummy data already appears; you'll need to replace all this data with your own accurate data. If you want to choose a different type of chart, click on the corresponding chart button on the Main toolbar. If you need to make changes to the structure or organization of the data, click on the corresponding chart data button in the Chart Data window.

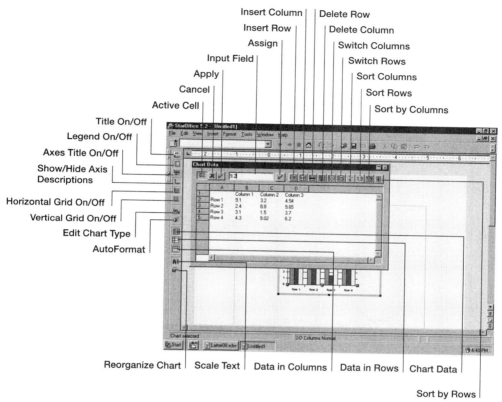

Figure 8.21   Insert data directly into the Chart Data window.

If you want to alter the chart data, double-click on the chart to activate the charting options on the Main toolbar. Click the Chart Data button to open the Chart Data window. Click the cell you want to modify. Type the alternate data into the cell contents field and click the green checkmark on the left of the field to accept the changes (click the red X to cancel any changes). Then, click the green checkmark on the right of the field to apply the change to the chart.

To Modify Chart Appearance

You can alter the appearance of your chart after you have created it. First, double-click on the chart to activate the charting options on the Main toolbar (refer to Figure 8.21). All the graphing tools and commands become visible again.

Formatting Frames, Graphics, and Objects

Frames, graphics, and objects are very similar elements in Writer where formatting is concerned. You can move and resize, arrange, align, anchor, and wrap each element. In addition, the sections earlier in this chapter that covered how to insert frames, graphics, and all kinds of objects described the tabs and options available to each element. Selecting the element and choosing the first command at the top of the Format menu (either Frame, Graphic, or Object) can access these same tabs. Also notice that when you click on an object to format it, specific buttons become available on the Object Bar (see Figure 8.22). These buttons can be used in the following sections (in addition to the corresponding menu commands).

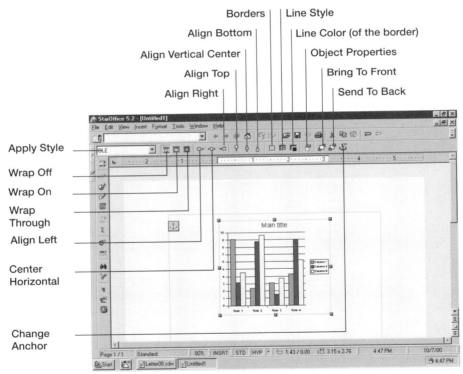

Figure 8.22   The formatting buttons available on the Object bar.

TO MOVE AND RESIZE ELEMENTS

When you insert elements (frames, graphics, or objects) into a document, Writer maintains the original size of the element. The easiest way to move and resize an element is by using the mouse. When you select an element, you activate sizing handles on all four sides and at all four corners. If you click and drag a sizing handle (when the mouse pointer changes to a double-headed arrow) at the corner, you can resize the element in two directions at the same time. In addition, moving an element is easy; you simply click and drag it to the new location.

When you move and size an element with the mouse, it is hard to be precise with the measurements. Use the Type tab on Frame, Graphic, or Object dialog boxes (by choosing the Format menu and selecting either Frame, Graphic, or Object depending on the type of element you are formatting). You can enter exact measurements in the Position area based upon how the element is anchored (page, paragraph, or character). Refer to the extensive breakdown of each tab and its contents in the section "To Insert a Frame (Text Box)."

TO ARRANGE ELEMENTS

When you have placed multiple elements into your document, you might find that they overlap each other. To make sure the elements are displayed as you like, you can arrange and rearrange them in layers.

1   Click once directly on the element to activate the sizing handles.

2   Choose Format, Arrange and choose from the following submenu of options:

- Bring to Front—This positions the element in front of all other elements that overlap. This option is also a button on the Object bar.
- Bring Forward—This positions the element one step forward.
- Send Backward—This positions the element one step backward.
- Send to Back—This positions the element in back of all other elements that overlap. This option is also a button on the Object bar.

The objects will rearrange accordingly.

TO ALIGN AN ELEMENT

1   Click once directly on the element to activate the sizing handles.

2   Choose Format, Alignment and choose from the following options (which are all also buttons available on the Object bar): Left, Centered, Right (horizontally) and Top, Centered, Bottom (vertically). The object will realign accordingly.

TO ANCHOR AN ELEMENT

An element that floats can be positioned anywhere in a document, including the margins, header or footer, or even moved in front or back of text and other elements. An anchor is used to keep an object in the same place with a particular page, paragraph, or character. This is convenient when you must have, for example, a graphic on a particular page. You can make sure it stays anchored to a particular page even if other text and objects are added and edited that would normally alter the location of the element.

1   Click once directly on the element to activate the sizing handles.

2   Choose Format, Anchor and choose from the following options:

   •To Page—Aligns the element with the specific page into which it is inserted.
   •To Paragraph—Aligns the element with the specific paragraph into which it is inserted.
   •To Character—Aligns the element with a specific character.
   •As Character—Aligns the element with the text like a letter (because the letter has a predetermined horizontal position, you can only vary the vertical position).

The element will anchor accordingly. You can also select the Change Anchor button on the Object bar and choose these options from the submenu.

TO WRAP ELEMENTS

Text wrapping is how text flows around an element in a document. When you insert an element into a document, by default, text automatically flows to the left and right around the *bounding box* (remember the Parallel setting), which is a box around a frame, graphic, or object. If you choose to wrap text around the form of the element, the text is placed next to the actual outline of the element, not the bounding box. Writer allows you to change the way that text wraps around an element, and even control the distance between the element and the text.

1   Click once directly on the element to activate the sizing handles.

2   Choose Format, Wrap and choose from the following options:

   •No Wrap—Text will not wrap around the element; it will appear above and below the element. The Wrap Off button is also available on the Object bar.
   •Page Wrap—Text will appear to the left and right of the element. The Wrap On button is also available on the Object bar.
   •Optimal Page Wrap—Depending upon the width and position of the element, text will appear to the left or right of the element (or perhaps not at all, if it doesn't optimize the space).
   •Wrap Through—Text will fall behind the element, and not be visible. The Wrap Through button is also available on the Object bar.

- In Background—Text will fall behind the element, but it will be visible in the background.

3 Select from the contour options available depending on the type of element you have selected to wrap:

- Contour—If selected, text will flow around the contour of the element.
- Edit Contour—This opens the Contour Editor window in which you can alter the element contour, define a new wrap region according to the area you indicate (using objects like ellipses and rectangles), apply the new wrap region, alter the color tolerance, and so on.

4 Select the First Paragraph if you want to begin a new paragraph below the element after you press <Enter>.

The element will display the selected wrap options accordingly.

TO EDIT OBJECTS

1 Select an object that you have entered into your document (either an OLE Object, Plug-In, Sound, Video, Applet, Formula, or Chart). For example, if you inserted an OLE Object that was a StarOffice 5.2 Spreadsheet, you can edit or open the object.

2 If the object was originally created in StarOffice, you can select from the following options:

Choose Edit, Object, Open to open the object in a separate window and make modifications.

Choose Edit, Object, Edit to make modifications to the object directly in the current document.

Choose the Cut, Copy, and Paste buttons on the Function bar just like you would with text, if you need to move the object to another location.

3 If the object was originally created in another application, you need to edit the object directly in that application. If it is an OLE object, the application will open automatically when you double-click on the object.

Inserting Captions

Once you have inserted frames, graphics, and objects into your documents, it may be convenient to have accompanying captions. These can be used to navigate elements in large documents and to keep descriptions with the appropriate element.

To Insert Captions

1 Click on the element to which you want to add a caption.

2 Choose Insert, Caption to open the Caption dialog box.

   The Category and the Object name list boxes should already display according to the graphic or object you selected in Step 1.

3 Select the type of numbering system to arrange the captions from the Numbering drop-down list box.

4 Type the text you want displayed in the Caption text box.

NOTE   If you press the <Spacebar> to add a space before you type the caption text, it will keep the caption number from running directly into the caption text.

5 Click the Options button if you prefer to assign specific numbering according to a range of options (for example, chapter number separated by a period and then caption number, 1.1).

6 Select the Position of the caption in relation to the graphic or object (Above or Below). Note that this option will be available only to certain element types (for example, tables).

7 Click the OK button (see Figure 8.23) and the caption will be added to your document, next to the graphic or object.

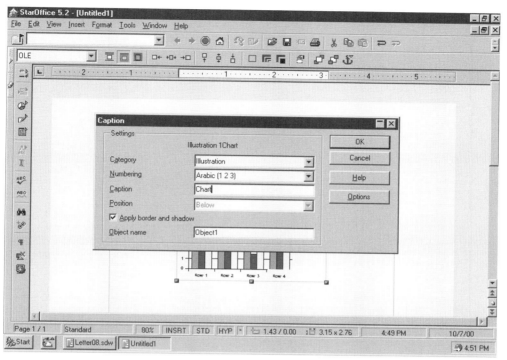

Figure 8.23 You can add accompanying captions.

NOTE You can have captions inserted into your documents automatically when you create a new element (table, frame, graphic, or object). Choose Tools, Options and click on the Text document item available in the options list on the left of the Options dialog box. Click the Insert submenu and click the Automatic option in the Captions section. Click the Object selection button, and indicate which caption options and settings you prefer to be automatically created from the Caption dialog box that opens. Click the OK button and the next time you create a new element, a caption will accompany the element automatically. Keep in mind that it doesn't go back and automatically caption any elements already in the document.

Working with Tables

Creating a Table

You can organize data within a table using rows and columns. The intersection of a row and column is called a cell. Rows are numbered from top to bottom (numerically), and columns are labeled from left to right (alphabetically). Each cell has a unique cell address, which consists of the column letter combined with the row number (for example, the top left cell is A1).

Writer tables can help you organize data and perform basic calculations. If you need to apply advanced formulas, you might instead consider using StarOffice Calc.

TO CREATE A TABLE USING THE INSERT MENU

1   Create a new blank text document (File, New, Text Document).

2   Choose Insert, Table to open the Insert Table dialog box.

3   Type a name for the table; you can choose something more informative than Table1, for example, "CreditCardTerms" (pertaining to the data it will contain).

4   Choose the number of Columns and Rows using the spin boxes in the Size area (or type the number directly into each box).

5   Choose from the available Options (see Figure 9.1):

   • Header—Designates the top-most row as the header row for the table. It is a good idea to set a header row in case you later want to AutoFormat the table (Writer might suggest applying a format that will emphasize that row).

   • Repeat header—Repeats the header row at the top of a new page, if the table runs over to multiple pages.

   • Don't split table—Forces the entire table to fit on one page; i.e., not to be split at the bottom and top. In other words, if there is insufficient space on the page where the table begins, the entire table jumps to the following page. This option is not selected by default when you create a new table.

   • Border—Places a border around the table.

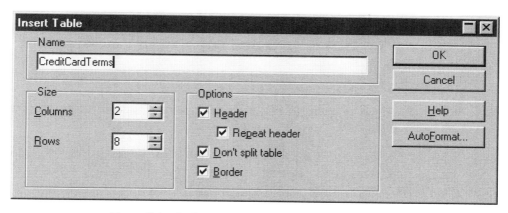

Figure 9.1 Assign a table name, size, and other options.

6   Click the OK button when finished entering the options (see Figure 9.2).

Writer creates the table at the cursor location, within the margins of the document. Writer creates evenly spaced (width) table columns between the available margin space, by default. If you want to change the column widths, refer to the section "To Change the Column Width."

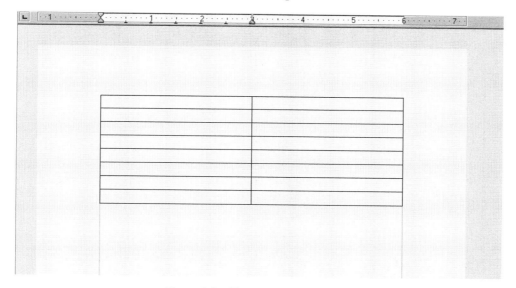

Figure 9.2 The newly created table.

To Create a Table Using the Main Toolbar

1   Open a document in which you want to insert a table (or you can create a new document). In this example, you will see how to place the table below the table created using the Insert Menu in the previous section (at the location of the cursor).

2   Click and hold the mouse pointer on the Insert button located on the Main Toolbar, and move the mouse pointer to the Insert Table button. Then, drag the mouse pointer to select the number of columns and rows you would like in your table: 2 x 8, for example (see Figure 9.3). Release the mouse pointer over the table dimensions and the table will be created using Writer's default name and options ("Table2," because Table1 was renamed as "CreditCardTerms" in the previous section).

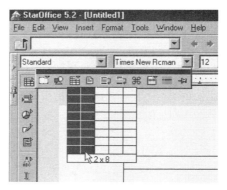

Figure 9.3   Creating a table via the Insert Table option on the Main toolbar.

To change the table defaults either choose Format, Table and click on the Table tab or click once directly on the Insert button on the Main Toolbar (which now displays the Insert Table button as its default) and choose the Table tab. Or, you can also right-click on the table and choose Table from the shortcut menu. More table formatting options can be found in the section "Altering the Table Format."

Entering Text into a Table

Typing text into a table is similar to typing text into a document. One difference is that you use the arrow keys and the <Tab> key to move from one cell to another in a table. <Tab> moves you one cell to the right and <Shift+Tab> moves you one cell to the left.

> **NOTE** To indicate a number as text in a cell, place the "at" symbol (@) in front of the number; for example, if you want to display an actual formula in the text, without Writer trying to calculate the formula in the table.

TO ENTER TEXT INTO A TABLE

1   Type the information into the first cell of your table (upper left cell). Notice that the text is in bold italics by default. This is because the top-most row is assigned as the Header row by default (refer to the section "To Create a Table Using the Insert Menu").

2   Press <Tab> to move to the next cell to the right (press <Shift+Tab> to move to the left).

Pressing the tab key moves the insertion point one cell to the right. If there are no more cells to the right, the cursor moves to the left-most cell on the next row down. You may also use the mouse to position the insertion point within a table. To move the insertion point to a specific cell, position the mouse pointer on the cell and click the left mouse button.

3   Type the rest of the information you would like in your table. Figure 9.4 is an example of text that has been entered.

There are a couple of things you should note about the information entered in this figure:

• Note 1—The information ran over to two pages; because the Headers row repeated by default, it's still easy to determine what the columns represent.

• Note 2—A cell that contains only numerical data automatically falls flush right, just like a number would in a Calc spreadsheet (not flush left, like text in a Calc spreadsheet). Refer to the next section for alignment options.

• Note 3—Text that fills multiple lines of a cell automatically wraps around within the cell.

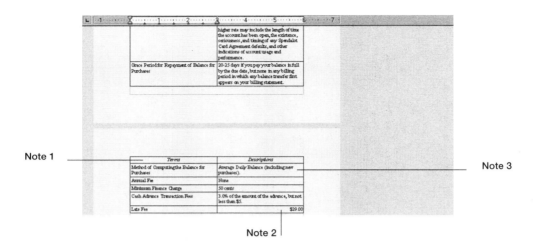

Note 1

Note 3

Note 2

Figure 9.4 Text entered into a new table.

NOTE Pressing <Enter> while in a cell will begin the text on a new line within the cell. Press <Control+Tab> if you need to insert a tab stop within a table cell (because simply pressing the <Tab> key will move you through the table).

Aligning Cell Text and Data

You can align text in the center, on the right side, or on the left side of a cell.

TO ALIGN CELL INFORMATION

1   Place the insertion point in the cell (for a single cell). To select multiple cells, click and drag over all the cells you want to select.

2   Click the Text Object Bar button to return the Table Object Bar to display the text options. (Refer to Figure 9.5 for the location of the Text Object Bar button.)

3   Click the Align Left, Centered, Align Right, or Justify buttons.

     This is similar to formatting a paragraph in the section "Changing Text Alignment" in Chapter 5. You would choose Format, Paragraph and select the alignment options from the Alignment tab.

Inserting, Deleting, and Moving Rows and Columns

Many times you will find that you need to add or remove rows and columns after you have created the original table. In addition, if you entered a row or column of data and find that you need to move it to a different row or column in the table, you can do this easily with Writer.

TO INSERT AND DELETE ROWS AND COLUMNS

1   To add a row, place the cursor in the row above where you want a new row.

2   Click the Insert Rows button on the Table Object Bar (see Figure 9.5).

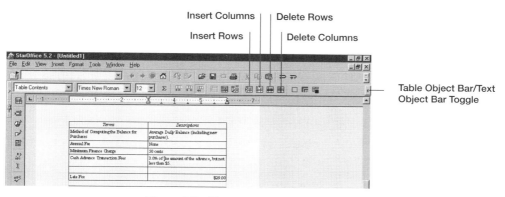

Figure 9.5   Text entered into a new table.

3   To add a column, place the cursor in the column where you want a new column added to the right.

4   Click the Insert Columns button on the Table Object Bar.

5   To delete a row, place the cursor in the row that you want deleted.

If you prefer multiple rows deleted, select the rows with the mouse pointer first.

6   Click the Delete Row button on the Table Object Bar.

7   To delete a column, place the cursor in the column that you want deleted.

If you want multiple columns deleted, select the columns with the mouse pointer first.

8   Click the Delete Column button on the Table Object Bar.

NOTE   To append a new row at the end of a table, you can also press <Tab> while in the bottom right-most cell. A new row will automatically be added and you can continue to add text and data.

TO INSERT ROWS OR COLUMNS BEFORE A ROW OR COLUMN

When you insert a row or column, by default Writer places the new row below your current insertion point, and a new column to the right of your current insertion point. You must perform a few extra steps in order to add a new first row or column to a table (because you need to add that row or column above or to the left of your cursor). To insert rows or columns before the current row or column, perform the following:

- To insert a row before, place the insertion point in the first row in the table and choose Format, Row, Insert to open the InsertRows dialog box. Select the number of rows you want to append, select the Position option Before, and click OK.

- To insert a column before, place the insertion point in the first column in the table and choose Format, Column, Insert to open the InsertColumns dialog box. Select the number of columns you want to append, select the Position option Before, and click OK.

You can also use this dialog box to add multiple rows or columns at once, which can save you time when working in a small existing table.

NOTE   To delete rows and columns quickly, select them with your mouse and right-click to activate the shortcut menu; then choose Row, Delete or Column, Delete.

TO MOVE A ROW OR COLUMN

1   Select the row or column you would like to move.

If you are having a hard time selecting rows or columns, you can place the cursor in a cell within the Row or Column and choose Format, Row (or Column), Select.

2   Click the mouse pointer on the selected row or column and drag it to the new location, and then release the mouse button.

The mouse pointer will change to an arrow with a little gray box to indicate you are moving information.

You cannot use the Copy/Cut and Paste features to move rows or columns; they only cut and paste the data contained in the row or column, not the row or column itself.

Changing Column Width

By default, Writer creates columns of equal width in tables that fill the space between the left and right margins. If you need one column to be larger or smaller, you can easily alter the width in several different ways.

To Change Column Width Using the Ruler

Once you get the hang of working with tables, you will find it more convenient at times to alter the column widths using the Ruler.

1   Click the first cell of the first column.

With the insertion point inside the table, the ruler changes to display the boundary markers for each column.

2   Move the mouse pointer over the boundary marker for the right edge of the column you want to change.

You can also move the cursor over the line between the columns in the table itself. Either way, the cursor will change to a double-headed arrow.

3   Drag the marker to the width you prefer the column to be (see Figure 9.6).

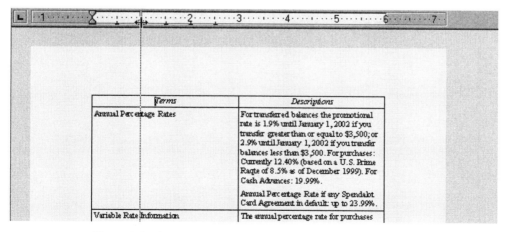

Figure 9.6   Drag a column boundary marker to change its width.

4   Notice that the ruler starts at zero. If you drag the marker to the 1 on the ruler, you make the column 1-inch wide (see Figure 9.7).

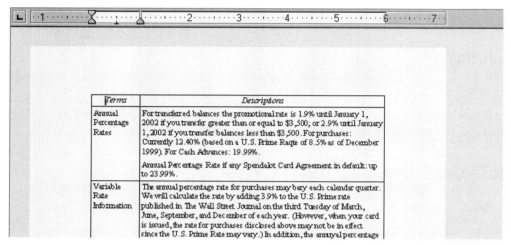

Figure 9.7   The new column width.

TO CHANGE COLUMNS TO THE OPTIMAL WIDTH

Writer can resize your column(s) based on the amount of text in each column. Keep in mind, though, that if you add more text to a cell, the column does *not* readjust to the optimal width automatically, and you will have to perform the steps again. That is why the optimal feature is best used when you have finished entering the text and data into your table.

1   Select the column(s) that you want to resize.

2   Choose Format, Column, Optimal Width.

TO CHANGE COLUMN WIDTH MANUALLY

1   Select the column(s) that you want to resize.

2   Choose Format, Column, Width to open the Column Width dialog box (see Figure 9.8).

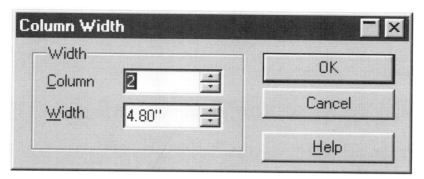

Figure 9.8   Set the column width.

3   Select the specific Column number, type in the Width you prefer, and click the OK button.

Writer resizes your column(s) based on the specific size you indicate.

NOTE   You cannot resize multiple columns at the same time with the Column Width dialog box; this prevents you from entering widths that add up to more or less than the space between the margins.

Changing Row Height

By default, Writer bases row height on the size of the font (or the greatest number of lines in any cell in that row). You can set a specific row height, but keep in mind that if you set the height too small, some of the text in the row's cells may not be visible. A red arrow will display in the cell to indicate that there is more information that is not visible.

TO CHANGE ROW HEIGHT

1   Select the row(s) that you want to resize.

2   Choose Format, Row, Height to open the Row Height dialog box (see Figure 9.9).

NOTE   If you have set row height to be shorter than the contents of the row, one easy way to make everything visible again is to choose Format, Row, Optimal Height. The Optimal Height command will only be available on the Format, Row submenu if the height of the row is smaller than the space the contents require.

If you want to adjust the height of the cells to the height of the contents, make sure the Fit to size option is selected in the Row Height dialog box (it should be by default). This will prevent you from making the row height smaller than the space that the contents require. You can, though, have this option selected and set the row height larger than the contents.

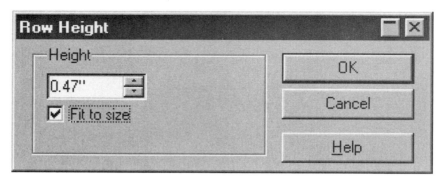

Figure 9.9 Set the row height.

3 Type in the Height you prefer and click the OK button.

Writer resizes your row(s) based on the specific size you indicate.

TO SPACE ROWS EVENLY

1 Select the rows that you want to space evenly. This means that each row will be the same height regardless of the amount of text the row contains.

2 Choose Format, Row, Space Equally and the rows will be spaced automatically to the size of the tallest row (based on the largest cell contents).

Working with Cells in a Table

In addition to working with rows and columns in tables, you can manipulate individual cells in a table. For example, you can split a cell into two or more cells so that you have vertical or horizontal cells within the original cell area. You can also merge cells that contain all the information you prefer in one cell. In addition, you can format the text and data within a cell to be aligned at the top, bottom, or centered within the area of the cell. And last, but not least, you can protect cells so that the cell data cannot be modified or deleted.

To Split Cells

1   Select the cells that you want to split.

2   Click the Split Cells button on the Table Object Bar or choose Format, Cell, Split. Either method opens the Split Cells dialog box (see Figure 9.10).

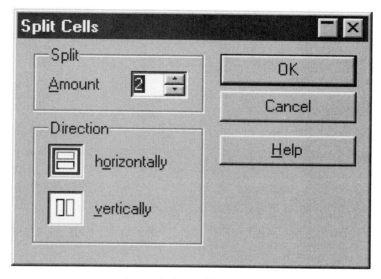

Figure 9.10   Split a cell into multiple cells.

If the original cell has multiple separate paragraph sections (you pressed <Enter> when typing in the text), the cells split horizontally will be divided between the paragraphs, which will look like multiple cells within the original cell (row/column intersection). This won't apply if split vertically. Refer to Figure 9.11.

If the original cell has only one paragraph section (you didn't press <Enter> when typing in the text), the horizontal split(s) will be inserted at the end of the text, which will look like a new cell (or new multiple cells) within the original cell (row/column intersection). Refer to Figure 9.11.

3   Select the Amount into which you want to split the cell.

4   Choose the Direction of the split(s) to be placed either horizontally or vertically in the original cell.

5   Click the OK button and the cells will be split.

New Split Column Indicator

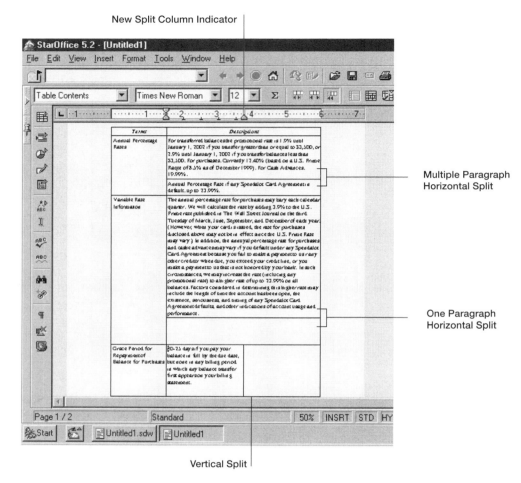

Multiple Paragraph
Horizontal Split

One Paragraph
Horizontal Split

Vertical Split

Figure 9.11   Cells split horizontally and vertically.

NOTE   Keep in mind that when you split cells in a table, it can be tricky to indicate the correct cells names in formulas. For example, the contents of a split cell would be summed together as follows: "=sum(<C2.1.1> | <C2.1.2>)". The decimal points indicate the splits within a cell.

TO MERGE CELLS

1   Select the cells that you want to merge.

2   Click the Merge Cells button on the Table Object Bar or choose Format, Cell, Merge (see Figure 9.12).

    The Merge Cells button is active only if you have multiple cells selected.

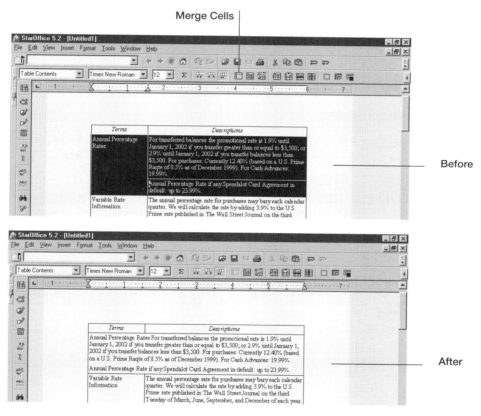

Figure 9.12   Before and after cells are merged.

TO ALIGN TEXT AND DATA WITHIN A CELL

1   Select the cell(s) in which you want to manipulate the text and data alignment within the cell (or you can place the cursor anywhere in the cell).

2   Choose Format, Cell, and choose either Top, Center, or Bottom from the submenu.

    The text and data within the cell will align accordingly (see Figure 9.13).

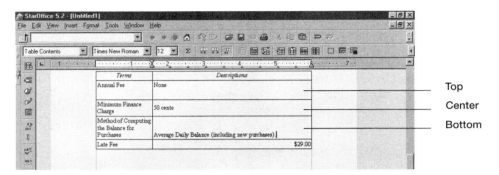

Figure 9.13   Aligning the text and data within a cell.

To Protect and Unprotect Cells

1   Select the cell(s) in which you want to protect the text and data from being modified or deleted (or you can place the cursor anywhere in the cell).

2   Choose Format, Cell, and select Protect from the submenu.

If you return to the cell and attempt to modify or delete the cell, you will receive a message explaining that the read only data cannot be changed or modified.

Choose Format, Cell and select Unprotect from the submenu if you want to be able to make modifications to the cell again. Notice that the Format menu has fewer options available to you when a cell is protected. Also note that this in no way keeps others who have access to your documents from making changes. They can simply choose to unprotect the cells. A better way of enforcing the protection of cells in a document is to assign a password to your entire document (choose Save with password on the Save As dialog box). Refer to the section "To Save a Document the First Time" in Chapter 1 for more information.

Formatting Numbers in a Table

Even though StarOffice Writer is a word processing application, tables inserted in documents have features that are similar to spreadsheet applications like StarOffice Calc. For example, you can format the numbers so that they are displayed according to the category of number (dollars/cents, dates, percentages, and so on).

To Format Numbers in Tables

1   Select the cells that contain numerical data that you want to format.

2   Choose Format, Number Format to open the Number Format dialog box (see Figure 9.14).

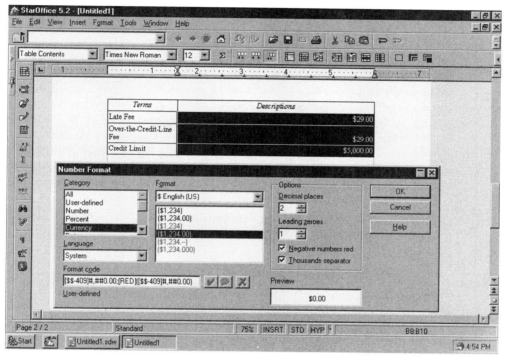

Figure 9.14   Altering the number format in a table.

3   Select the number type Category from the list box and the options available:

- All—You can choose from a list of all the available number formatting options.
- User-defined—You can create your own number format. When you type the Format code in the text box, the Add, Edit Comment, and Remove buttons are activated; these help you define your number.
- Number—You can choose to display general numbers, positive/negative; decimal places, leading zeroes, negative numbers in red, and a thousands separator (usually a comma) are also available.
- Percent—You can choose to display positive/negative percents; decimal places, leading zeroes, negative numbers in red, and a thousands separator (usually a comma) are also available.

- Currency—You can choose to display the number in $ English (U.S.) by default or choose an alternative currency from the Format drop-down list box. You can also indicate how to display positive/negative numbers, decimal places, leading zeroes, negative numbers in red, and a thousands separator (usually a comma).
- Date—You can display the date in numerous different formats.
- Time—You can display the time in numerous different formats.
- Scientific—You can display numbers exponentially to ten or one hundred times.
- Fraction—You can display numbers rounded off to the nearest 1-digit or 2-digit decimal depending on the format you choose. For example, if you enter "45.13", the 1-digit fraction displays as "45 1/8", but the 2-digit fraction displays as "45 7/53".
- Boolean value—You can display true or false values.
- Text—You can display a number as text, which will left-align the number. To indicate a number as text in a cell, place the "at" symbol (@) in front of the number. For example, if you want to display an actual formula in the text, without Writer trying to calculate the formula in the table.

4   Click the OK button when the number format displays appropriately in the Preview area.

Calculating Values in a Table

Writer can perform calculations in a table by using the built-in spreadsheet functions. For example, you can use SUM to add numbers or values together to calculate a total. In addition, you can create your own formulas and functions using the Function bar.

TO SUM VALUES IN A TABLE

1   Place the cursor in a cell in which you want to calculate a total for a set of cells (see Figure 9.15).

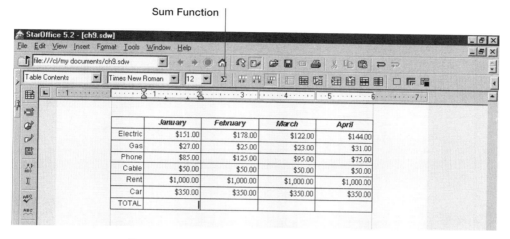

Figure 9.15   You can calculate cells within a table.

2   Click the Sum Function button on the Table Object Bar.

A Function bar appears with a suggested formula that Writer predicts you want to perform (see Figure 9.16).

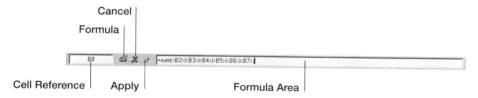

Figure 9.16   Select the formulas or functions you want to perform.

If you want to perform another type of formula, refer to the next section.

3   Click the Apply button on the Function bar or press <Enter> to accept the cells that Writer suggests calculating. If you prefer to change the cell references in the calculation, do so in the Formula Area text box.

The sum of the cells provides a total for the column. Repeat this procedure for each column you want to total (see Figure 9.17). You can move the mouse pointer over the cell and the formula will appear in a Help tip.

Refer to the previous section on applying number formats in order for the summed cells to contain the same number format as the cells in the table; for example, if you want to display the numbers as Currency.

	January	February	March	April
Electric	$151.00	$178.00	$122.00	$144.00
Gas	$27.00	$25.00	$23.00	$31.00
Phone	$85.00	$125.00	$95.00	$75.00
Cable	$50.00	$50.00	$50.00	$50.00
Rent	$1,000.00	$1,000.00	$1,000.00	$1,000.00
Car	$350.00	$350.00	$350.00	$350.00
TOTAL	$1,663.00	$1,728.00	$1,640.00	$1,650.00

Figure 9.17   The columns totaled using SUM.

NOTE   If you see an "***Expression is faulty***" message in the cell, it means there is an error in your formula and you must correct it by clicking the Sum Function button again. If you change any of the values in cells that are included in a formula or function, or if you alter a formula, Writer will automatically recalculate the answer.

TO ENTER A FORMULA OR FUNCTION DIRECTLY INTO A CELL

You can type formulas and functions directly into a cell or use the submenus on the Function bar (via the Formula button) to create your own formulas and functions.

1   Place the cursor in a cell in which you want to place the formula or function.

2   Press the <F2> key to activate the Function bar. Notice that an equals sign (=) appears in the Formula Area. If you already have a formula or function in a cell, it will display in the Formula Area; this is how you can edit a formula or function at a later time.

   If you want to cancel this procedure, you can press the <Esc> key at any time to return to the document and deactivate the Function bar.

3   Click the Formula button and select one from the submenu list of options (if you already know the syntax for the formula, you can type it directly into the Formula Area):

   •Sum—Calculates a total of the indicated cells.
   •Round—Rounds the cell number to an indicated number of decimals.
   •Percent—Calculates a percent value on the specified cell.

- •Square Root—Calculates a square root on the specified cell.
- •Power—Calculates the power on the specified cell.
- •Operators—Allows you to select from a list of operators to insert into your cell's formula.
- •Statistical Functions—Calculates the mean, maximum, or minimum on a specified cell.
- •Functions—Allows you to select from the trigonometric functions of sign, cosign, tangent, arcsign, arccosign, and arctangent.

4 Type the name of the cells that you want to include in the formula or function; you can also click the mouse pointer directly on the cells that you want to include and their reference names will automatically be added to the Formula Area.

You can click the cells one at a time and place operators between them by choosing the Operators submenu on the Formula button; you can also click and drag to select multiple cells.

5 Click the Apply button on the Function bar or press <Enter> to accept the formula or function. If you prefer to change the cell references in the calculation, do so in the Formula Area text box.

Sorting Rows and Columns in a Table

Once you type the text and data into your table, you might find that you prefer to have the information alphabetized or sorted numerically. Writer allows you to quickly sort your table rows or columns so that you don't need to copy and paste the information in your table to get it into a specific order.

To Sort Rows or Columns

1   Select the rows or columns you want to sort.

2   Choose Tools, Sort to open the Sort dialog box (see Figure 9.18).

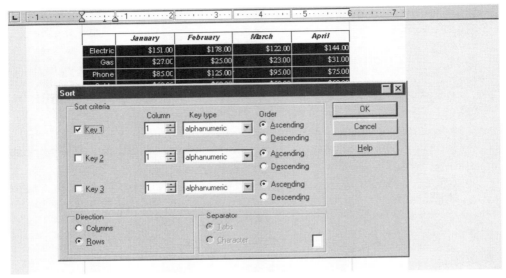

Figure 9.18   The sort options available for tables.

3   Select the Direction you would like to sort—by Columns or Rows.

4   Choose the Sort criteria according to the row or column you want to sort on. In this example, we are going to sort all the rows of text alphabetically in ascending order, according to the text in Column 1. You could add up to three sort criteria and alter the order to descending.

5   Click the OK button and the table will automatically sort according to the criteria (see Figure 9.19).

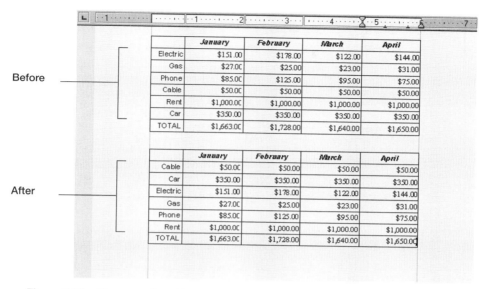

Figure 9.19 The rows of a table sorted alphabetically according to the text in Column 1.

Converting Tables and Text

Sometimes you will find that a text-based table would be better suited in paragraph form; or perhaps you need to export the information in a table in order to use it in other applications (export to a database application, for example). In these cases, Writer allows you to convert a table back into regular text or delimited (separated by a specific character) text. In addition, Writer can work in the reverse direction: you can transform regular text into a table quickly (though you might need to make some modifications to the table's cell entries and formatting).

To Convert a Table to Text

1 Select the table that you want to change to regular text.

2 Choose Tools, Text <-> Table to open the Convert Table to Text dialog box.

3 Select the option as to how you prefer the text to be separated. Tabs are convenient for keeping the data similar to the original look, and create data that can be used by applications that import tab-delimited text. Paragraph can make a text-heavy table look like regular text paragraphs; Semicolons can format text ready to be exported to another

application; and Other allows you to place a separator of your choice (also convenient for exporting). For this example, choose Tabs.

4   Click the OK button and the table will be converted to text (see Figure 9.20).

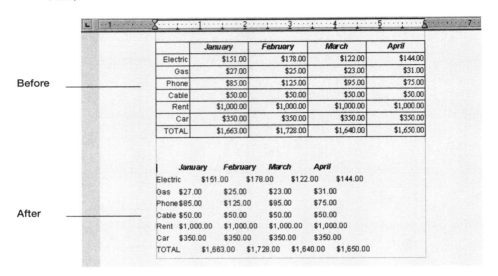

Figure 9.20   Changing a table to regular text.

To CONVERT TEXT TO A TABLE

1   Select the text that you want to change into a table. It helps for the text you would like as part of a table to be separated consistently by tabs or some type of import/export character (for example, a colon ":").

2   Choose Tools, Text <-> Table to open the Convert Text to Table dialog box (see Figure 9.21).

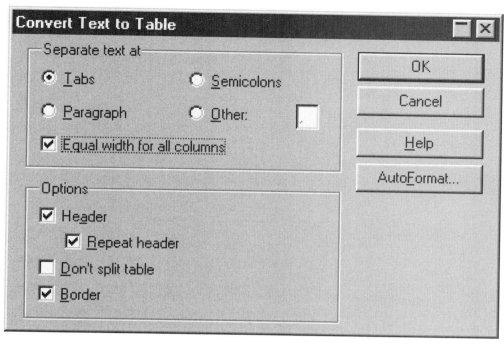

Figure 9.21 Changing regular text to a table.

3   Select the option as to how Writer will identify what to put in each cell, and where to end each row. You determined this when you typed the information into your document or perhaps the file you received has a particular delimiter (separation character). Indicate whether you separated your tabular information with Tabs, Paragraphs, Semicolons, or something else (Other). This example uses Tabs.

The equal width for all columns option will help the table look more uniform. The Options area in the dialog box is similar to when you create a new table; select these as you see fit.

4   Click the OK button and the text will be converted to a table (see Figure 9.22).

Notice, in our example, that some of the text will need to be rearranged in the table. The table header row needs to have the text entries shifted one column to the right; but this is much better than creating a new table and then copying and pasting all the information into each cell.

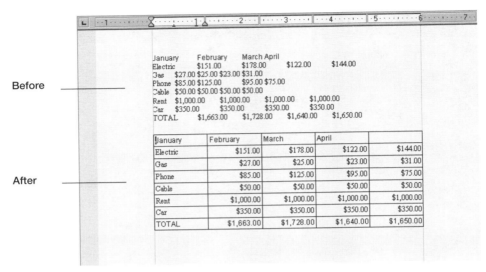

Figure 9.22   Changing regular text to a table.

Altering the Table Format

Once you have created a table and formatted the rows, columns, and cells to your liking, there are still more ways you can alter your table. For example, you can apply bold, underline, and add other formatting just as you would to regular text and paragraphs. In addition, you can format specific words within a cell, or format multiple cells, rows, or columns. Refer to Chapter 5, "Formatting Paragraphs," for help with each of the formatting options. This section will concentrate on formatting the table and the main elements within the table, such as the text flow, columns, and borders and backgrounds.

TO ALTER TABLE PROPERTIES

1   Click in a cell somewhere in the table.

2   Choose Format, Table to open the Table Format dialog box.

3   Select the Table tab (see Figure 9.23).

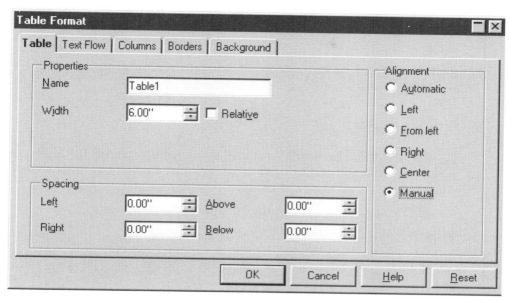

Figure 9.23 Changing the table properties.

4 Click the Manual option in the Alignment area. The following are the options you can change (Automatic is the default Alignment table format):

- Name—Alter or assign the table name. You can use the table name with the Navigator (refer to the section "Working with Master Documents" in Chapter 11 for more information on the Navigator).
- Width—Change the overall width of the table; the total width is based upon the column widths in the Columns tab (refer to the section "To Alter Table Columns"). Note that Width cannot be changed if you use Automatic alignment.
- Spacing Above and Below—Specify how far away the table is from paragraphs above and below the table.

5 Select from the options in the Alignment area and the Spacing area:

- Automatic—The default setting in which the table extends to the left and right margins.
- Left—The table will align with the left margin.
- From left—Set the left margin (Left Spacing) and the width (Width Properties) at the same time.
- Right—The table will align with the right margin.
- Center—The table will be centered between the left and right margins.
- Manual—The table aligns according to the Left and Right Spacing fields.

Notice that all the alignment options (except Automatic) allow you to alter the overall table Width or choose a percentage of the page width using the Relative option.

6   Click the OK button and the table will update with the changes automatically.

TO ALTER TABLE TEXTFLOW

1   Click in a cell in the table. Note that if you want to add a Break in the table text flow, you would need to click in the exact place in the table where you want to insert the break.

2   Choose Format, Table to open the Table Format dialog box.

3   Select the Text Flow tab (see Figure 9.24).

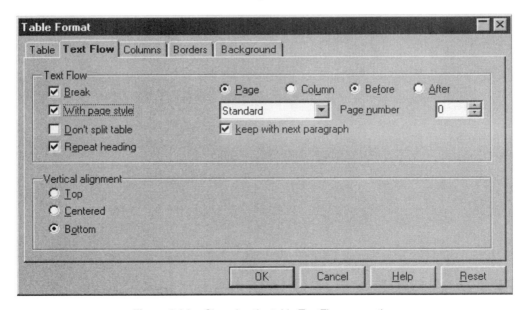

Figure 9.24   Changing the table TextFlow properties.

4   Select from the available Text Flow options:

•Break—Allows you to break a table into a new page or column; Before and After relate to the location of the table in conjunction with a paragraph of text (for example, to add a table caption, refer to the later section "Adding a Table Caption").

•With page style—If you have selected a Page Break Before option, you can specify a particular page style that the table will accompany.

- •Don't split table—This will keep an entire table on a same page, even if the entire table must be jumped to the following page in the document.
- •Repeat heading—This will repeat the table heading row if the table runs over to another page so you can easily identify the column information.
- •Keep with next paragraph—This will keep the table with the very next paragraph; it is convenient if you have assigned a table caption to accompany the table (refer to the section "Adding a Table Caption" for more on table captions).

5   Select the Vertical alignment options to set the cell text and data alignment (also refer to the section "Aligning Cell Text and Data").

6   Click the OK button and the table will automatically update with the changes.

To Alter Table Columns

1   Click in a cell in the table.

2   Choose Format, Table to open the Table Format dialog box.

3   Select the Table tab and choose the Manual Alignment option. This must be selected in order for the Column tab options to be available (otherwise only the Column widths can be adjusted).

4   Select the Columns tab and review the options (see Figure 9.25):

- •Fit to table width—The table will expand proportionately according to the amount of space in the Remaining space text box.
- •Adjust columns proportionally—This automatically adjusts the width of all the remaining columns when you adjust any one column.
- •Remaining space—The amount of space remaining into which the table can expand according to the Width box in the Table tab. When zero space is left, the columns can no longer be widened without narrowing a different column.
- •Column width—Allows you to adjust the width of specific columns, as long as you have remaining space or a different column is adjusted proportionately.

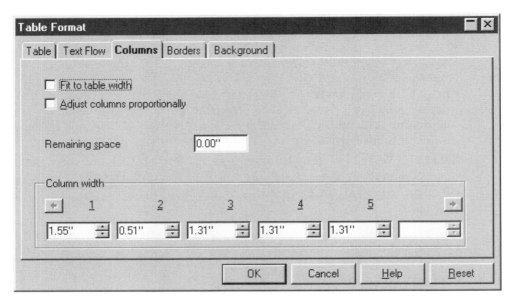

Figure 9.25   Changing the table column properties.

5   Click the OK button and the table will update with the changes automatically.

TO ADD BORDERS TO A TABLE

1   Select the cells to which you want to add a border.

By default, new tables have a .05-point, black, single-line border.

2   Click the Borders button on the Table Object Bar and select from the Borders toolbar (click and drag the toolbar to make it remain on your workspace).

3   Click the Line Style button on the Table Object Bar and select from the Border Style toolbar (you can click and drag this toolbar to keep it in the workspace as well).

You could have also chosen Format, Table and selected the Borders tab (see Figure 9.26). This is the one-stop location for selecting Presets, a Frame, the Line Style, Color, and Shadow Style Position, Size, and Color.

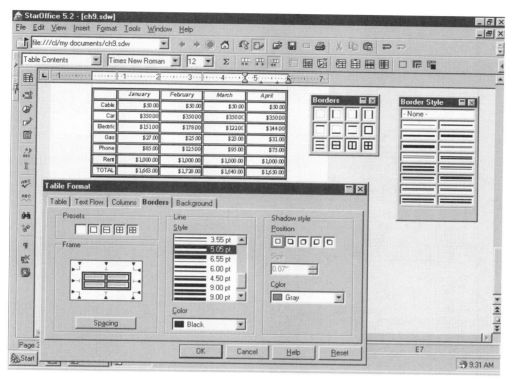

Figure 9.26 Use the Borders tab to apply border options.

TO ADD BACKGROUNDS TO A TABLE

1 Select the cells to which you want to apply a background color.

2 Click the Background Color button on the Table Object Bar and select from the Background toolbar (click and drag the toolbar to make it remain on your workspace).

You could also have chosen Format, Table and selected the Background tab (see Figure 9.27). This is the one-stop location for selecting background colors or graphics for cells, rows, or tables. Refer to the section "Adding Paragraph Backgrounds" in Chapter 5 for more information on applying background graphics.

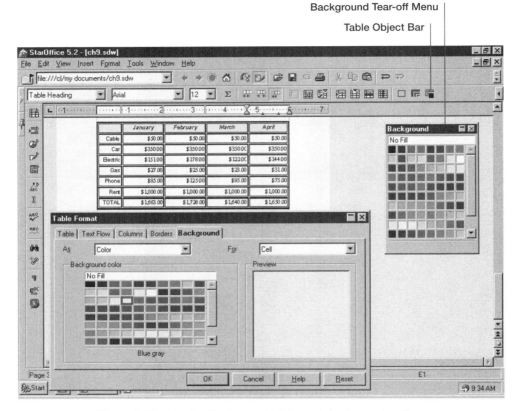

Figure 9.27   Use the Background tab to apply background options.

Applying a Table AutoFormat

One of the most efficient methods for formatting a table is to use the AutoFormat formatting option. You can choose from numerous preset table formats or even create your own format to use again and again.

To Apply a Table AutoFormat

1   Select the cells to which you want to apply a standard format.

2   Choose Format, AutoFormat to open the AutoFormat dialog box (see Figure 9.28).

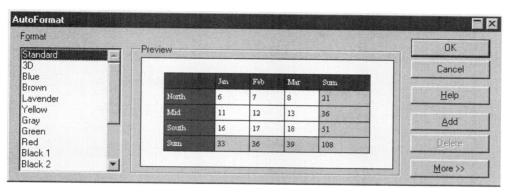

Figure 9.28 Select from available AutoFormat options.

3 Select the Format and review its appearance in the Preview area.

4 Click the OK button and your table will automatically format (see Figure 9.29).

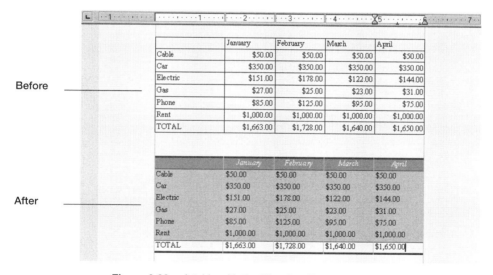

Figure 9.29 A table with the Blue AutoFormat applied.

NOTE   You can always alter the formatting options in a table that has an AutoFormat applied. For example, in Figure 9.29, you may want the monthly columns to have the currency aligned by decimal place instead of flush left. You can make this change, and even assign this as a new AutoFormat. In the AutoFormat dialog box, simply click the Add button, assign the new table formatting a name, and click the OK button. The named AutoFormat will now be available to apply to other tables.

Adding a Table Caption

Once you have inserted the table into your documents, it may be convenient to have an accompanying caption. These can be used to navigate tables in large documents and keep table descriptions with the appropriate table.

TO ADD A TABLE CAPTION

1   Click in the table in which you want to have a caption.

2   Choose Insert, Caption to open the Caption dialog box.

The Category and the Object name list boxes should already display according to the table you selected in Step 1.

3   Select the type of numbering system to order the captions from the Numbering drop-down list box.

4   Type the text you would like displayed in the Caption text box.

5   Click the Options button if you want to assign specific numbering according to a range of options (for example, chapter number separated by a period and then caption number, 1.1).

6   Select the Position of the caption in relation to the table (Above or Below).

7 Click the OK button and the caption will be added to your document, next to the table.

NOTE You can have captions automatically inserted into your documents when you create a new table. Choose Tools, Options and click on the Text document item available in the options list on the left of the Options dialog box. Click the Insert submenu and click the Automatic option in the Captions section. Click the Object selection button and select the StarOffice Writer Table (or other frames, graphics, or objects if you desire) options and Settings you prefer to be automatically created from the Caption dialog box that opens. Click the OK button and the next time you create a table, a caption will automatically accompany the table.

chapter 10

Reviewing, Collaborating, and Merging Documents

IN THIS CHAPTER:

Finding and Replacing Text

The Find and Replace features in Writer can search for specific text and formatting in a document and replace them. You can search using all kinds of search options available to you, including searching for formats, attributes, and styles (covered in the following section). You can even search for items using a set of wildcard and placeholder characters that allow you to search for items by using a portion of the text as the search string.

Choose Edit, Find & Replace to open the Find & Replace dialog box (see Figure 10.1). You could also press <Ctrl+F>.

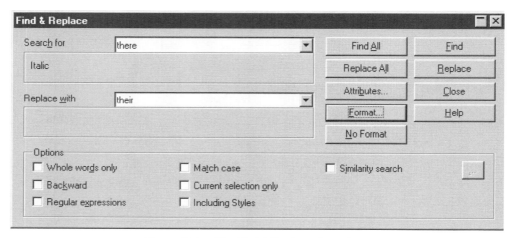

Figure 10.1   The Find & Replace dialog box.

To Use Search

To search for particular text (known as a *string*), type the information in the Search for box. To search for the string you entered, click the Find button. The find feature will search out the first occurrence of the item in the document and then select it.

> **NOTE**   When you are working with the Find & Replace feature, you may have to move the Find & Replace dialog box (drag it out of the way) to view the results of a particular search.

Once the search is complete, you can close the Find & Replace dialog box using the Close button. Even after you close the dialog box, you can quickly repeat the last search that you did. Press <Shift+Ctrl+F>, and the next occurrence of the search item will be selected.

You can also search for all the occurrences of the item that you are searching for. Just click the Find All button. All occurrences of the search string will be highlighted on the current document.

TO USE THE SEARCH OPTIONS

A number of different search options are provided by the Find & Replace dialog box. These options are:

- Attributes—Click this button to access the Attributes dialog box (see Figure 10.2); here you can select and deselect the attributes to be searched for in the current search. For example, Page Style, Tab Stops, Spacing, and so on.

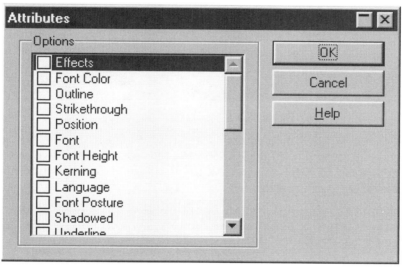

Figure 10.2 The Attributes dialog box.

- Format—Click this button to access the Text Format(Search) dialog box (see Figure 10.3); here you can select and deselect the formatting options to be searched for in the current search. For example, Font Effects, Alignment, and so on.

NOTE If you previously performed a search, it will still appear in the dialog box until you exit the Writer application. If there are any formats (for example, bold) or attributes (for example, Alignment) that accompany the Search for or Replace with drop-down list boxes, they will be displayed below the individual text box.

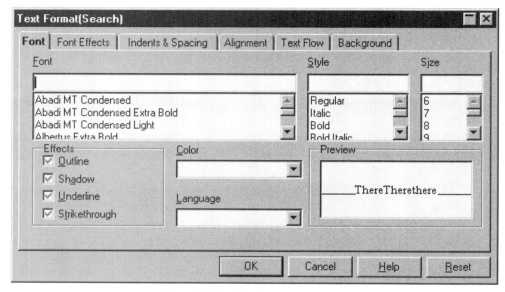

Figure 10.3   The Format dialog box.

- No Format—Click this button to deselect all the formats and attributes in the Search for and/or Replace with fields. If you want to only remove specific attributes, you must select the Format or Attributes buttons and deselect the specific options.

- Whole words only—If this check box is selected, the result will find only the Search for text if it is part of a whole word. For example, Search for "hat" will only find "hat", not "that" or "hatch".

- Backward—If this check box is selected, the search will be performed from the point of the cursor to the beginning of the document. When it reaches the beginning, a message box will appear asking if you want to continue searching at the bottom of the document; click Yes to continue or No to stop.

- Regular expressions—If this check box is selected, you can use placeholders (also known as wildcards) in your search criteria string. A number of different placeholders are available. Table 10.1 lists some of the more useful placeholders available.

- Match case—If this check box is selected, the result will only find the Search for text as it appears exactly in the text box (case sensitive). For example, "Hat" will only find "Hat", not "hat".

- Current selection only—For this check box to be active, you must select a specific portion of the document prior to opening the Search & Replace dialog box. This will perform the search and/or replace only within the selected area.

- Search for Styles—If this check box is selected, you can use this to search for and replace specific paragraph styles in the document. Select the paragraph style while in the Search for box. The Search for styles option changes to Including styles when you select an option from the Attributes or Format buttons (for example, Line Spacing). More information on replacing styles in a document in the section that follows, "Finding and Replacing Styles."

- Similarity Search—If this check box is selected, you can search for entries that are similar to the search criteria. Once this option is selected, the Settings button (...) becomes active. Click the button and use the Similarity Search dialog box to specify the number of characters that the entries can vary (Exchange characters) and the number of additional or fewer characters that will be allowed for a match (Add characters and Remove characters respectively).

Table 10.1 Regular Expression Search Placeholders

CHARACTER	RESULT
. (period)	This will return any character; for example, Search for "l.ck" finds "lick", "lock", "lack", and "luck".
^Sid	Finds the word only if it appears at the *beginning* of a paragraph.
Sid$	Finds the word only if it appears at the *end* of a paragraph.
.*	Any text or characters before the .* may appear in unlimited instances or not at all: "Sid .*home", for example, finds the text "Sid will go home", "Sid is at home", and "Sidhome".
?	Any text or characters preceding the ? may occur never or only once. "Lakes?", for example, finds the words "Lake" and "Lakes".
\C	Finds any specific text or character after the slash; for example, to search for all ampersands in a document, enter: \&.
\n	Finds a hard row break that has been inserted with <Shift+Enter> (this expression can also be used in Replace with).
\t	Finds a <Tab> (this expression can also be used in Replace with).

Table 10.1   Regular Expression Search Placeholders (Continued)

\>	The search term must appear at the end of a word: "cent\>", for example, finds "percent", but not "century".
\<	The search term must appear at the beginning of a word: "\>cent", for example, finds "century", but not "percent".
^$	Searches for blank paragraphs.
$	Searches for the end of a paragraph.
^.	Searches for the first character of a paragraph.
&	This symbol can be used to attach the replacement term to the search term. For example, "percentage" in the Search for field and "&rate" in the Replace with field returns "percentage rate" with Replace.
[xyz53]	Finds all the characters between the brackets.
[n-z]	Finds all characters between the letters n and z.
[n-pw-z]	Finds all characters between the letters n through p and w through z.
[^n-w]	Finds all characters except for the letters n through w.

TO USE REPLACE

You can also search for items in your documents and then replace them with another entry. To do a search and replace, enter a search string in the Search for box and then enter the replacement string in the Replace with box. You can apply formats and attributes to the replaced text using the search options described in the previous section.

You can then conduct your search and replace by clicking the Replace button. The first occurrence of the search string (in relation to where the cursor was in the document before you invoked the Find & Replace dialog box) will be replaced by the Replace with string.

> **NOTE**   When using search and replace: press <Ctrl+Home> to go to the beginning of the current document before you open the Find & Replace dialog box. This will start the search at the beginning of the document.

If you wish to replace all occurrences of the search string, click the Replace All button.

Finding and Replacing Styles

You can use the Find and Replace feature to actually find styles in a document and then replace them with another style. This can be particularly useful in cases where you've assigned a style and then completely rethought the look that you want for the document. Rather than modifying the style currently assigned you can replace it with another of your styles.

TO FIND AND REPLACE A STYLE

To find and replace styles, you use the same Find & Replace dialog box that you use to find and replace text in your documents.

1   Choose Edit, Find & Replace to open the Find & Replace dialog box. You could also press <Ctrl+F>. If you previously performed a search, it will still appear in the dialog box until you exit the Writer application.

2   Click the Search for Styles check box at the bottom of the dialog box.

3   Click the Search for drop-down list box and select the appropriate style you want to search for.

4   Click the Replace with drop-down list box and select the appropriate style that will serve as the replacement.

5   Click the Find button to locate the first occurrence of the style in the document.

6   To replace the occurrence of the style that was found, click the Replace button.

   If you wish to find all the occurrences of the style in the document, click the Find All button. All the occurrences of the style will be selected.

If you wish to replace all the occurrences of the style in the document, click the Replace All button.

7   Click the Close button when you are finished working with the Find & Replace dialog box.

Inserting Notes in a Document

With Writer, you can make comments to yourself (or the original author of a document) by inserting notes directly into the document. This is similar to writing comments in a printed document's margins. Writer marks the location in the document where the note is inserted.

To Insert Notes in a Document

1   Place the cursor in the text where you want to insert a note.

2   Choose Insert, Note to open the Insert Note dialog box.

3   Type the Text that you want the note to contain; the initials of the author of the note will be listed in the dialog box (see Figure 10.4).

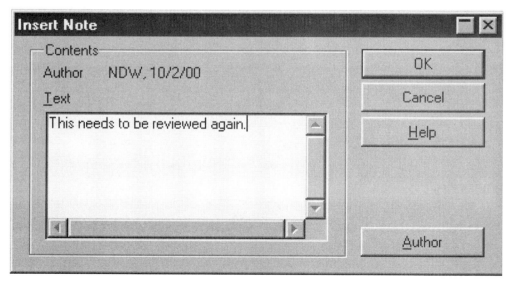

Figure 10.4   The Insert Note dialog box.

4   Click the Author button if you would like the author's initials and date the note was added to accompany the note.

5   Click the OK button to insert the note indicator into the text; it will appear as a yellow vertical bar.

TO WORK WITH NOTES

To review the note, double-click on the yellow bar and you can edit the note in the Edit Note dialog box. If there are multiple notes, arrows appear in the dialog box so you can move to previous or later notes in the document.

> **NOTE**   There is no security associated with notes; anyone can edit your notes if they wish. A better way of enforcing the protection of notes in a document is to assign a password to your entire document (choose Save with password on the Save As dialog box). Refer to the section "To Save a Document the First Time" in Chapter 1 for more information.

To delete a note, place the cursor next to the note indicator in the text and press the <Delete> or <Backspace> key, depending on where you are in relation to the note.

To print the notes that accompany your document, choose File, Print to open the Printer Options dialog box. Click the Options button in the Notes area: Notes only will print only the document notes, not the document; End of document will print the notes at the end of the printed document; End of page will print the notes that accompany each page at the bottom of the particular page when printing the document.

Including Document Properties Information

You learned how to add document properties information in Chapter 1, in the section "To Add Document Properties.". This information can be useful when different people review and collaborate on your documents. You can include document properties information in the document itself by inserting a field directly in the document.

Document properties include the file specifications (General tab); Title, Subject, Keywords, and any Comments (Description tab); individual user-defined information (User Defined tab); automatic Internet page reloading (Internet tab); and document statistics (Statistics tab).

To Insert Document Properties Information

1   Place the cursor in the text at the location where you want to add a document properties field.

2   Choose Insert, Fields and select from the available fields on the submenu. If the Document Property you want to insert isn't available from the Insert, Fields submenu, or if you need to customize how the document property appears in your document, choose the Other command (or press <Ctrl+F2>) to open the Fields dialog box.

3   Click the DocInformation tab and choose properties available according to the Type, Select, and Format list boxes (see Figure 10.5). There are also fields on the Document tab, which are used for entering content referring directly to the current document (for example, chapter number and chapter name).

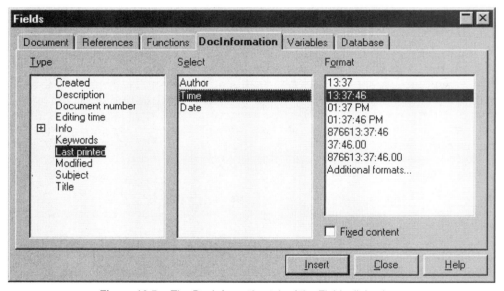

Figure 10.5   The DocInformation tab of the Fields dialog box.

4   Click the Insert button and the properties information you chose will be inserted as a field in your document.

Recording Changes to a Document

You can record changes while you edit, which will help you keep track of changes you've made to a document. When you record changes, Writer indicates all changes made to a document by applying colored text. Insertions are marked with underline, by default, and deletions are marked with strikethrough.

After you record changes in your document, you can review them and decide whether to accept the change (incorporate it into the document) or reject the change (delete it from the document).

To Record Changes to a Document

1   Choose Edit, Changes, Record to activate the recording feature (and add a checkmark next to the menu command).

2   Make some changes to your document and notice that the changes are made in a different color. This indicates that they were made since you started recording changes.

   If you move the mouse pointer over the changed text, a Help tip will display who inserted the change and when.

3   Choose Edit, Changes, Show to toggle this command on and off. This will display the altered text, but without the recording marks displayed (sometimes it is more convenient to make the changes while the recording marks are invisible). Changes are automatically shown by default.

To Add Comments to Recorded Changes

The date, time, and the individual who recorded a change in a document are displayed, by default, as a Help tip when the mouse pointer is moved over a recorded change. In order to provide more information about the change in the Help tip, you can add comments to accompany the default information.

1   Select the text in which you want to insert a comment (it must be text that indicates a recorded change).

2   Choose Edit, Changes, Comment to open the Comment: Insert dialog box.

3   Type in your commentary text and click the OK button. You can also move to previous and later comments with this dialog box (as long as you have more than one comment).

   Now when you move the mouse pointer over a recorded change to which you added a comment, the comment will appear with the default information. Note that this information does not have an option to allow it to be printed; it is in Help tip form only.

To Accept or Reject Recorded Changes

1   Choose Edit, Changes, Accept or Reject to open the Accept or Reject Changes window (see Figure 10.6).

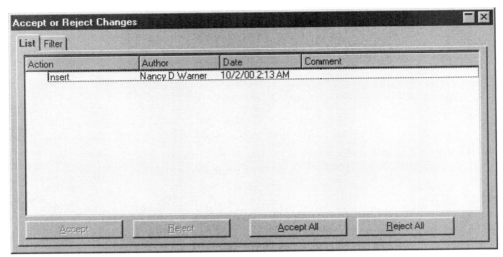

Figure 10.6   The Accept or Reject Changes dialog box.

2   Click the Accept All or Reject All buttons to accept or reject all the changes that appear in the document, or click each individual Action and click the Accept or Reject buttons.

NOTE   If Writer reaches the end or the beginning of the document while selecting changes (depending on the direction you are searching), a message will ask whether you want to continue. Choose Yes to continue, or No to stop.

3   Click the Filter tab if there are so many changes recorded that you need to filter the list (see Figure 10.7).

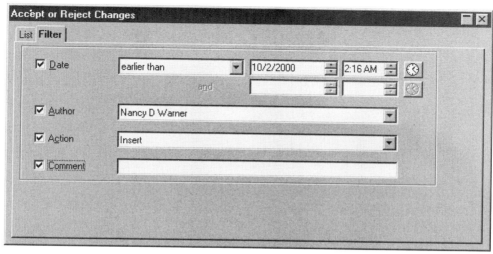

Figure 10.7 The Filter tab.

You can choose to filter the list of recorded changes by Date (date the change was made), Author (who made the change), Action (what type of change was made), or Comment (comments about the change). Then, click back to the List tab and the list will contain only the items by which you filtered the list.

4   Whenever you're ready to return to your document, click the X Close button on the Accept or Reject Changes window.

NOTE   Saving different versions of a document is another way to keep track of review and collaboration on a document. Review the sections "To Save Document Versions" and "To Review Document Versions" in Chapter 1 to learn how to save and review document versions.

TO ALTER HOW RECORDED CHANGES DISPLAY

1   Choose Tools, Options to open the Options window; click on Text document and select the Changes register (see Figure 10.8).

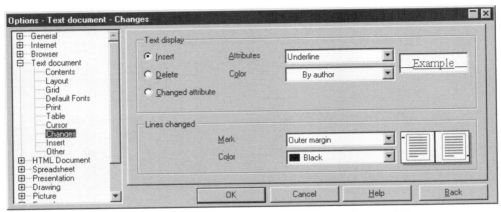

Figure 10.8   Alter the text display and line changes in the Options dialog box.

2   To control how additions to the document are displayed, click the Insert option and select from the various Attributes and Color drop-down list boxes; the changes will display in the Example area. By default, inserted text is underlined and the color displays according to the author, so each person's additions will appear in a different color.

3   To control how deletions from the document are displayed, click the Delete option and select from the various Attributes and Color drop-down list boxes; the changes will display in the Example area. By default, deleted text shows as strikethrough and the color displays according to the author, so each person's deletions will appear in a different color.

4   To display how changes to document attributes (for example, italics) display, select from the various Attributes and Color drop-down list boxes; the changes will display in the Example area. By default, changed text is bold and the color is black.

5   To help reviewers quickly locate changes, Writer places a vertical black line, called a Mark, in the outer margin of any line with a change. To specify a different location, choose the new location from the Mark drop-down list box. To change the Mark's color, choose from the Color drop-down list box.

6   Click the OK button to accept the changes and return to your StarOffice Writer text document.

Merging Multiple Documents

If you sent a copy of your document to your partner for updates to the document and they *recorded* the changes or deletions he or she made, Writer allows you to merge the documents.

TO MERGE MULTIPLE DOCUMENTS

1 Open your original document.

2 Choose Edit, Changes, Merge Documents to open the Insert dialog box.

3 Select the file with which you want to merge the original and click the Insert button.

   Writer merges the two documents and displays the differences between the two as recorded changes. The effect is as if you had tracked the changes while editing—text that appears in the original document but not in the new document is marked as a deletion, while text that appears in the new document but not in the original document is marked as an insertion.

Comparing Documents

If you sent a copy of your document to your partner for updates to the document and they *did not record* the changes or deletions he or she made, Writer allows you to compare the documents, displaying the differences between the documents as recorded changes.

> **NOTE**   If *you* also made changes to the document you sent for review to your partner, you must merge the two documents before you compare them. Otherwise, additions in your document will appear as deletions when you compare the documents (because obviously the partner-reviewed document won't have your additions). Refer to the previous section "Merging Documents" for more information.

TO COMPARE DOCUMENTS

1 Open the original document.

2 Choose Edit, Compare Document to open the Insert dialog box.

3   Select the file with which you want to compare the original and click the Insert button.

Writer compares the two documents and records the differences between the two by displaying the recorded changes. The effect is as if you had tracked the changes while editing—text that appears in the original document but not in the new document is marked as a deletion, while text that appears in the new document but not in the original document is marked as an insertion.

The Accept or Reject Changes window will open automatically so you can indicate which changes to accept and which to delete.

4   Click the Accept All or Reject All buttons to accept or reject all the changes apparent in the original document, or click each individual Action and click the Accept or Reject buttons.

5   Click the Filter tab if there are so many changes recorded that you need to filter the list.

You can choose to filter the list of recorded changes by Date (date the change was made), Author (who made the change), Action (what type of change was made), or Comment (comments about the change). Then, click back to the List tab and the list will only contain the items by which you filtered the list.

6   Click the X Close button on the Accept or Reject Changes window to return to your document.

Sending a Document as Email

Instead of having multiple people make changes, notes, and comments to the same document, send the document via email, so each recipient gets his or her own copy to work from. Later, you can merge the comments into a single document reflecting all of them.

To do this, you must have an email system installed on your computer and Writer must be configured to send information to your email program (you must first create an Outbox).

To Send a Document as Email

1   Open the document you plan to route, or select the text in the document you want to send.

2   Choose File, Send, Document as Email to open the Send Mail dialog box (see Figure 10.9).

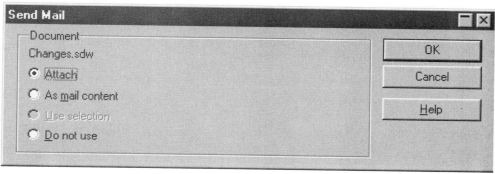

Figure 10.9   The Send Mail dialog box.

3   Select from the options to Attach the Document, send it As mail content, Use selection to send (for this option, you must select the specific part of the document prior to opening the Send Mail dialog box), or Do not use. For this example, choose Attach.

4   Click the OK button to open the email message window.

If you instead get a message box telling you that you need to first create an Outbox, follow the steps in the section "To Create an Outbox to Use with Writer" and then return to this section.

If you click the Attachments tab (see Figure 10.10) in the upper right of the message, you will see the document you attached to this email (if you chose the Attach option). You can click the Attach File button if you need to attach additional files.

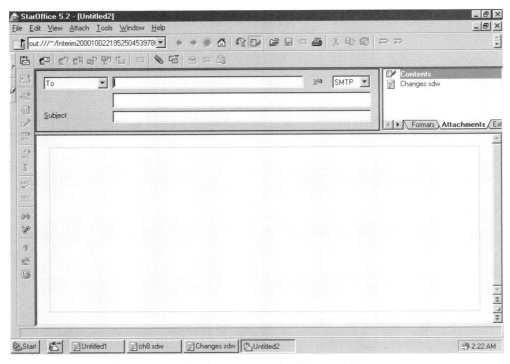

Figure 10.10   The document attached in an email message.

5   Type in the address for whom you would like to route the document.

Make sure to indicate SMTP if you are sending the message to a person's email address. You can click the Show Address Book button to select an email address from your address book. If you are sending the email to a newsgroup, you will want to select via NNTP.

6   Press the <Tab> key to move to the Subject line and type in a subject of the email.

7   Click the mouse pointer once directly in the message body below the email header information.

8   Type in any message information that you want to accompany the document you are sending.

9   Click the Send Message button, and the message will be sent; you will return to the document you were working in (and that you wanted to send via email).

To Create an Outbox to Use with Writer

1   Choose Window, Desktop to return to the desktop. Click the Show button if you need to see the Explorer window.

2   Or, choose View, Explorer. Click on the E-mail & News section (see Figure 10.11).

You must create an outbox if you want to be able to send email and news postings within StarOffice Writer. When you send a document via email, it is automatically placed in your Outbox. You can start your email application and after you connect online, the action of sending and receiving messages will automatically send the document you wanted to send as an email message via the Outbox.

Figure 10.11
The Explorer window.

3   Right-click in the Explorer window and choose New, Outbox to open the Properties of Outbox dialog box.

4   Click the General tab and type in a Name for the Outbox.

You can add other information on the other tabs of the dialog box (for example, SMTP for email or NNTP for newsgroups). If you have already filled in everything under Tools, Options, Internet, Mail/News, the entries are automatically applied to the Outbox. If you need this information, check with your Internet Service Provider or review the email account properties in your email application (typically from the Tools, Account or Account, Properties commands).

> **NOTE**   You can create separate views of your Outbox—perhaps for business and personal mail. However, the Outbox Properties settings you choose will be the same for all views of the Outbox.

5   Click the OK button and a new Outbox will be created at your location in the Explorer window.

Performing a Form Letter Mail Merge

A mail merge in StarOffice Writer requires that you use a database you already have (containing fields in a table) to merge with a document you set up (form letter). Basically, you merge the fields in a document that correspond to the same fields in a database table. For example, you can have the name and address of the clients in the Address Book File table automatically merged into a form letter containing corresponding name and address fields.

- **Step 1:** Assemble Your Data—This is where you create new data or import data to correspond to the specific information you want inserted into each form letter. For example, the name and address fields for the people to whom you are mailing your form letters.

- **Step 2:** Create the Form Letter—Using the AutoPilot or by creating a new letter for the mail merge, the body of the letter must contain the fields that correspond to your data, as well as any specific text you want in each letter. For example, if you want to send letters to all the people in your office, you must type the letter and insert fields that correspond to their names and addresses.

- **Step 3:** Perform the Form Letter Mail Merge—This is essentially where you combine the data and the letter to create as many letters as you have data records. For example, if there are 10 people in your office to whom you are mailing, you will actually be creating and printing 10 separate letter documents (or if you are emailing them, sending 10 separate emails; or if you are saving them to file, creating 10 separate text document files).

> **NOTE**   Depending on how much you know about databases, or whether you already have a database that you want to use in the form letter mail merge, you might want to read through each of the sections that follow before you begin performing the steps in StarOffice.

To Review Your Explorer Database Tables

If you already have database tables that contain the data fields you want to use in your form letter mail merge, the following steps will show you how to quickly review them.

1   Choose Window, Desktop to return to the Explorer window.

2   Click the Show button if you need to see the Explorer areas. Or choose View, Explorer.

3   Click on the Explorer section.

4   Click the + to the left of the Address Book option to display the forms, reports, queries, and tables available in your address book (that you created or existing samples).

5   Click the + to the left of the Tables option to display the tables available in your address book (that you created or existing samples). See Figure 10.12.

Do not be alarmed if there are no tables listed, because you will create one based on the Address Book data in the very next section.

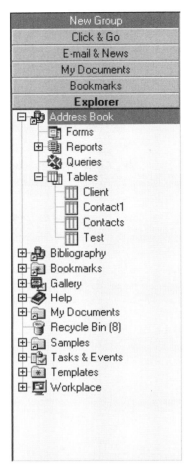

Figure 10.12   The Address Book
tables in the Explorer window.

TO CREATE A DATABASE BASED ON A TEXT FILE

This set of steps applies if you have a text file that contains the data you want to use in your form letter mail merge, but you first need to import it into your database (perhaps the data originated from a non-StarOffice application). You are basically telling Writer what file to use to assemble your data in a database table.

> **NOTE**   Before you start, you might need to tweak your source document to improve the likelihood of a successful import. For example, check your source document with a Text-to-Table conversion, based on the delimiter used in your text file. Refer to the section "To Convert Text to a Table" for more information. Fix any problems with the text file before converting it into a database.

1   Choose File, New, Database to open the properties of the <Database> dialog box. If you get a "database failure to connect message", ignore it by clicking OK, and continue on with the steps.

2   Type in a name for the database on the General tab. For example, type Clients.

3   Click the Type tab and select Text from the Database type drop-down list box.

> **NOTE**   You can select from any of the Database types you prefer, and each of the tabs will vary accordingly. Select and input the various options and then continue with step 6.

4   Click the Browse button and indicate the location of the text file to be created as a new database (by choosing the location of the file and clicking the Select button).

5   Click the Text tab and indicate the separators used in your text file. If your text file contains information on specific tables, click the Tables tab and Select the tables to be displayed from the list.

6   Click the OK button to create the database based on the StarOffice defaults contained in the remaining tabs. This is simply a way for you to get started in creating a personal clients database based on a text file you already have (perhaps from a file saved by a different database application), not to teach you how to use databases.

7   Notice that the Clients database appears in the Explorer list just as the Address Book database from the previous section "To Review Your Explorer Database Tables."

Click on the Clients +, click the Tables +, and double-click on the table that was created from the text file. You can edit or add more clients to your database table as you like; or, you can create a completely new table (see the following section).

TO CREATE A TABLE BASED ON THE ADDRESS BOOK FILE

If you have the data you need for your form letter mail merge saved in your Address Book file, this procedure will get you working with your data a lot faster. Also, if there are additional records you need to add to the database file, you can enter the records one at a time.

1 Choose File, AutoPilot, Table to open the AutoPilot Table dialog box to the Table type page.

2 Click the Databases drop-down list box and select Address Book File (this will base any new tables on the Address Book formats). Leave the Table set to Business by default. Click on the Contacts information, and then click the Next button to move to the Field selection page.

3 Press the <Ctrl> key while you click on each of the Proposed Fields from the list. These will be the fields that are used, for example, from the Address Book File, in your newly created Clients table. Or, to transfer all the fields to the Applied area, click the double-right-arrow button. Then, click the Next button to move to the Customization page.

4 Type in a name for the Table. It is probably a good idea for now to simply accept the Field name defaults and skip this page by clicking the Next button to move to the Create Table page.

5 Choose to Enter data into the table After completion option (instead of the Do not show table option) and click the Create button. This way you can review your new Client table and add clients immediately.

6 Type in each field and press the arrow keys to move through each record. A record contains all the fields in the list; you can add, delete, and edit fields within a record. When finished, simply click the X close button.

TO CREATE AN AUTOPILOT TEMPLATE AND LETTER FOR THE MAIL MERGE

This and the section that follows are intended to contrast building a letter with the AutoPilot with creating one from scratch. This set of steps creates a letter using the AutoPilot.

1 Choose File, AutoPilot, Letter to open the AutoPilot Letter dialog box. If you receive the message "Error reading data from database", simply click the OK button and continue on with the steps.

2 Choose whether you want to create a Business letter or Personal letter; choose the Modern, Classic, or Decorative style you prefer. Then, click the Next button to move to the next page in the AutoPilot.

3 Select whether you want a logo to display as a graphic or as text you enter (or No logo at all—if so, move to step 4). Select the Position of the logo on the letter (Left, Center, Right) and how far From left or From top.

You can also choose the Size Height and Width of the logo. Click the Next button to move to the next page in the AutoPilot.

4   Make sure the Enter sender address is correct (it will display according to the information you provided StarOffice when you installed the software; otherwise, you can enter it again in the Tools, Options, General, User Data dialog box). Indicate whether you would like it to Repeat in addressee field (select Yes or No and you can see where it displays on the template). Indicate the Position and Size of the sender address information and click the Next button to move to the next page in the AutoPilot.

5   Select the Database name from the drop-down list and then choose the table from the drop-down list to the right. If you receive an "Error reading data from database" message, you might need to check to make sure that you are properly connected to your database. Click on each of the Database fields listed below the database table, and click the left arrow button (after you select each one) to add the fields to the Address area according to how you want them to display in the letter (you can add spaces with the <Spacebar>, delete fields with the <Backspace> key, and press the <Enter> key to move fields to the next line; or use the return arrow button to insert a paragraph break in the Address area). Type in a Salutation for the letter and select the specific Address field for the salutation text from the drop-down list, for example, <database.table.first-name>. Click the Next button to move to the next page in the AutoPilot.

6   Choose each checkbox field option according to the elements that you would like your letter to contain. Each option will display in the preview area on the left to help you determine where the information will be on your letter. Click the Next button to move to the next page in the AutoPilot.

7   Choose from the Footer options and type in any information you would like to include in the footer. You can also alter the From left and From right Page margins on this page. Click the Next button to move to the next page in the AutoPilot.

8   Choose the continuation page Header and Footer information you would like to include in case your letter flows over to more than one page. Click the Next button to move to the next page in the AutoPilot.

9   Choose from the Doc Information drop-down Title and Subject list boxes (or leave None as the default) to save as properties of your template. Select the Automatic option in the File name area if you would like StarOffice to assign a file name automatically. (If you do so, the Destination button is activated; click it to specify where the file should be saved.) Type the Name and Info you prefer to be assigned to the Template file name (by default it is saved to your standard StarOffice templates folder—just as when you created new templates in Chapter 7). Click the Next button to move to the next page in the AutoPilot.

10   Select where the Logo and Sender address should be printed; the drop-down list options are Always, First page, Continuation pages, and Don't print. Alter the printer setup and location (if the defaults aren't correct). Click the Create button to create the AutoPilot letter template and display the fields that you indicated in the Letter AutoPilot that would be integrated into the letter. The newly created document will open as an Untitled document based on the template.

This template can be accessed later by choosing File, New, From Template, and then choosing the Template name from the Standard section of document template Categories.

11   Type any additional text you would like in your letter. You can click the Save button on the Main toolbar to save the letter template as a document. If you don't resave the letter, you will have to type the additional text you want in the letter again, after you open the original letter template you created.

NOTE   The text you add to your document is not saved with the template. To alter the template, you would need to open a new document based on the template, add the boilerplate text, and save the document as a template in the new template folder location (Office52\User\Template).

12   Follow along steps 1–4 in the section "To Perform the Letter Mail Merge" to perform the mail merge.

NOTE   If you make any changes to the data in the records displayed, you will be asked whether or not you want to save those changes.

To Create a New Letter for the Mail Merge

This and the preceding section are intended to contrast building a letter with the AutoPilot with creating one from scratch. This set of steps creates a letter from scratch.

1   Choose File, New Text Document to open a blank document.

2   Type the letter as you want it to appear in the final mail merge document. Place the cursor at the location where you would like to insert the first field in your document.

3   Choose Insert, Fields, Other (or press <Ctrl+F2>) to open the Fields dialog box.

4   Click the Database tab and choose Form letter field from the Type list box.

5   Click the Database selection option by clicking the + sign on the database to expand it into tables, then click the + sign on the table to expand it into fields.

6   Select the specific field you want inserted into your document and click the Insert button. Move the cursor to the next location in your document (the Fields dialog box remains visible). Repeat this step for each field you would like inserted. The field name will appear in the document unless you have chosen View, Fields (or pressed <Ctrl+F9>) to view the field contents instead—though it will end up being the same information in the form letter.

NOTE   Don't forget to add the necessary spaces between fields that you insert into your document. For example, you would need to type a space between FirstName and LastName fields.

7   Click the Close button in the Fields dialog box when you have finished inserting fields.

8   Save the document and follow along steps 1–4 in the section "To Perform the Letter Mail Merge" to perform the mail merge.

TO PERFORM THE LETTER MAIL MERGE

1   Open the letter you created to use in the mail merge. You can either use the saved version of the letter or choose File, New, From Template, and then select the Template name from the Standard section of Categories. The document will open based on the document template you created for the form letter.

If you opened the file as a template (like the one you created in the section "To Create the AutoPilot Letter Template for the Mail Merge"), only the basic template information will appear, so you will need to retype the actual letter information before you move on to Step 2.

If you opened the file that you saved as a document (like the one you created in the section "To Create a New Letter for the Mail Merge"), only the letter will appear, so you may need to press <F4> or choose View, Current Database to see the records associated with the letter.

2   Choose File, Form Letter to open the Form Letter dialog box.

If you selected specific records in the table before you clicked the Form Letter button, the Selected records option will be available. You can select records from the table by holding the <Ctrl> key and clicking the mouse pointer on the gray rectangle to the left of the left-most field column.

NOTE   You can also perform a sort or filter on the records in the table to perform the mail merge on specific records. For example, sort the records alphabetically by the second field—last name, or perhaps you want to filter records so that only people with the last name "Smith" received the letter.

3   Choose how you would like the record to Output:

- Printer—Select the Single print jobs option if you don't want all the records to be sent to the printer as one print job. The advantage of this is that if you find an error while printing, you can stop the print job easier. Otherwise this option will open the Print dialog box.
- Mailing—If an email address is contained as a field in the table you are working with, you can select the email Address field from the table, type in a Subject, indicate and select any attachments, and choose the Mail Format.
- File—If you want to perform the mail merge, but print the letters later, you can save the records as separate files. Indicate the Path of the files and either type a file name in the Manual setting text box or select the Database field from the drop-down list box to generate the file names.

4   Click the OK button to send the form letter to the appropriate Output location (printer, email, or file name).

NOTE   If you want to create a set of labels for these letters (or a few envelopes if your mail merge is small), refer to the sections "Preparing and Printing Labels" or "Preparing and Printing Envelopes" in Chapter 2.

Working with Long Document Features

Inserting Headers and Footers

You can insert all types of things into your headers and footers, such as graphics, frames, and objects. You can also insert fields like dates, times, page numbers, and even chapter numbers of the specific chapter in which you are working.

Keep in mind that headers and footers are page styles, so if you want to alter them uniformly throughout your document, you must modify the page style in the Stylist. You can even modify them specifically for left- and right-hand pages, and to create a separate header or footer (or to eliminate the header or footer) on the first page of your document.

TO INSERT AND DELETE A HEADER OR FOOTER

Choose Format, Page to open the Page Style dialog box and click the Header (or Footer) tab. If you already have a header (or footer) in your document, the Header on (or Footer on) option will be active. Otherwise, select this option to activate the header (or footer) area in your document (see Figure 11.1).

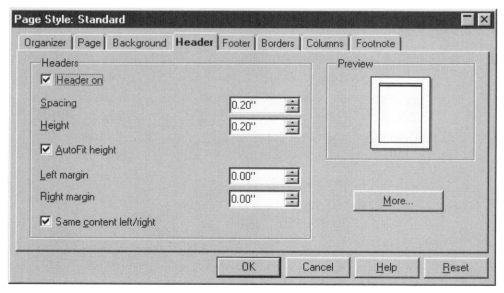

Figure 11.1   Insert a header or footer using the appropriate tabs on the Page Style dialog box.

You can also choose Insert, Header (or Footer) to activate either the Standard or HTML header (or footer) for the document.

> **NOTE** HTML documents have some commands available for headers and footers (for example, Author and Sender). Headers and footers are exported as special tags and interpreted when viewing the HTML page in StarOffice. StarOffice inserts a field command and updates it as necessary, while other Web browsers display the header and footer contents exactly as they were when you performed the HTML export. Keep in mind that you must activate the headers and footers in Online Layout mode in order to export them in HTML documents.

If there is already a header or footer in the document, there will be a checkmark next to the Standard command (unless your header or footer has a different page style assigned, in which case the checkmark would be next to the current style). If you choose Insert, Header (or Footer) again (in essence, deselecting the checkmark), you will be prompted as to whether you prefer to remove the header (or footer).

TO USE DIFFERENT LEFT PAGE AND RIGHT PAGE HEADERS OR FOOTERS

If you need, you can type different content in an odd-numbered left page header (or footer) versus an even-numbered right page header (or footer).

1   Choose Format, Page to open the Page Style dialog box and click the Header (or Footer) tab.

2   Click to deselect the Same content left/right option and click the OK button.

> **NOTE** You could also create two separate page styles using the Stylist and assign them to the respective pages (or headers and footers).

TO ESTABLISH DIFFERENT HEADERS OR FOOTERS IN A DOCUMENT

This section is slightly different than simply inserting a Standard style header or footer into your document. When you insert a header or footer, it will appear in all the pages that have the same Page style. If you need the first page in your document to have a different header (or no header), or if you need left and right pages (verso and recto in printing) to be different, you must specify this using the Page styles: First Page, Left Page, and Right Page.

1   Choose File, New, Text Document to open a new, blank text document. This is for the purposes of this example, but you could also open a document you have already created.

2   Press <F11> to open the Stylist and click the Page Styles icon.

3   Select the style First Page to use as the basis for your own page style.

4   Right-click in the Stylist and choose New from the shortcut menu to open the Page Style dialog box (see Figure 11.2).

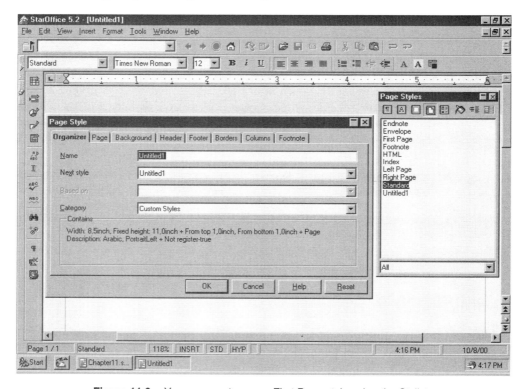

Figure 11.2   You can create a new First Page style using the Stylist.

5   Click the Organizer tab of the Page Style dialog box if it does not already appear; then type a Name for the new page style, for example "Page-1," and choose Left Page from the Next style drop-down list box. Then, click the OK button.

6   If you don't do the next steps exactly, you won't get the correct styles on following pages. Click the Left Page style in the Stylist; right-click and choose Modify from the shortcut menu to open the Page Styles dialog box. Click the Next style drop-down list box, and choose Right Page. Click the Right Page style in the Stylist; right-click and choose Modify

from the shortcut menu to open the Page Styles dialog box. Click the Next style drop-down list box, choose Left Page, and click the OK button.

7   Choose Format, Page; select the Header (or Footer) tab and click the Header on (or Footer on) option, and click the OK button.

8   Place the cursor in the header (or footer) area in the document.

9   Choose Insert, Header (or Insert, Footer) and apply the appropriate style from the list you made available on the submenu (see Figure 11.3). Then, enter the information you would like in your header or footer.

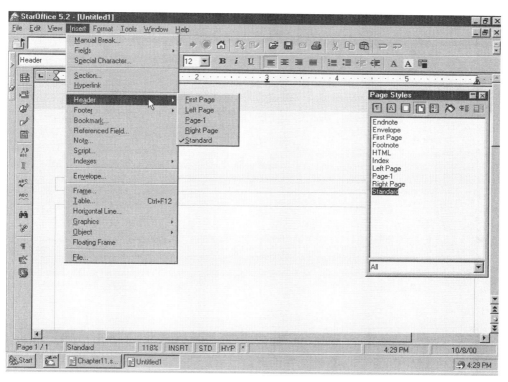

Figure 11.3   Apply the header or footer style you made available.

TO ASSIGN A SINGLE PAGE A DIFFERENT HEADER OR FOOTER

This is a very handy feature for first pages (like cover pages in a document) that you don't want a header or footer on; or if you don't want to take the time to complete the steps to change the page styles in the previous section, "To Establish Different Headers or Footers in a Document."

1   Place the cursor in the header (or footer) on the exact page on which you prefer not to have a header (or footer).

2   Choose Insert, Frame to open the Frame dialog box to the Type tab.

3   Click the Wrap tab and select the Through option.

4   Click the Background tab and select the White color (do not choose No Fill; actually select the small box that is white).

5   Click the OK button to return to the document header (or footer). Frames default to the centered position, so you may need to click the Align Left button on the Frame Object bar.

6   Select the sizing handles and resize the frame so that it covers up the text in the header (or footer) that you don't want to show (see Figure 11.4).

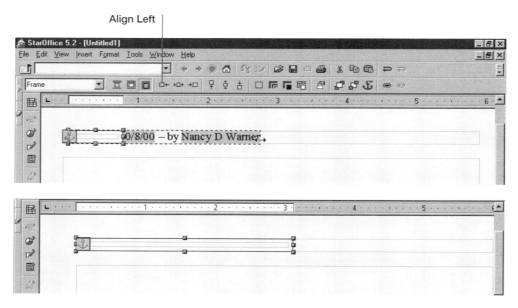

Figure 11.4   You can add a frame to cover up information in a header or footer.

To Add a Border to a Header or Footer

1   Choose Format, Page to open the Page Style dialog box and click the Header (or Footer) tab.

    You can choose Insert, Header (or Footer) and apply a Standard or other available page style if the document doesn't already have a header (or footer) inserted.

2   Click the More button to open the Border/Background dialog box.

3   To specify which sides of the header or footer should be bordered, use the Presets, or click on each side you want to border in the Frame area.

4   Choose the Line Style from the list and select the Color from the drop-down list box.

    You could also choose a Shadow style Position, Size, and Color, though these are rarely used in headers (or footers).

5   Click the OK button on both dialog boxes to return to the document (see Figure 11.5).

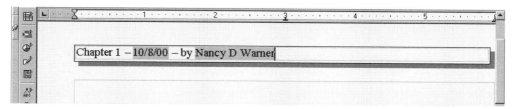

Figure 11.5   You can apply a border and background options to your header or footer.

To Add Chapter Information to a Header or Footer

1   Enter text in a long document and apply the style "Heading 1" to chapter headings.

2   Choose Format, Page to open the Page Style dialog box and click the Header (or Footer) tab; make sure the Header on (or Footer on) option is selected and click the OK button.

    You can choose Insert, Header (or Footer) if the document doesn't already have a header (or footer) inserted.

3   Click in the header (or footer) to place the cursor there; then type the text you want to appear adjacent to the automated chapter number. For example, type: "Chapter:".

4   Choose Insert, Fields, Other to open the Fields dialog box and click the Document tab (see Figure 11.6).

You could also choose the common fields from the Fields submenu, or available options from the other tabs in the Fields dialog box. Refer to the section "Inserting Fields" for more information on adding fields to documents when you want to add fields to a header or footer.

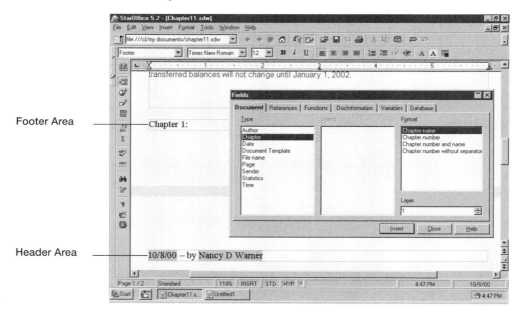

Footer Area

Header Area

Figure 11.6   You can apply specific fields to your headers or footers.

5   Select Chapter in the Type list and Chapter name in the Format list.

If you prefer the text to be drawn from a different style heading level (for example, if you would like the section name in the header that corresponds to text on the page styled as Heading 3), simply change the Level value to the corresponding style heading number. This only works if you haven't changed the level associated with these built-in styles. You also have to add numbering in the chapter first if you want to add a chapter number to the header or footer.

6   Click the Insert button to place the chapter number field in the header (or footer) and click the Close button on the dialog box to return to the document.

Inserting Footnotes and Endnotes

Footnotes can be displayed at the bottom of a page, at the end of a document, or even at the bottom of a column if you are using multiple columns. Endnotes are always displayed as the last page of the document, even after footnotes that may be displayed at the end of a document.

When you insert a footnote or endnote into your document, a marker is placed in the text at the location of your cursor. This marker identifies the presence of a footnote or endnote. After you type the footnote or endnote text, you can return to the information by clicking directly on the specific marker in the text. To return to working in the document, click directly in the document body (or press the page up or down keys).

You can change the formatting of all footnotes and/or endnotes in your document at the same time by modifying the corresponding Footnote and/or Endnote paragraph style through the Stylist, or through Format, Styles, Style Catalog. If you insert footnotes as endnotes at the end of a document, you can apply a separate page style (in advance) to the pages where they are inserted automatically.

TO INSERT A FOOTNOTE OR ENDNOTE

1   Open a document in which you want to add a footnote or endnote.

   To add a footnote or endnote immediately—without first reviewing or changing the settings for that footnote—click the Insert Endnote Directly or Insert Footnote Directly option on the Insert submenu off the Main toolbar (see Figure 11.7). By default the footnote or endnote marker will be inserted into the document with automatic numbering, and the cursor will be in the footnote or endnote area for you to enter the information.

Insert Endnote Directly

Insert Footnote Directly

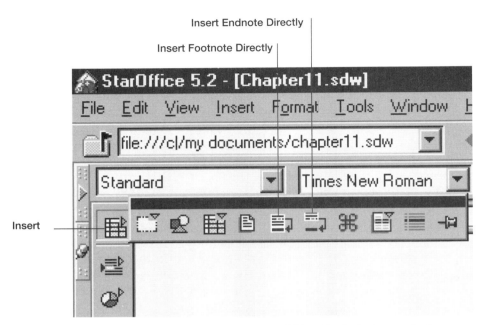

Insert

Figure 11.7   You can use the Insert menu to quickly add a footnote or endnote.

2   Choose Insert, Footnote to open the Insert Footnote dialog box.

3   Select either the Footnote or Endnote Type option (see Figure 11.8).

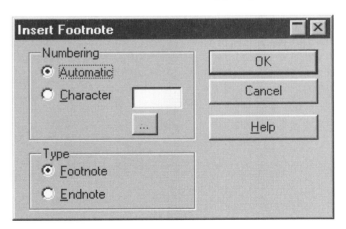

Figure 11.8   Indicate the type and numbering you want for your
footnotes or endnotes.

4   Choose from the following Numbering options; this will determine the type of marker that displays in your document to indicate a footnote or endnote:

- Automatically—Ensures that footnotes or endnotes appear consecutively numbered in your document, making automatic adjustments to numbering as you add or move new footnotes or endnotes. For example, if you have inserted two footnotes (or endnotes) in the text and then decide you would like to add a footnote or endnote somewhere in the text between them, all reference markers will automatically renumber consecutively from the beginning of the document to the end.
- Character—Displays a character of your choice. You can also click on the (…) button to select a character from the Special Characters dialog box.

5   Click the OK button to insert the footnote or endnote marker and move the cursor to the footnote or endnote text location (see Figure 11.9). Type in your footnote or endnote text and then click elsewhere in the document to return to the document body (or click the page up or page down keys).

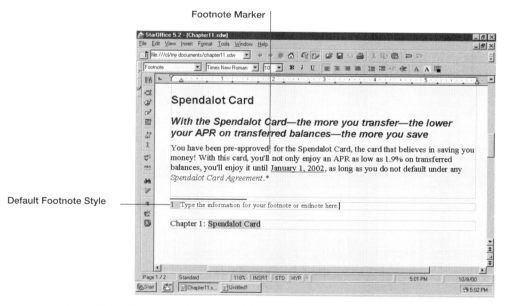

Figure 11.9   This is what a default style footnote looks like in your document.

To Edit or Delete a Footnote or Endnote

If you want to edit the *text* directly in a footnote or endnote, place the cursor in the footnote or endnote area and edit the text as necessary. You can also add formatting to each footnote. For example, you could boldface one footnote, or italicize a book title mentioned within a specific footnote.

If you want to edit the footnote or endnote *marker*, place the cursor before the marker and choose Edit, Footnote to open the Edit Footnote dialog box. Here you can alter the Numbering (from Automatic to a Character), alter the Type (in case you want to change a footnote to an endnote), or simply click the left and right arrow buttons to move through and edit the other footnotes or endnotes.

If you want to delete a footnote or endnote, simply delete the corresponding marker directly in the text (by pressing <Delete> or <Backspace> on the keyboard).

To Alter Footnote or Endnote Options

1   Choose Tools, Footnotes to open the Footnote Options dialog box. Perform steps 2 and/or 3, depending upon whether you want to alter a footnote, an endnote, or both.

2   Click the Footnotes tab to select from the following options (see Figure 11.10):

   • AutoNumbering—Indicate the type of numbering in the drop-down list box (1,2,3, A,B,C, and so on) and choose whether you would like the footnote numbering to be per document, per chapter, or even for a specific page (if you indicated a page style for a specific page). Select the number it should Start at (for example, if you choose the Per document option, you can start the numbering where the previous chapter left off). If you want to begin or end the footnote marker with additional characters, type them in the Before and After text boxes.

   • Styles—Indicate the Paragraph or Page Styles for the footnote *text* (how the actual footnote will appear in the document in the footnote area). This can depend upon whether you are formatting a footnote or page styled footnote.

   • Character styles—Indicate the Text area or Footnote area Character styles for the footnote *symbol* (how the footnote marker will appear in the document).

   • Position—Select whether to Position the footnote or endnote text at the End of page or End of document. Notice that if you select the End of page option, you can no longer format the Page Style.

   • Continuation notice—Indicate the specific text to use when telling the reader that a footnote or endnote is continued on the next page. For example, you may use "continued on next page" in the End of footnote text box and "continued from previous page" in the Start of next page text box.

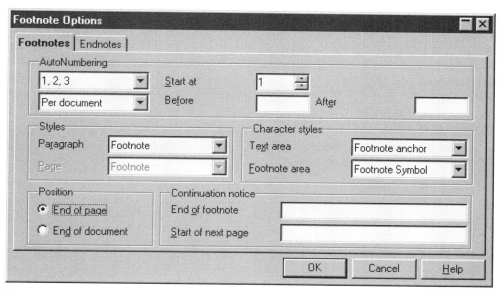

Figure 11.10   You can alter the way footnotes will appear at the bottom of the pages in your document.

3   Click the Endnotes tab to select from the following options (see Figure 11.11):

  •AutoNumbering—Indicate the type of numbering in the drop-down list box and choose the number it should Start at (for example, if you want to continue the numbering where a previous chapter left off). If you would like to begin or end the footnote marker with additional characters, type them in the Before and After text boxes.

  •Styles—Indicate the Paragraph or Page Styles for the endnote *text* (how the actual endnote will appear in the document). This will depend upon whether you are formatting an endnote or page styled endnote.

  •Character styles—Indicate the Text area or Endnote area Character styles for the endnote *symbol* (how the endnote marker will appear in the document).

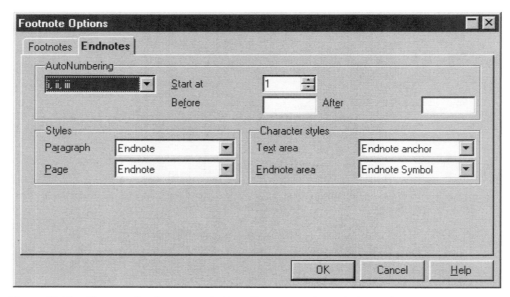

Figure 11.11   You can alter the way endnotes will appear at the end of your document.

4   Click the OK button to apply the changes and return to the document.

TO ADJUST SPACING BETWEEN FOOTNOTES AND ENDNOTES

The spacing adjustments in this section refer to the distance between each foot-note or endnote in the footnote or endnote area.

1   Place the cursor in a footnote (or endnote) area (not the marker) and press <F11> to open the Stylist.

2   Click the Paragraph Style button and choose Footnote (or Endnote).

3   Right-click in the Stylist and choose Modify from the shortcut menu to open the Paragraph Style dialog box.

4   Click the Borders tab and click between the lower brackets in the Frame area to designate a border below the text in the header (or footer).

5   Choose the Line Style from the list and select White from the Color drop-down list box.

6   Click the Spacing button to open the Spacing dialog box and click to turn the Synchronize option off (unless it is already deselected). Click the spin box controls for the Bottom Settings and increase the value (for example, to .06).

7   Click the OK button on both dialog boxes to return to the document.

Working with Indexes and Tables of Contents

When working in longer documents, it can be extremely convenient to create indexes that can help readers move through the document and find specific locations for terms in documents. Writer allows you to create a few different types of indexes to enable this type of document referencing. Indexes use page numbers as references to locations in documents, which are listed in ascending order.

Creating an index is a two-step process; create the entries, then create the index. For a Table of Contents, create the headings (with heading styles or use the Writer default styles), then create the Table of Contents.

The following is a list of descriptions for each of the indexes available:

- Table of Contents—Lists the headers assigned with paragraph styles throughout a document as well as any added entries.
- Alphabetical Index—Lists the entries that have been assigned throughout the document, in alphabetical order.
- Illustration Index—Lists the illustration captions or object names that have been assigned as entries throughout the document.
- Index of Tables—Lists the table captions or object names that have been assigned as entries throughout the document.
- User-Defined—Lists any or all of the styles, index marks, tables, graphics, text frames, or OLE objects that have been assigned as entries throughout the document.
- Table of Objects—Lists the StarOffice objects and or OLE objects that have been assigned as entries throughout the document.
- Bibliography—Lists bibliographic entries that have been assigned throughout the document.

Keep in mind that you cannot automatically create Indexes that encompass more than one document unless you are working with a master document (covered at the end of the chapter). Another way to do this is to paste each index into a separate document and edit them all. But, of course, there is a way to manipulate this as well. Select the indexes of individual documents and define them as sections (refer to the section "Working with Section Breaks," in Chapter 6). You can then insert each of the sections into a single index document, one after the other, and create the index on all of them at the same time. If you are working with a master document, common indexes are possible across all parts of documents. Also note that you can have multiple types of indexes in one document.

To Define Index Entries in a Document

Entries for an alphabetical (key word-based) index and for user-defined indexes must be defined as entries in the text before you can compile the index.

1   Select the word(s) or elements in your document you want to have listed in an index. You can indicate multiple words by pressing <Shift> as you select them (if they are listed one after the other), or by pressing <Ctrl> (if they are spaced apart).

2   Position the cursor somewhere in the word to select it.

To indicate all occurrences of a word, press <Ctrl+F> to open the Search and Replace dialog box and type the text into the Search for box; then click the Find All button. You will then need to perform step 2 each time the Search and Replace dialog box moves you to the next occurrence of the term. In addition, you can use the Apply to All Similar Texts check-box in the Insert Index Entry dialog box to flag all similar entries at once.

3   Choose Insert, Indexes, Entry to open the Insert Index Entry dialog box (see Figure 11.12). The text will already be inserted into the Entry text box whether you simply placed the cursor in the text or if you performed a search to find the text.

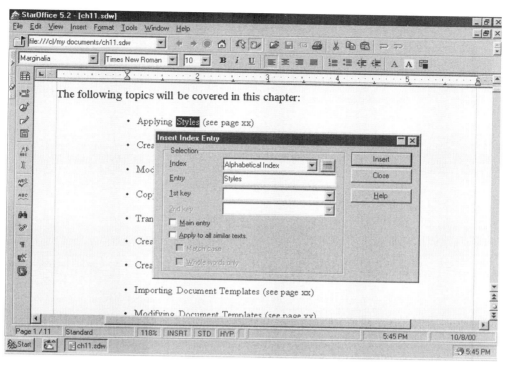

Figure 11.12   Select the term and choose to insert it as an index entry.

4   Click the Index drop-down list box and choose whether you want to create an entry for a Table of Contents, Alphabetical Index, or a User-
Defined Index. When you make your selection, the Insert Index Entry
dialog box will change to reflect the options available in that type of
index. Perform the steps associated with the paragraph corresponding to
the index you choose.

User-Defined Index: In the Entry text box, type the text that you want
to actually display in the index (this can, and often will be, different than
the text you selected). You will be able to specify the appearance of your
entries when you create the user-defined index (refer to the section "To
Create a User-Defined Index").

NOTE   If you prefer entries to fall under a different term in the
index, type the new term into the Entry text box. For example, if the
selected term is "bunny", you might want the Entry to instead be
found under "rabbit" in the index.

Alphabetical Index: In the Entry text box, type the text that you want
to actually display in the index. The Apply to all similar texts option is

available. If this option is selected, you can indicate whether to include terms similar to the Entry field: Match case—The Entry term must match exactly by case; Whole words only—The Entry term must match by the whole word.

In addition, to provide more information about the Entry term in the index, you can type a first key in to the text box. You can also apply a second key, for example, the text entered into the dialog box as:

Entry:as alphabetical
1st key:index
2nd key:creating

will display as follows in an index (assuming your index uses default display and formatting options):

```
index
  creating
    as alphabetical 5
```

This will make your index more robust and detailed for the people who use it. As you create more 1st and 2nd key entries, they will accumulate in the drop-down list boxes of the Insert Index Entry dialog box, allowing you to select existing keys rather than creating new ones, and making it easier to build a more consistent index. If you select the Main entry option, the page number of the currently selected text is inserted into the index in a different number format than the page numbers of the other entries of this text.

Table of Contents: Here, you can add an index entry to a table of contents. However, before doing so, keep in mind that you typically build a table of contents from the headings in your document, using heading styles. You would typically only use the Index Entry dialog box to supplement those headings. Define the entries you want to include in the table of contents before you create an index. To do so, you simply apply the paragraph style for text and headers that you want to include as entries. For example, label your different heading levels (Heading 1, Heading 2, and so on) to indicate the organizational sections in your document. Essentially, applying paragraph styles to your document will automatically define your table of contents entries. If you have numerous header levels and prefer to include only some of them in your table of contents, you will be able to specify this when you create the table of contents index (refer to the section "To Create a Table of Contents").

New User-Defined Index: If you want to create your own type of user-defined index to select from this list, click the New user-defined index button, located to the right of the Index drop-down list box. Simply type the new index name into the Create new user-defined index dialog box and click the OK button; you will return to the Insert Index Entry dialog box with the new index name automatically selected from the drop-down list. This new index name will appear as the title of the index, and it can be altered at any time without affecting the actual contents of the index.

5   Click the Insert button to add the entry to the document. If you want to assign more entries, click the mouse pointer in the document and locate the next term you would like to include, then click back in the Insert Index Entry dialog box and the new term automatically appears in the Entry field (this will remain open until you click the Close button).

Index entries that you define will appear as shaded gray (like fields) in your document, though this shading will not print. Again, as with fields, you can choose View, Field Shadings to toggle the shading on or off.

If you modified the displayed text of the entry (as compared to the actual text in the document), the altered text will automatically be inserted into the generated index. You will now see only a thin gray mark to the left of the entry term in the document (instead of the entire term highlighted). To edit this type of modified entry, place the cursor directly after the gray mark and choose Edit, Index Entry.

At this point, the index has not yet been created, you are simply telling Writer to flag these terms as index entries that you will compile later. The following sections give you specific instructions for creating each type of index once you've created entries that will appear in them.

TO EDIT OR DELETE THE INDEX ENTRIES

1   Place the text cursor directly in front of or inside text that has already been marked as an index entry.

2   Choose Edit, Index Entry (see Figure 11.13), and one of two things will happen:

   • If there is more than one entry assigned to this word (for example, if you assign two separate entries for rabbit as "rabbit" and as "bunny"), they will both appear as a list in the Index Entry dialog box. Select the specific entry and click the OK button to open the Edit Index Entry dialog box.

   • If there is only one entry assigned to the word, the Edit Index Entry dialog box will automatically open.

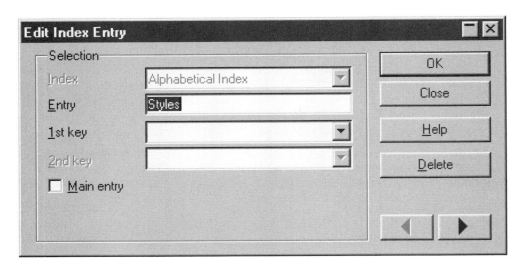

Figure 11.13   You can edit index entries later if necessary.

3   Select from the available options, which depend upon the type of index entry you already created. You can also click the right and left arrow buttons to quickly move through and edit the other entries in the document.

4   Click the OK button when finished editing the entry, or you can click the Delete button to remove this entry from the list of all marked entries.

5   Click the Close button to close the Edit Index Entry dialog box and return to the document.

NOTE   To delete a short index entry, you can simply double-click on the word to select it and then simply type over it (or retype the word).

To CREATE A TABLE OF CONTENTS

You can define the document entries that you want to include in the table of contents before you create one. Refer to the section "To Define Index Entries in a Document" for more information. Or, you can simply choose Insert, Indexes, Indexes; choose Table of Contents from the Type drop-down box (it's selected by default); and click OK. You'll get a TOC based on the heading styles in your document.

1   Place the cursor where you would like to create the table of contents—for example, in a frame to the right of your text (for a Web page), or at the beginning or end of your document.

2   Choose Insert, Indexes to open the Insert Index dialog box and select the Indexes tab.

3   Select Table of Contents from the Type drop-down list box if it isn't already selected (see Figure 11.14).

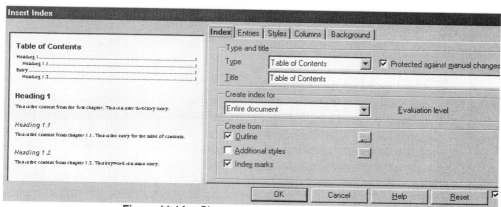

Figure 11.14   Choose to create a table of contents.

4   Type the name you prefer for the table of contents in the Title text box. If you leave the default text alone, the words Table of Contents will appear at the top of your table of contents.

5   Click the Create index for drop-down list box to select whether you want the table of contents created for the Entire document or for only the Chapter you are currently in.

6   Select the number from the Evaluation level box to indicate the number of heading levels deep the table of contents will be.

7   Select the Create from options you prefer:

•Outline—Allows you to create the table of contents based upon outline numbering that you have assigned to your document. Refer to the section "Using Outline Numbering" in Chapter 12 for more information. If you have not yet created outline numbering, click the adjacent button containing three dots, and the Outline Numbering dialog box opens. Here, you can set outline numbering for the entire document or any portion of it you have selected.

•Additional styles—Allows you to include styles in the table of contents that aren't necessarily headers, or that are specific types of headers (you created) that you want to include. Select this option and the (...) button will activate; click on the button and select the Styles from the Assign Styles dialog box. You can then click on the specific style and assign it a level between 1 and 10 by clicking the right and left arrow buttons; click OK to return to the Insert Index dialog box.

• Index marks—Allows you to include all the index entries that you marked throughout the document (for example, entries for user-defined and keyword indexes).

NOTE   You can also automatically assign hyperlinks to the entries in a table of contents as long as they have been generated from the document headings. In the Insert Indexes dialog box, choose the Entries tab. Place the cursor in the Structure line (blank box) in front of the entry E#, click the Hyperlink button, position the cursor behind E (blank box), and click the Hyperlink button again. You can click on a hyperlink in the table of contents to immediately jump to the location of the entry.

The other tabs in the Insert Index will allow you to specify the structure and format of your entries (Entries tab); assign levels and paragraph styles (Styles tab); decide whether you prefer the index to be displayed in columns (Columns tab); and decide whether there should be a color or graphical background behind the index (Background tab). You can see what the table of contents will look like in the preview area to the left. If you make changes, you will have to update the table of contents (refer to the section "To Edit, Update, or Delete an Index").

8   Click the OK button to generate the table of contents (see Figure 11.15).

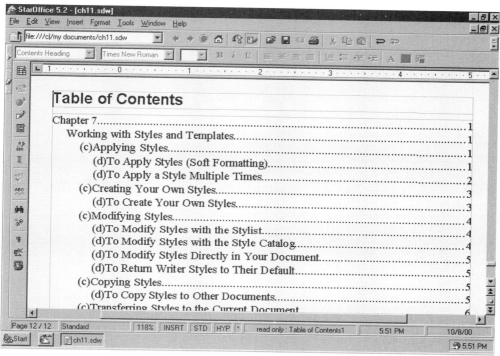

Figure 11.15   How a default style table of contents appears.

TO CREATE AN ALPHABETICAL KEY WORD INDEX

You must define the document entries that you want to include in the alphabetical key word index before you can create an index (unless you want to create a blank one and update it later). Refer to the section "To Define Index Entries in a Document" for more information.

1   Place the cursor where you would like to create the index.

2   Choose Insert, Indexes, Indexes and click on the Index tab of the Insert Index dialog box.

3   Select Alphabetical Index from the Type drop-down list box (see Figure 11.16).

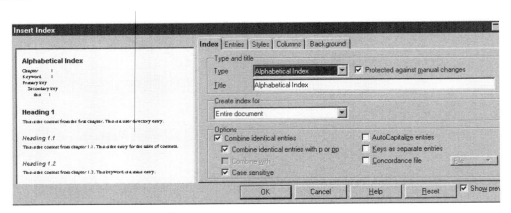

Figure 11.16   Choose to create an alphabetical index.

If you want to create a simple index without all the bells and whistles, move to step 4; otherwise, you can manipulate some of the following options:

• Combine identical entries—Consolidate multiple identical entries onto a single line of the compiled index.

For example, if as you go through your document and assign index entries, perhaps you assign an entry to "bunny" twice. Select the Combine identical entries option to make the bunny reference from page 2 appear with the bunny reference on page 4:

```
alligator  3
bunny  2,4
cow  2
```

Combine identical entries with p or pp—For example, "Bunny 13, 14, 15" would become "Bunny 13pp" (where each "p" referred to each additional page—pages 14 and 15).

Combine with—For example, "Bunny 13, 14, 15" would become "Bunny 13-15".

Case sensitive—For example, the terms "Writer" for StarOffice Writer would show up in a different location than "writer" as in the author of this book.

• AutoCapitalize entries—All entries in the index will begin with capital letters.

If you would like the entry and each of the keys to be included in the index, select the Keys as separate entries option. This way bunny, rabbit, and Peter Cottontail will all have references to the selected entry page location:

```
alligator  3
```
bunny 4
```
cow  2
lamb  5
```
Peter Cottontail 4
rabbit 4
```
zebra  1
```

- Keys as separate entries—The different first key and second key fields you assigned will be listed as separate entries in the index, instead of subentries off the main Entry term.
- Concordance file—Open or create a new file in which you can compare your index entries. A *true* concordance lists every reference to every word in a document. It's often done with Bibles and in literary criticism. However, in StarOffice Writer it means a file you can use to automate the creation of an index. You enter the index entries you want Writer to look for, the appropriate keys and settings you want to use, and so on, then you open the concordance file, and Writer indexes your document automatically.

The other tabs in the Insert Index will allow you to specify the structure and format of your entries (Entries tab), assign levels and paragraph styles (Styles tab), decide whether you prefer the index to be displayed in columns (Columns tab), and decide whether there should be a color or graphical background behind the index (Background tab).

4   Click the OK button to insert the alphabetical key word index using the standard formatting settings (see Figure 11.17).

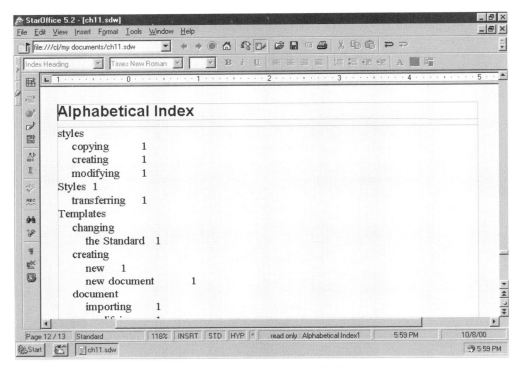

Figure 11.17   How a default style alphabetical index appears.

> **NOTE**   By default, indexes and tables of contents are protected
> against manual changes. This means users cannot edit the text of an
> index or table of contents directly; they must edit relevant entries
> and update the index or table of contents by right-clicking on it and
> choosing Update Index from the shortcut menu. However, in some
> cases you may wish to permit manual changes; clear the Protected
> against manual changes checkbox in the Index tab of the Insert Index
> dialog box. Note that if you permit manual text changes, but then use
> Update Index to update the index or table of contents, your manual
> changes will be eliminated. In addition, you can click the Create
> index for drop-down list if you want to create the index for only one
> chapter (within, for example, a master document) instead of the
> entire document.

To Create a User-Defined Index

You must define the document entries that you want to include in the user-
defined index before you can create an index. This will allow you to index any

entries you like. Refer to the section "To Define Index Entries in a Document" for more information.

1   Place the cursor where you would like to create the index.

2   Choose Insert, Indexes, Indexes and click on the Index tab of the Insert Index dialog box.

3   Select User-Defined Index from the Type drop-down list box (see Figure 11.18). If you have created a new user-defined index, select the specific name.

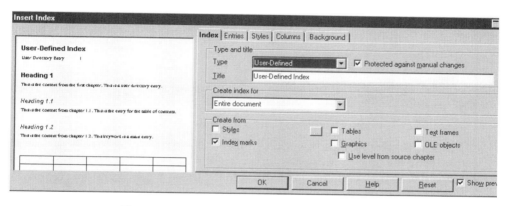

Figure 11.18   Choose to create a user-defined index.

4   Select the Create index for drop-down list box and choose whether you want to create the index for the Entire document or a specific chapter.

Choose from the following Create from options to base your index:

Select the Styles option and click the (...) button to open the Assign Styles dialog box (see Figure 11.19). Click on one of the styles used in your document and click the right or left arrow buttons to indicate the level that the style should represent. For example, if you created new paragraph styles in the document (such as chapter name, chapter head 1, chapter head 2, and so on), you can assign them each a different level (such as level 1, level 2, level 3, and so on). The index will be based on the designated levels. Click the OK button to return to the Insert Index dialog box.

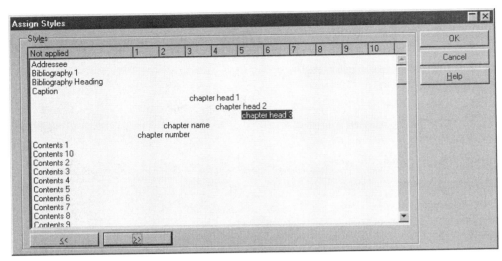

Figure 11.19   Assign the styles to the desired level.

Select the Index marks option to insert the terms designated as entries in your document into your index (refer to the section "To Define Index Entries in a Document" for more information).

You can also select any or all of the Tables, Graphics, Text frames, and OLE objects options (in the document) to list them in your index. If you select the Use level from source chapter option, these objects will be indented in the index according to the designated document level (for example, a heading paragraph style) in which the object resides.

5   Type a title name into the Title text box for the index. You can also alter the title directly in the document, but if you do so, it will revert back to the title specified in this text box whenever you update the index.

The other tabs in the Insert Index will allow you to specify the structure and format of your entries (Entries tab), assign levels and paragraph styles (Styles tab), decide whether you prefer the index to be displayed in columns (Columns tab), and decide whether there should be a color or graphical background behind the index (Background tab).

6   Click the OK button to insert the user-defined index into your document using the standard formatting settings (see Figure 11.20).

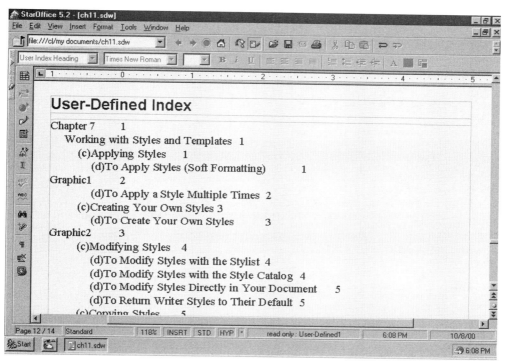

Figure 11.20 How a default style user-defined index appears.

To Edit, Update, or Delete an Index

The most common use for updating an index or table of contents is making sure it reflects edits and new content in the document, much more so than making sure it reflects changes to the settings associated with the index itself (though that certainly happens).

1 Place the cursor within the index in the document.

2 Right-click and select Edit Index from the shortcut menu. This will open the Insert Index dialog box; make your changes and click the OK button. At this point you must update your index for the changes to apply.

3 Again, place the cursor within the index in the document. Right-click the index and choose Update Index from the shortcut menu.

You can also choose Tools, Update, All Indexes to update all the indexes in a document. Or select Current Index from the submenu if you have more than one (for example, a table of contents and an alphabetical index) index in your document.

If you want to delete an index, place the cursor within the index in the document. Right-click the index and choose Remove Index from the shortcut menu.

Creating a Bibliography

Many publications contain references to literary sources within the text. For example, "Lewis [Lewis 2001] has written extensively on this software." Lewis is the author, and 2001 is the publication date. In this example, the bracketed text refers to a bibliography containing more detailed information, listed by the key word [Lewis 2001], containing names, titles, publishers, and dates of the literary sources used in the document. The Bibliography index is a storehouse of bibliography information that you can draw upon in all your documents (or only with a single document if you prefer).

TO ADD A BIBLIOGRAPHY ENTRY TO THE BIBLIOGRAPHY DATABASE

1   Choose Edit, Bibliography Database to open the biblio table in the [Bibliography Database] window (see Figure 11.21). StarOffice has already created this database for you as part of the installation; notice the entries that already exist.

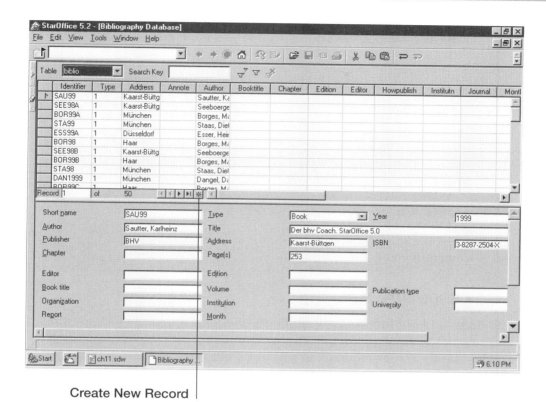

Create New Record

Figure 11.21   The Biblio table in the Bibliography Database.

2   Click the Create New Record button (appears as small yellow starburst)
    to move the cursor to the end of the list and place the cursor in the first
    entry cell. If you prefer, you can click directly on the Short name text box
    and enter the bibliographical record using the record form (appears as a
    form document) instead of using the tabular form (appears as a table).
    You still press the <Tab> key to move through the fields when you enter
    the bibliography data.

3   Choose File, Close to exit the database when you have finished entering in the bibliography records.

> **NOTE**   The Type field corresponds to new bibliography entries created in a document and in the Bibliography Database as follows: Book (1), Brochure (2), Conference report (3), Book excerpt (4), Book excerpt with title (5), Conference proceedings (6), Journal (7), Manual (8), Thesis (9), Miscellaneous (10), Dissertation (11), Conference proceedings (12), Research report (13), Unpublished (14), email (15), WWW document (16), User-Defined 1 (17), User-Defined 2 (18), User-Defined 3 (19), User-Defined 4 (20), and User-Defined 5 (21).

To Add a Bibliography Entry to the Document

1   Choose Insert, Indexes, Bibliography Entry to open the Insert bibliography entry dialog box.

Adding a bibliography entry this way will save it only with this document (not to the Bibliography Database), and you will not be able to use it in other documents.

2   Choose the From document content option.

3   Click the New button (see Figure 11.22). This will open the Define Bibliography Entry dialog box in which you can type the information.

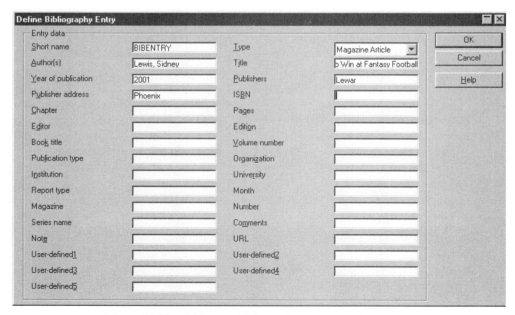

Figure 11.22   Add a new bibliography entry to the document.

4   When you've finished entering the information you have, click OK to
    return to the dialog box (see Figure 11.23). You do not, of course, need to
    enter information in every text box.

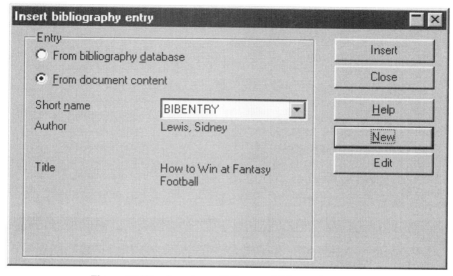

Figure 11.23   Insert or edit the new bibliography entry.

5   Click the Insert button to insert the new bibliography entry into your
    document at the location of the cursor (see Figure 11.24). You can also
    click the Edit button and edit the entry.

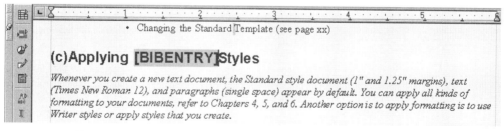

Figure 11.24   How the new bibliography entry appears in the document.

TO INSERT A BIBLIOGRAPHY REFERENCE

Now that you have created a bibliography reference, here's how to include it in
your document.

1   Choose Insert, Indexes, Bibliography Entry to open the Insert bibliogra-
    phy entry dialog box (see Figure 11.25).

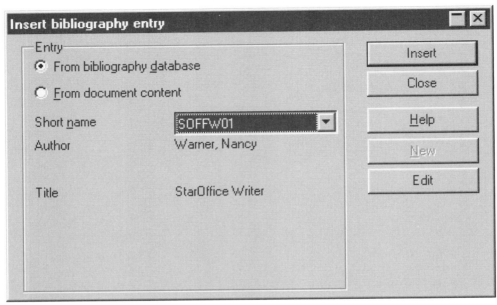

Figure 11.25   Insert a bibliography entry reference.

2   Select where you want the bibliography Entry to come from:

   • From bibliography database—If there are no entries, the database no
     longer resides in the office52\user\database and biblio folders, or the
     Bibliography Database is empty (refer to the section "To Add a
     Bibliography Entry to the Bibliography Database").

   • From document content—If there are no entries, you haven't created
     any in your document yet. Refer the section "To Add a Bibliography
     Entry to the Document." If you choose an entry from the Bibliography
     Database now, and click Edit to edit it, you get a screen that looks just
     like the From Document Content screen. Your edits will be reflected in
     the biblio database.

3   Click the Short name drop-down list box and select the bibliography; the
    corresponding Author name and Title should display in the dialog box.

4   Click the Insert button and the reference will be inserted into the document at the location of the cursor.

NOTE   When you save a document that contains a bibliography entry, the information is saved along with the document so that you can copy the file to a different location (or send it via email) and the entries will still be intact. This is true regardless of whether the bibliography entry was inserted from the Bibliography Database or created directly in the document.

TO CREATE A BIBLIOGRAPHY INDEX

1   Place the cursor where you would like to create the index.

2   Choose Insert, Indexes, Indexes and click on the Index tab of the Insert Index dialog box.

3   Select Bibliography from the Type drop-down list box.

4   Click the Number entries if you want a number to accompany the entries in the bibliography list. If you check Number entries, StarOffice Writer numbers your bibliography items consecutively, in the order of their appearance in your document, but does *not* show the entries' short names.

5   Click the Brackets drop-down list to choose how you would like the entries displayed. This only affects how the short names are displayed, and only if these appear in your bibliography.

6   Click the Entries tab and select from the following options:

- Type—The Structure fields will change according to the typical bibliographical information for that type.
- Structure—The default structure will appear, but you can place the cursor in an empty Structure box, select the entry drop-down list box (directly below the Structure boxes), and click the Insert button to add more bibliographical information to the index list (or click the Remove button). You can also click the Tab Stop button to insert tab in the entry.
- Character style—This is the format for the actual bibliographical entries in the index list.
- Sort by—You can choose to sort by Document position, which lists the entries in order according to where they are entered in the document; or Content (see Figure 11.26), which lists the entries according to the Sort keys (you can indicate alphabetical ascending or descending order according to the Structure fields).

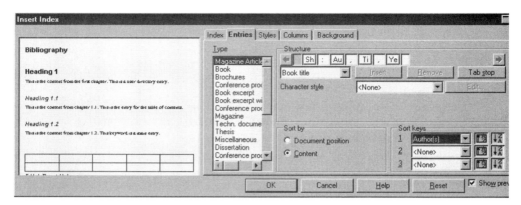

Figure 11.26   Insert a bibliography index and sort the information as you prefer.

The other tabs in the Insert Index will allow you to assign levels and paragraph styles (Styles tab), decide whether you would like the index to be displayed in columns (Columns tab), and decide whether there should be a color or graphical background behind the index (Background tab).

7   Click the OK button to insert the bibliography index into your document (see Figure 11.27).

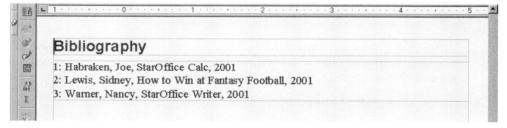

Figure 11.27   How a bibliography index can appear.

Using Custom Number Sequences

You can define separate number sequences for groups of similar elements. For example, you can assign a number sequence to all the tables, notes, and so on.

To Define Custom Number Sequences

1 Type "Table Number" in front of the first table.

2 Choose Insert, Fields, Other to open the Fields dialog box and click on the Variables tab.

3 Select the Number range option in the Type list, choose Table from the Selection list, and select the Format from the right-most list.

If you want to indicate the chapter or heading number with the table number, click the Level drop-down list box and select the level that corresponds to the chapter number or heading level (for example, Level 1 for a Heading 1 chapter number). You can also separate the level and table number by indicating the type of Separator in the list box.

4 Click the Insert button and click the Close button to return to your document.

NOTE The Value field allows you to indicate a new initial value for the entire number sequence. You would do this if you were dealing with a particular document that related to a group of other documents.

Inserting Cross-References

Cross-references allow you to jump to different locations within a single document, but not multiple documents. For example, you can create a cross-reference from a word in the text to a graphic caption, table, headings, other words in the document, or other references you define.

You insert field commands for references and define the reference target. You can define all kinds of references; for example, "See also chapter 3, page 24"; "As already shown in Figure 2.16"; or "Compare this to Table 4 on page 2". Writer automatically places the correct reference in the document; updates the reference as you add, move, or delete content throughout the document; and numbers will update accordingly.

Cross-references are also displayed in the Navigator, and you can click on the links to jump directly to the target location in the document.

To Insert Referenced Fields

1 Position the cursor at the location you want to *refer to* (the target destination of the reference). For example, select a word as a destination for

the reference. This will enable you to find the position in the document more easily in the future.

2   Choose Insert, Referenced Field to open the Fields dialog box to the References tab.

3   Click the Set Reference Type and type a unique Name for the reference in this document (see Figure 11.28).

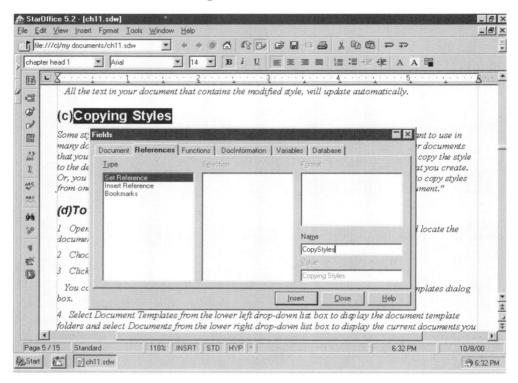

Figure 11.28   Select the text where you want to insert a referenced field and open the Fields dialog box.

4   Click Insert and click the Close button to return to the document.

5   Position the cursor at the location where you would like the cross-reference to appear and *reference from* (the origination of the reference). For example, your text here might read: "For further information see page".

6   Choose Insert, Referenced Field to open the Fields dialog box to the References tab.

7   Click the Insert Reference Type and choose the term from the Select list of names that you have set as references (as in step 3).

8 From the Selection list, choose the name of the cross-reference you set in Step 3, choose a Format option, and click the Insert button to add the reference to the document (see Figure 11.29).

Now when you click on the original reference, it will immediately jump your cursor to the target reference.

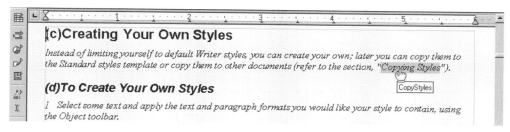

(c)Creating Your Own Styles

Instead of limiting yourself to default Writer styles, you can create your own; later you can copy them to the Standard styles template or copy them to other documents (refer to the section, "Copying Styles").

(d)To Create Your Own Styles

CopyStyles

1 Select some text and apply the text and paragraph formats you would like your style to contain, using the Object toolbar.

Figure 11.29 How the reference appears in the document.

NOTE If you prefer to assign a reference to a picture or table caption in the current document, you would first need to insert a caption and indicate the caption as the referenced field (Set Reference from step 3).

TO INSERT CROSS-REFERENCES AS WEB HYPERLINKS

1 Open the document in which you want to insert hyperlink cross-references.

2 If SEL appears in the status bar, click on it to switch into HYP (hyperlink) mode. This will make the hyperlinks you add *active*, instead of editable. You can later edit the text of the hyperlink if you like, using SEL mode. In this procedure, you need to drag and drop hyperlinks, and you can't do so in SEL mode.

3 Choose Edit, Navigator to open the Navigator (or press <F5>). Click the Content View button to view all the contents of the document in the Navigator.

4 Click the Drag mode button on the Navigator and make sure that Insert as Hyperlink is the command selected (see Figure 11.30). This will allow you to drag and drop the hyperlinks from the Navigator to the document.

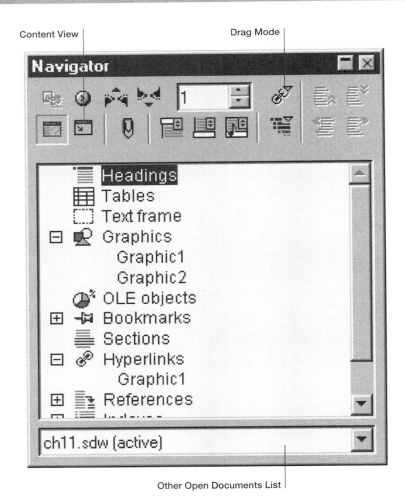

Figure 11.30   Make sure the Drag mode on the Navigator is set to Insert as Hyperlink.

5   Click the + to the left of the elements within the document (for example, Headings, Graphics, Bookmarks, and so on). This will display each individual occurrence of the particular element, if you have multiples.

If you have other documents open in StarOffice, you can select a different document to link to by clicking the drop-down list box at the bottom of the Navigator. You can also drag a document from the Beamer into the Navigator to make the elements in another document active.

6   Click the specific element expanded in the Navigator list. For example, click on a specific graphic contained in the document.

NOTE   If you prefer not to see all the document elements, only the types of element you are looking to hyperlink, select the element, and then click the Content View button on the Navigator toolbar. Refer to the section "Using the Navigator" for more information on the buttons and commands available on the Navigator.

7   Click and drag the graphic hyperlink (see Figure 11.31) to the desired location in the document (perhaps where you reference the graphic in the text). The inserted hyperlink reference is automatically underlined and highlighted. Remember that a visited hyperlink that you have clicked on in the same session is indicated by a different color.

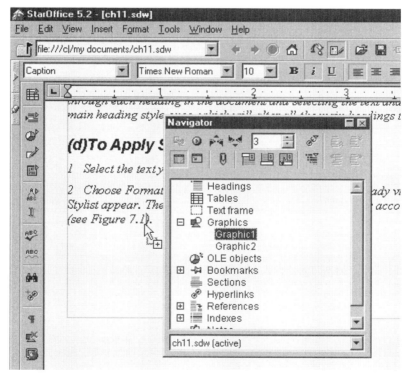

Figure 11.31   Click and drag a target link from the Navigator to the reference location.

Now when you click on the reference link (see Figure 11.32), your cursor will automatically jump to the graphic (or target link you choose from the Navigator).

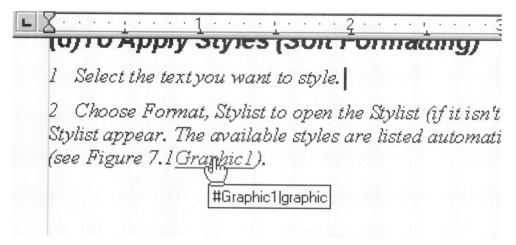

Figure 11.32   Click the reference to jump to the target destination location in your document.

Using Bookmarks

You can assign bookmarks within your documents to identify specific places in the document. For example, you can insert a bookmark and use the Navigator to quickly move to the bookmark. Simply place the cursor at the location in the document where you would like a bookmark. Choose Insert, Bookmark to open the Insert Bookmarks dialog box. Type the name you prefer for the bookmark and click the OK button. You can also delete bookmarks on this dialog box, for example, if you added a bookmark to a place in your document that you needed to update. Once you made the update, you can delete the bookmark to that location.

In addition, Bookmarks can link you to files on your hard drive or to your local network, as well as to HTML pages on the Internet. You can even set a bookmark at a certain position in a document and, after clicking the bookmark, the document will be loaded and the cursor will be set at this exact position (for example, an HTML anchor or a StarOffice Writer bookmark).

To place a bookmark link in the Bookmarks group of the Explorer, you can drag the Bookmark icon (on the Function bar) into the Bookmark group in the Explorer. The Bookmarks group in the Explorer represents a link to the current Bookmark folder in your system. StarOffice also has a Bookmark folder in which various subfolders are contained. This is a normal folder and can be found under the path Office52/Share/Bookmark. These two folders do not necessarily coincide. The link in the StarOffice Windows version can refer to the "Favorites" folder in the Windows directory and be completely independent of the Bookmark folder beneath the StarOffice directory. Such a folder is defined as "Bookmarks" when you choose Tools, Options, and select the General, Paths register.

You can create a link to this folder, for example, to your favorite Web sites, or if you want to refer to a specific file that you want to edit later. Click the Link icon in the opened Hyperlink bar (choose View, Toolbars, Hyperlink Bar to display). This will automatically create the link (or bookmark) within the bookmark folder.

To assign a destination for a hyperlink within a document, insert a bookmark by choosing Insert, Bookmark to open the Insert Bookmark dialog box; type a name and click OK to create a tag for the Internet anchor. The bookmark will appear automatically at the beginning of the paragraph as <A name="Name_of_Bookmark"></A> when you save the document in HTML format. You can also jump to other documents or any location in a document using hyperlinks. To do this, add a "#" sign, along with the name of the bookmark, to the file name in the URL address of the destination Web site.

NOTE   If a text document contains bookmarks, you can right-click to choose from a list of existing bookmarks on the shortcut menu. In addition, you can right-click Page in the status bar and select a bookmark from the list.

Working with Master Documents

Master documents are a convenient way to maintain and organize long documents so files aren't so large. Instead of writing a whole document (for example, a book) in one file, you can maintain them in smaller chunks (for example, separate chapters). In addition, you can create cross-references and indexes across all your documents instead of having to combine them later or maintain separate elements.

If you are learning about master documents for the first time, it is a good idea to know that you can either create a new master document, create a master document out of an existing document, or even insert (add) documents that you have already written into a master document.

To maintain consistency across your entire master document, you will want to assign styles (paragraph, character, frame, page, and numbering) in the master document and then apply them within the documents. This will enable you to create a uniform look and feel across documents and ensure that elements like captions, indexes, and cross-references are consistent. If you create a style in a subdocument and then create a slightly different style (but named the same thing) in the master document, the master document style will overwrite the subdocument style.

In addition, changes you make to templates (or ones you create) in the master document will have priority over the templates in your subdocuments. If a new template is needed in your documents immediately, you can add it to the document template and reload the master document. Then the new template can be applied to all documents automatically.

You can work in subdocuments without the master document being open. Likewise, you can work in the master document without having the subdocuments open. And last, but not least, when you print a master document, all the subdocuments, text within the master document, and corresponding indexes will print at once.

TO CREATE A NEW MASTER DOCUMENT

1   Choose File, New, Master Document to open up a new master document (notice that master documents have an .sgl extension after the file name, versus the .sdw extension for a regular Writer text document).

NOTE   If you installed the sample files with your StarOffice installation, there is a Master Document sample. You can review this file at \office52\share\samples\English\texts\book.sgl, also labeled "My House".

The Navigator will appear automatically, looking slightly different than usual, to aid in moving through your document.

2   Click the Insert button on the Navigator and select whether you want to insert an Index, File, New Document, or Text.

NOTE   New documents, files, or blocks of text are always inserted above the location of the cursor. You can change the order of the master document elements by dragging and dropping the entries in the Navigator or by clicking the Move Up or Move Down buttons on the Navigator.

If you choose New Document, an Untitled document will open, and you will immediately be asked to save the file. Type in a file name and click the Save button to return to the document. It is a good idea to maintain a specific folder location for the master document and subdocuments. The

Navigator will now appear as it usually does in a text document, with all the elements available to you.

> **NOTE**   All Indexes are created directly in the master document and automatically include all the subdocuments. If you changed one or more subdocuments after creating an index, you should update the indexes in the master document. Click the Update button on the master document Navigator and choose from the submenu to update the Selection (if you have the index selected), Indexes (if that is all you want to update), or All (to update all elements). Choose the Links option if you prefer to update the links within the entire master document.

3   Create the document as you normally would and save the file. When you want to view the document in your master document, click the master document file in the taskbar.

4   Choose File, Save As and save the master document to the desired location (don't forget to create a new folder structure to coordinate the master and subdocuments).

5   Place the cursor in the area in the master document that is designated as the new document you just created. If you don't yet see your file, right-click on the file name in the Navigator and choose Update, All from the shortcut menu. This will update the information in the file and make it active in the master document.

6   Click in the Text area of the master document and type in the information you would like it to contain.

7   Click the Insert button on the Navigator and choose File from the menu. This will allow you to incorporate an already existing file in the master document.

The file will appear as read-only in the master document. To edit the file, you must right-click on the file name in the Navigator and choose Edit from the shortcut menu. Notice that you could also choose Delete to delete the file, or Insert to select from a submenu in which you can insert an Index, File, New Document, or Text within the file. Essentially, you can maintain multiple documents within multiple documents, if you so desire.

TO CREATE A MASTER DOCUMENT AND SUBDOCUMENTS FROM AN EXISTING FILE

This section will show you how to create both a master document and subdocuments.

1. Open the document in which you would like to create a master document.

2. Choose File, Send, Create Master Document to open the Name and Path of Master Document dialog box. This is how you indicate where you want the new master document saved.

3. Type in a file name for the master document and choose the path where you would like the files to be saved. Note that each subdocument will begin with whatever name you type here.

4. Click the Style button to indicate the style that separates the "sections" in your original document. For example, if you have Heading 1 styles applied to all the chapter numbers in your document, this style will be where the master document separates each of the subdocuments.

5. Click the "separator" style in the Select Style dialog box and click the OK button. If you don't have a separator style, you will want to put these into your current document before you perform this procedure. Writer has to have some indication of where the subdocuments need to begin and end.

6. Click the Save button when you return to the Name and Path of Master Document dialog box. The master document and subdocuments will create automatically. They will appear in the Navigator, and you can perform all the tasks that were covered in the previous sections.

Using Document Automation

Working with AutoText Entries

AutoText entries can save you typing time by allowing you to insert commonly used text and text blocks (with or without formatting) into your text. StarOffice comes with numerous built-in AutoText entries to simplify the creation of letters and many other types of documents. You can also create your own.

TO CREATE AN AUTOTEXT ENTRY

1   Select the text that you would like to become an AutoText entry. You must do this, or some of the AutoText options won't be available.

2   Choose Edit, AutoText (or press <Ctrl+F3>) to open the AutoText dialog box (see Figure 12.1). You can also click the Edit AutoText button on the Main toolbar.

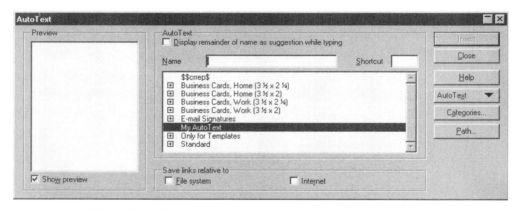

Figure 12.1   The AutoText dialog box where you create new entries.

Choose from the options available:

- Display remainder of name as suggestion while typing—If you check this box, when you begin typing the first few characters of your AutoText name in your document, the full name of the AutoText entry will appear near the text in a small yellow Help Tip. If you want to use the AutoText entry, press the <Enter> key.
- Name—Type a name you want this AutoText entry to be identified by.

3   Select a category list for this AutoText entry. When you click the Auto-Text button on the Main toolbar, you can select in the list box below the Name field to indicate the submenu (for example, My AutoText).

- Shortcut—Type the initials you would like to serve as the key combination for selecting the AutoText within the text.

- •Save links relative to—This will save them relatively to the File system and/or the Internet.

4   Click the AutoText button and choose New from the list. This will add the new AutoText entry to the selected submenu list. Double-click on the category list submenu you indicated (for example, My AutoText), click once on the new AutoText entry (which you named), and the entry will appear in the Preview area for you to review.

If the text you selected had formatting applied, but you didn't want that included with the AutoText entry, you could always choose the AutoText button and select New (text only) from the list.

If you would like to create a new category for the entry list, click the Categories button; type in a new name for a Category and click the New button. If you want to rename a category, select the Category from the list and click the Rename button. If you want to delete a category, select the Category from the list and click the Delete button.

If you don't want to modify the AutoText entry you just created, refer to the following section, "To Modify an AutoText Entry."

5   Click the Close button to return to your document.

To Modify an AutoText Entry

If, for example, a proper name or slang term has changed slightly, you can always modify the AutoText entry.

1   Choose Edit, AutoText (or press <Ctrl+F3>) to open the AutoText dialog box. You can also click the Edit AutoText button on the Main toolbar.

2   Select the AutoText entry you want to modify in the category list (see Figure 12.2). Notice that the AutoText entry you added in the previous section is now available when you expand the My AutoText list.

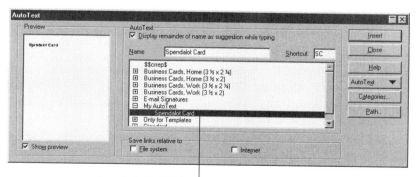

New AutoText Entry

Figure 12.2   You can modify AutoText entries.

3   Click the AutoText button and choose from the available modification options on the submenu:

• Replace—If you selected specific text in the document before you opened the AutoText dialog box, the Replace command will be active on the AutoText submenu; the text selected will replace the AutoText you have selected in the list. The Name and Shortcut information won't change, but when you click the Insert button, the new text will be inserted instead of the previous text.

• Rename—Choose this command to alter the AutoText entry Name or Shortcut.

• Delete—Choose this command to delete an AutoText entry; you will be asked Yes or No as to whether you indeed want to delete the entry.

• Edit—Select this option to edit the AutoText entry. Writer displays the contents of the entry within a new document window. When you finish making the changes, choose File, Save Text Block (this menu command won't be an option if you didn't actually make any changes to it); then choose File, Close to return to your original document.

NOTE   If you select the Macro command from the AutoText submenu, you can assign a macro to your selected AutoText entry (either one of StarOffice's many existing macros or one you write yourself). You can specify whether the macro runs before or after Writer inserts the text stored in your AutoText entry. For example, you might create an AutoText entry that enters new subheads into an existing document, and attach a macro that selects the entire document and updates all indexes and tables of contents.

4   Click the Close button when finished making the modifications to the AutoText entries.

TO INSERT AN AUTOTEXT ENTRY IN A DOCUMENT

1   Place the cursor in a document where you would like the AutoText entry to be inserted.

2   You can click the Edit AutoText Entry button on the Main toolbar to display the AutoText entry Categories submenu. Select the desired submenu and click on the AutoText entry to insert it directly into the document (see Figure 12.3).

Another way to insert an AutoText entry is to choose Edit, AutoText (or press <Ctrl+F3>) to open the AutoText dialog box. Then, double-click on the AutoText entry Categories list and double-click on the specific Auto-

Text entry (or click the Insert button). The dialog box will close, and the AutoText entry will be inserted directly into the document.

NOTE If you created an AutoText entry with a keyboard shortcut, you can use that keyboard shortcut.

Edit AutoText Entry

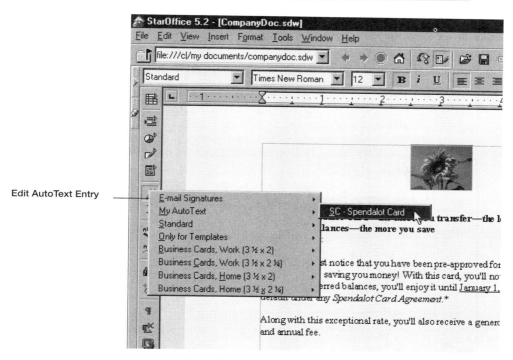

Figure 12.3 The AutoText entry submenus.

Using AutoCorrect Features

AutoCorrect is a very convenient feature within Writer. This section is going to open your eyes to the power of AutoCorrect by demonstrating how you can replace words, allow for exceptions, apply typing and modification options, and even complete words before you are finished typing them. I love this feature because I am so tired of discovering that I typed my name "Nnacy" instead of "Nancy".

TO ADD AUTOCORRECT REPLACEMENT TEXT

You can designate text you frequently type wrong to automatically replace with the correct text.

1   Choose Tools, AutoCorrect/AutoFormat to open the AutoCorrect dialog box.

2   Click the Replace tab and review the available options.

3   Type the Replace text into the Replacement table along with the corre-sponding With text (see Figure 12.4). For example, you could replace your common name misspellings like "Nnacy" with "Nancy" (because this wouldn't be in the dictionary, unless you added it via the Spellcheck dia-log box by clicking the Add button when it found the proper name).

If the text you want to replace is already in the replacement table of com-mon replacements, you don't need to insert it again. You will automati-cally be moved to the alphabetical location in which the text you replace would be in the Replacement table.

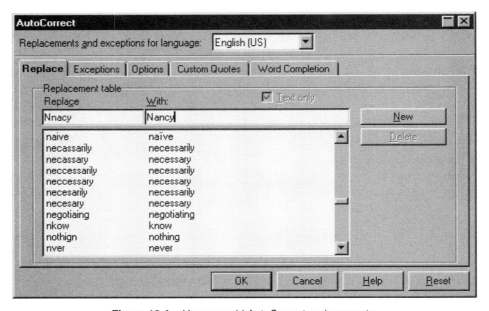

Figure 12.4   You can add AutoCorrect replacements.

4   Click the New button to insert the new AutoCorrect entry.

If you change your mind and want to delete an entry in the Replacement table, select the entry and click the Delete button.

5   Click the OK button to accept your changes and return to your docu-ment.

NOTE If you prefer not to accept your changes, and you haven't yet clicked the OK button on the AutoCorrect dialog box, you can click the Reset button to return the settings to before you opened the dialog box. You can also click Cancel to immediately return to the document.

6 Type the incorrect text in your document, and it will automatically change to the replacement text.

TO ADD AUTOCORRECT EXCEPTIONS

Sometimes when you type words as abbreviations or with multiple capital letters, Writer tries to automatically correct these "typos." If they aren't really typos, it can get annoying trying to correct the AutoCorrect. In these situations, you need to designate *exceptions* to the AutoCorrect rules.

1 Choose Tools, AutoCorrect/AutoFormat to open the AutoCorrect dialog box.

2 Click the Exceptions tab and review the available options.

3 Type the Abbreviations (no subsequent capital) text into the text box (see Figure 12.5). For example, you could add your initials like "n.d.w." if you use them frequently in documents (capitalization doesn't apply).

If the exception text is already in the list of common exceptions, you don't need to insert it again. You will automatically be moved to the alphabetical location in which your abbreviation would be listed.

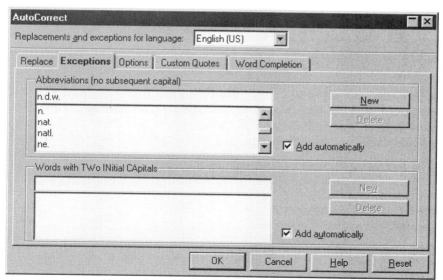

Figure 12.5 You can add AutoCorrect exceptions.

4   Click the New button to insert the new AutoCorrect abbreviation entry.

     If you change your mind and want to delete an entry in the Abbreviation
     list, select the entry and click the Delete button.

5   Type the Words with TWo INitial CApitals text into the text box. For
     example, you could add a company name like "NWarner".

     If the initial capitals text is already in the list of common initial capitals
     (which is doubtful because the default listing is empty), you don't need to
     insert it again. You will automatically be moved to the alphabetical loca-
     tion in which the text your initial capitals would be listed.

6   Click the New button to insert the new AutoCorrect initial capitals entry.

     If you change your mind and want to delete an entry in the Abbreviation
     list, select the entry and click the Delete button.

7   Click the OK button to accept your changes and return to your docu-
     ment. If you prefer not to accept your changes, and you haven't yet
     clicked the OK button, you can click the Reset button to return to the
     previous settings. You can also click Cancel to immediately return to the
     document.

TO MODIFY THE AUTOCORRECT REPLACEMENT OPTIONS

1   Choose Tools, AutoCorrect/AutoFormat to open the AutoCorrect dialog box.

2   Click the Options tab (see Figure 12.6) to review the available options:

     (M): Replace while modifying existing text—This option means that a
     replacement should occur only when you choose Format, AutoFormat,
     Apply to automatically format the document.

     (T): AutoFormat/AutoCorrect while typing—This option means that the
     option will apply automatically when you are typing in a document.

3   Click the OK button to accept your changes and return to your document.
     If you prefer not to accept your changes, and you haven't yet clicked the
     OK button, you can click the Reset button to return to the previous set-
     tings. You can also click Cancel to immediately return to the document.

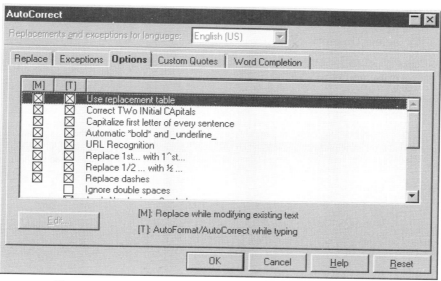

Figure 12.6 You can modify the AutoCorrect replacement options.

TO APPLY CUSTOM QUOTES WITH AUTOCORRECT

The primary application of Custom Quotes in the U.S. is to replace straight quotes with curly quotes.

1   Choose Tools, AutoCorrect/AutoFormat to open the AutoCorrect dialog box.

2   Click the Custom Quotes tab to review the available options (see Figure 12.7). You may change your custom quotes for an advertisement or logo that you create.

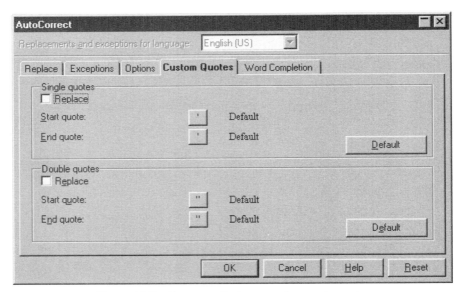

Figure 12.7   You can adjust your custom quote marks.

3   Click the Single quotes Replace option and click the Start quote and End quote buttons to open a dialog box that allows you to specify new start and end quote characters (similar to the Special Characters dialog box).

4   Click the Double quotes Replace option and click the Start quote and End quote buttons to open a dialog box that allows you to specify new start and end quote characters (similar to the Special Characters dialog box).

5   Click the Default buttons if you want to convert the start and end quotes to the standard system quotes.

6   Click the OK button to accept your changes and return to your document. If you prefer not to accept your changes, and you haven't yet clicked the OK button, you can click the Reset button to return to the previous settings. You can also click Cancel to immediately return to the document.

To Add Words that Complete Automatically While Typing

If there are particularly long words that you type on a regular basis (or words that are cumbersome to type), you can tell Writer to automatically complete the long word for you once it recognizes the specific word.

1   Choose Tools, AutoCorrect/AutoFormat to open the AutoCorrect dialog box.

2   Click the Word Completion tab to review the list of words that will automatically complete while typing (see Figure 12.8).

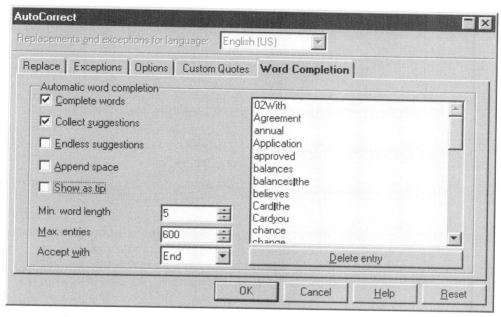

Figure 12.8 You can add words that will automatically complete as you type.

3   The Complete words option should be selected by default. Begin typing the first letters of a word from this list, for example, "perforation", into your text document. A word completion suggestion will appear either as highlighted text or as a Help Tip in the document—depending upon whether or not you have the Show as tip option selected. If you select this option, it will show as a tip (see Figure 12.9).

4   You must have the Collect suggestions option selected for the list on the right to automatically compile. Select this option and any words that you type into your StarOffice documents that meet the Min. word length (the default is 10, but can only be decreased to 5) will automatically be added to the list in this dialog box.

5   Select the Endless suggestions option so that the number of suggestions will continue to repeat in the tip list in your document (or as a highlight). For example, if you have the words "performance", "perforation", and "performed" in your list, when you type _perf_ in your document, you can press <Ctrl+Shift+Tab> to toggle through the available words from the list. If this is not selected, you will see only one word until, as you continue typing, the correct word suggestion appears.

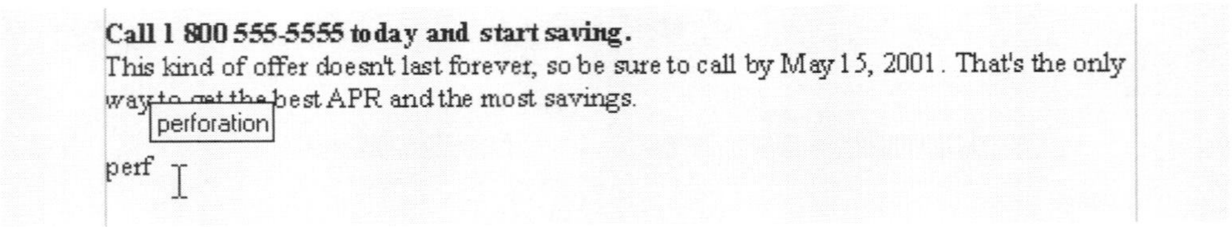

Call 1 800 555-5555 today and start saving.
This kind of offer doesn't last forever, so be sure to call by May 15, 2001. That's the only way to get the best APR and the most savings.

perforation

perf

Figure 12.9   The automatic completion word is displayed as a Help tip.

6   Select the Append space option so that a space is automatically added after the word completion tip (or highlight) is selected (depending upon what you have selected in the Accept with list box).

7   Choose the Accept with drop-down list box option that you want to use to accept the word completion tip (or highlight) by pressing <End>, <Enter>, <Space>bar, or <Right> arrow.

8   You can change the Max. entries option to establish the maximum number of words to be in the list of this dialog box. This will be the number of words that can be recalled at a time. The more word entries allowed, the more Writer has to remember, and the more resources used by your computer.

9   Click the OK button to accept your changes and return to your document. If you prefer not to accept your changes, and you haven't yet clicked the OK button, you can click the Reset button to return to the previous settings. You can also click Cancel to immediately return to the document.

NOTE Because the word completion list in the Word Completion tab of the AutoCorrect dialog box goes away and resets each time you close StarOffice, you may want to maintain a word completion list of your own. When working in a document that contains a lot of words for your compilation list, choose Tools, AutoCorrect/AutoFormat to open the AutoCorrect dialog box and click the Word Completion tab. Click once on the first word in the list, press and hold the <Shift> key, and scroll down and click the last word in the list (this will select all the words in the list). Copy all the selected words using <Ctrl+C>. Paste this list of words into a new text document and save it as a words reference list (for example, WordRefList.sdw). You can then extend or edit this text document manually by adding new words to it or removing words and saving it each time. Then, when you have started StarOffice Writer again, and want the words to be available in your Word Completion list, you can select the Collect suggestions check box contained in the Word Completion tab of the AutoCorrect dialog box, click the OK button on the dialog box, and open the WordRefList.sdw document (or whatever you named it). The words will automatically be included in the list on the dialog box. Choose the options from the list of steps in this section and click the OK button; the word completions will be available in all your text documents during this session with StarOffice.

Applying AutoFormat Functions

The AutoFormat function allows you to apply set formatting to specific areas of your document. Once you become familiar with ways to automatically apply formatting, it can minimize the time you take to apply multiple formats and styles. Pay special attention to the AutoFormat standards and apply them while you create your document.

TO APPLY VARIOUS AUTOFORMAT FUNCTIONS TO A DOCUMENT

1   Open a document into which you want to apply formatting features.

2   Choose Tools, AutoCorrect/AutoFormat and select the Options tab on the AutoCorrect dialog box. Then, scroll down and check the Apply Styles option in the [T] column, and click the OK button. This tells Writer to apply the various styles you indicate in your document.

Choose Format, AutoFormat, and make sure there is a checkmark next to the While Typing command. This will automatically format the current document while you are adding information.

Paragraphs headings are assigned if...

a) There is a blank paragraph above and below the paragraph.

b) The paragraph begins with a capital letter and does not have any ending punctuation.

Heading style formats are assigned as follows...

a)<Tab> at the beginning of your heading paragraph will assign it as a Heading1; <Tab><Tab> at the beginning will assign Heading2; and so on.

b) <Space> at the beginning of your heading paragraph will assign it as a Heading1; <Space><Space> at the beginning will assign Heading2; and so on.

c) A colon ":" at the end of a heading line will assign Heading3.

Bullets are assigned if you begin a paragraph with a hyphen "-", star "*" or a plus sign "+" (and if the paragraph is either already formatted as Standard, Text body, or Text body indent style). You must type text after the character for this to work.

Numbering is assigned if you begin a paragraph with a two-digit number (and if the paragraph is either already formatted as Standard, Text body, or Text body indent style). You must type text after the number for this to work.

Lines separators are added if a paragraph consists of...

a) Three hyphens "---" (the line will be .05 pt in thickness)

b) Three underscores "___" (the line will be 1 pt in thickness)

c) Three equal signs "===" (the line will be double and 1.10 pt in thickness)

If you type your document first (with the While Typing option deactivated) you can choose Format, AutoFormat, Apply and the document will automatically format the current document according to the above set of rules.

3   Choose Format, AutoFormat, Apply and Edit Changes to open the AutoFormat dialog box.

4   Click the Accept All or Reject All buttons to accept or reject all the AutoFormat changes in the document at once.

5   Click the Review Changes button to open the Accept or reject AutoFormat changes window, which is similar to the Accept or Reject Changes window in the "Recording Changes to a Document" section of Chapter 10.

6   Click the Accept All or Reject All buttons on the List tab to accept or reject all the changes apparent in the document; or click each individual Action and click the Accept or Reject buttons.

NOTE   You can click the Undo button if you accept or reject your changes, or if you decide that you want to reverse your changes. If you click the Undo button after you have accepted all or rejected all changes, *all* will be undone simultaneously.

7   Click the Filter tab if there are so many changes recorded that you need to filter the list. You can choose to filter the list of recorded changes by Date (date the change was made), Author (who made the change), Action (what type of change was made), or Comment (comments about the change). Then, click back to the List tab and the list will only contain the items by which you filtered the list.

8   Click the X Close button on the window to return to your document.

NOTE   You can also apply an AutoFormat to a table. Refer to the section "Applying a Table AutoFormat" in Chapter 9, "Working with Tables."

Using Outline Numbering

Outline numbering is linked to a Paragraph style in only the current document. If you define outline numbering for a Paragraph style, for example "HeadingX", these settings are valid wherever the style is assigned. For example, perhaps you have different sections within a chapter document. If you establish outline numbering, you can organize your illustrations and captions by chapter number, section number, and figure number. Keep in mind that you can create and assign up to 10 outline levels with the different numbering styles.

TO USE OUTLINE NUMBERING

You can organize your document automatically without having to constantly change numbering whenever you move or enter new subheads. And the numbering you include can be reflected automatically, for example, in tables of contents or captions.

1   Choose Tools, Outline Numbering to open the Outline Numbering dialog
    box. Select the Numbering tab (see Figure 12.10).

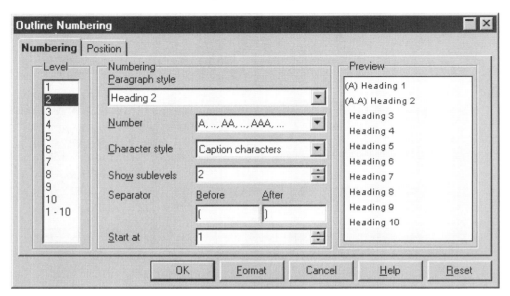

Figure 12.10   You can alter the outline numbering options.

2   You can set numbering styles and formats individually for each outline
    level in your document. To do so, choose the outline Level from the list
    box.

    If you select the "1-10" Level, the Numbering and Position tab settings are
    applied to all chapter levels; notice though, they will not be fixed to a cer-
    tain Paragraph style (that drop-down list box option appears grayed out).

3   Select from the Numbering options as follows (changes will automati-
    cally display in the Preview area):

    • Paragraph style—Where you designate the style of the paragraph for
      the outline number Level. For example, if you were writing a book, you
      might have multiple Section opener pages formatted as Heading 1, but
      want your Chapter names to behave as first-level paragraphs as well.

    • Number—Select how the actual numbers will appear at each outline
      level (for example, roman numerals or alphabetical).

    • Character style—Where you indicate the text style for the actual
      numbering, not the text itself. For example, the Page Number or
      Caption Characters styles.

    • Show sublevels—To display more than one level in a document (for
      example, if you designate captions to have more than one level in a
      document section like 2.1.5 for chapter 2, section 1, figure caption 5).

- Separator—Indicate a separator character to accompany the outline number, for example, adding parentheses before and after the number.
- Start at—Where you indicate the number to start at, for example, so you could continue numbering at a different position in the document, without interrupting the numbering sequence.

7   Click the Format button to save the specified chapter numbering (this allows you to reuse a complex numbering scheme without re-creating it from scratch). View the nine Untitled predetermined chapter numbering styles available or click Save As from the list to assign your own name to it.

NOTE   Click the Reset button if you want to revert the modified values back to their original settings. Keep in mind that once you click the OK button to save the settings, those become the new defaults.

8   Click the OK button to save the settings. You can then begin applying them to your document.

Inserting Scripts

Scripts are commands that can be executed with or without user interaction. These can be inserted directly into your documents so that the script will run.

To Insert Scripts

1   Place the cursor in the location of the document in which you would like the script inserted.

2   Choose Insert, Script to open the Insert Script dialog box.

The Script type will default to JavaScript. You could insert Live Script or VBScript as alternatives.

3   Choose either of the following:

- URL—Enter the URL of the script file to link to, or click the (...) button to select the specific script file to insert and link to.
- Text—Enter the script text in the window.

4   Click the OK button to insert the script at the current cursor position.

After the script is inserted, you can double-click on the green rectangle to open the Edit Script dialog box. You can edit the script and jump forward or backward between other scripts (if there are others inserted into the document).

NOTE   The green inserted script marker will be visible only if the Display notes option is selected under Tools, Options, Text Document (or Tools, Options, HTML Document) on the Contents page. In addition, you can choose File, Print and click the Options button to select whether you would like the scripts in your document to be printed at the end of the page or at the end of the document.

Working with Macros

A macro is a small program created in StarOffice Basic that allows you to simplify repetitive tasks. When you create a macro in Writer, you can create them manually or simply tell it to record all the actions (keystrokes and command selections) that you perform, until you tell it to stop recording.

To Record a Macro

For the macro we are going to record, run, and edit in this section, we are going to assume that your company wants its new company logo to be inserted at the top of all your documents.

1   Prepare the text document in which you want to record a macro. For example, open a new text document or open a document that you have already set up in which you want to record a macro (and essentially perform for the first time).

2   Choose Tools, Macro to open the Macro dialog box.

3   Type the name of the macro you would like to record into the Macro name text box (see Figure 12.11).

    By default, macros you record will be located within soffice, Standard, Module1.

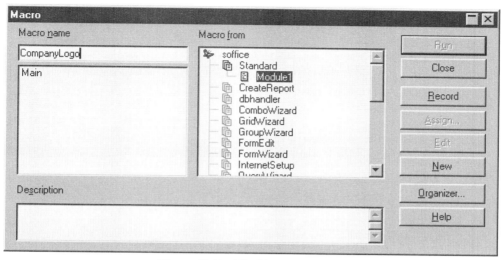

Figure 12.11   The Macro dialog box.

4   Press <Ctrl+Home> to move the cursor position to the beginning of the document.

5   Choose Insert, Graphic, From File to open the Insert Graphics dialog box. Locate and click once on the graphic; then click the Open button to insert the graphic into the document.

6   Click the Recording Off button and the macro has recorded the steps of moving to the beginning of the document and inserting the specific file.

If you accidentally make the mistake of typing text incorrectly while recording your macro, you can just backspace over the mistake and then type the correct information. Even the number of <Backspace> keystrokes are recorded in the macro; when the macro is run again, the text will be inserted and then deleted just as you did during the recording. Try to plan out your macro so that you don't include many unnecessary cursor movements; this takes the macro that much longer to run.

A commonly overlooked error when you are recording a macro is including the copying and pasting of text or objects. The tasks of copying and pasting are definitely recorded in the macro, but the text or objects that you select to be copied or pasted might differ when in a different document. This is because text or objects that are selected in a document to be copied are recorded as a selection *location* in the document, meaning the macro will try to select the text at the specific page x, section x, line x, and column x location. When in a different document than the one you recorded the macro in, completely different text or objects will be selected at that specified location; if the location doesn't exist (for example, if there is no page 20 in the second document) then you will receive a runtime error.

Another common error when recording a macro is to include inadvertent cursor movements. For example, if you press the arrow keys to move the cursor to the location in the document where you would like specific information typed, that cursor movement would be recorded and performed when the macro is run, potentially placing the cursor in an incorrect location for another document. If you accidentally include unnecessary cursor-movement actions in the macro, stop recording the macro and begin again.

TO RUN A MACRO

1   Choose Tools, Macro to open the Macro dialog box.

2   Type the name of the macro you would like to run into the Macro name text box or simply click on the macro name in the Macro from list box.

3   Click the Run button and the macro will begin.

    To cancel a macro while it is running, press <Shift+Ctrl+Q>. A message box will indicate that the macro has been canceled.

TO EDIT MACROS

When you record a macro, what you're really doing is writing code in a special computer language designed to work with StarOffice, called StarOffice Basic. This section will show only a very basic example of a macro in the Integrated Development Environment. In many cases it might be easier to simply re-record the macro and save it with the same name.

1   Choose Tools, Macro to open the Macro dialog box.

2   Type the name of the macro you would like to run into the Macro name text box or simply click on the macro name in the Macro from list box.

    If you wanted to delete the macro, you would click the Delete button. If you preferred to add the macro to a menu, keyboard keystroke, or tool-bar, you would click the Assign button (refer to Chapter 14, "Customizing the Writer Environment," for more information).

3   Click the Edit button to open the macro and review the code that has been generated in the StarOffice Basic programming language (see Figure 12.12).

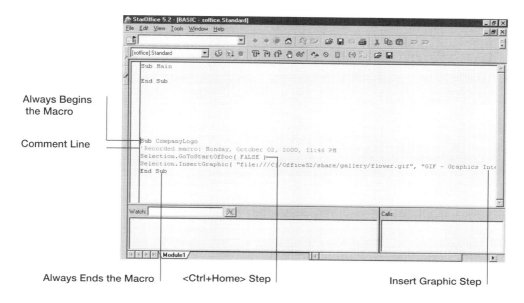

Always Begins the Macro

Comment Line

Always Ends the Macro   **<Ctrl+Home> Step**   **Insert Graphic Step**

Figure 12.12   The code appears in the IDE (Integrated Development Environment) programming interface.

7   Type any changes directly into the StarOffice Basic programming language macro. For example, you could alter the location of the inserted graphic file.

   If you want to add a comment to the macro, begin the line with an apostrophe ('), which will "remark out" the comment line statement so that StarOffice will not attempt to run it as a command.

8   Click the Save button and then choose File, Close to return to the text document (or whatever you have open in StarOffice).

Performing Calculations in Text

This might be an obscure feature in Writer, but I thought it was so nifty that I had to add a small section on it. Instead of grabbing a calculator or opening up StarOffice Calc to perform a calculation, you can calculate numbers right in the text of a Writer document.

To Perform a Calculation in Text

1   Type in the calculation you would like to have performed. For example, you can calculate 16 and 100 in numerous ways.

    `16 * 100 =`

2   Select the portion of the calculation you want performed:

    `16 * 100 =`

3   Choose Tools, Calculate.

4   Click the cursor at the location in the document where you would like the solution placed. For example, after the equals sign.

5   Click the Paste button on the Function bar and the solution will be entered in the document (see Figure 12.13).

    Notice that if you accidentally type a character that isn't a recognizable operator in Writer (line number 5 contains an em dash instead of an en dash minus sign), you will receive notification of a syntax error. Make the change to the formula and repeat steps 3 through 5 again.

Non-recognizable Character

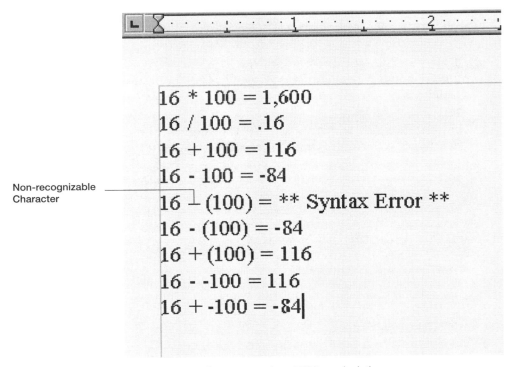

Figure 12.13   Some examples of Writer calculations.

Using the Microsoft Import AutoPilot

Writer offers a great way to import multiple Microsoft files into StarOffice without having to open each and every file and save it as a StarOffice document.

TO USE THE MICROSOFT IMPORT AUTOPILOT

1   Choose File, AutoPilot, Microsoft Import to open the Microsoft AutoPilot Import window. Read the introductory information and click the Continue>> button to begin.

2   Select either the Microsoft Word (documents), Excel (worksheets), or PowerPoint (presentations) icon. Depending on the icon you choose, you can choose to import Microsoft templates, documents, or both.

3   Click each appropriate Expand button (...) to open the Select a Directory dialog box. Locate the template and/or document path and click the Select button to return to the AutoPilot page.

4   Type the path of exported StarOffice Writer documents; or you can click the Expand button (...) or accept the default path by clicking the Continue>> button (see Figure 12.14).

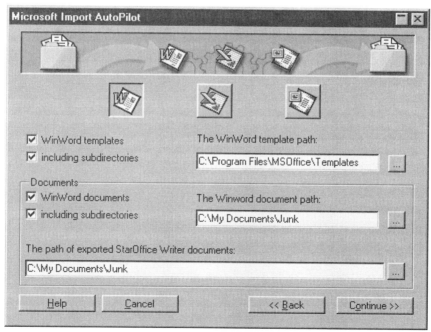

Figure 12.14   The second page of the Microsoft Import AutoPilot.

5   Review the information in the main Summary text box. If you find any errors, click the <<Back button and make the necessary changes. Also review the template groups of imported templates:

- Text template group—Insert a group name for your imported text templates (documents for Writer).

NOTE   You might see a message stating that, "The original VBA Basic Code contained in the document will not be saved." If this happens, you might need to open the document or document template and modify any macros or properties that do not translate to StarOffice.

- Calculation template group—Insert a group name for your imported calculation templates (spreadsheets for Calc).
- Presentation template group—Insert a group name for your imported presentation templates (presentations for Impress).

6   Click the Import button to begin the import procedures and review the progress.

If there are any errors with the import procedure, you will be notified that the file couldn't be imported and given the reason why.

The files that were imported are now in the directory you indicated and can be accessed and used at any time.

Working with StarOffice Tools

Understanding Web Pages

Before we take a look at how Writer can be used to create simple HTML documents, a brief explanation of how Web pages and Web sites work is in order. Even the simplest of Web site you find on the World Wide Web (WWW) consist of multiple HTML documents that are linked by a series of hyperlinks (more about hyperlinks in the section "Inserting Hyperlinks").

Web sites provide a home page that serves as the index for the rest of the Web site. All the navigation of the site is then handled by clicking on a particular link that takes you to another page on the site. In most Web page construction software, the first page created is actually titled index. All the pages that make up the Web site are saved in the HTML format.

The odd thing about Web pages is that all objects on a Web page such as graphics, backgrounds, or other design elements are actually separate files, even though the Web page appears to you in a Web browser. Before easy-to-use Web page creation software was available, building a Web page meant that each page would be created in a text editor using HTML codes. If the creator wanted to show a picture on a page, an HTML code would be placed on the page that referenced a graphic file. When the page was viewed using a Web browser, the HTML code would be interpreted by the Web browser and the graphic would appear on the page.

One other point about Web pages in general. Web pages are located on the WWW using URL (Uniform Resource Locator) addresses. A URL is a friendly name that is linked to the actual IP (Internet Protocol) address of the site on the Web. And the URL itself is derived from the actual domain name that has been assigned to a company. For example Sun Microsystems has the domain name sun.com. And its URL is www.sun.com.

To Create Web Pages

You can create Web pages using the StarOffice Web Page AutoPilot; it allows you to create numerous different Web page types, including special pages that include contact forms or a picture album. StarOffice Writer actually provides the workspace for working on Web pages created using the AutoPilot.

Once the different pages for the site have been created, you can insert links onto the pages that allow you to navigate to each of the pages that you have created. All you have to do is place the appropriate link on a page to navigate to another page in the Web site.

If you plan on creating a Web site of your own, keep the following points in mind:

- Create a folder on your computer that will hold all your HTML files, graphics, and other objects that make up the various Web pages for the site.

- Name the home page HTML file (the one that will contain the links to the other pages) index.html.

- Web pages that will actually be available on the WWW need to be hosted by a Web server. Most Internet Service Providers will provide you space for your Web pages on their Web server (some for free, most for a fee).

- If you plan on creating a Web page that will be available on the WWW, you may have to get your own domain name. For information on leasing (because you have to pay for it) a domain name (unless your Internet Service Provider takes care of that for you), check out the Web site at www.internic.com. It provides information on getting your own domain name.

- If you are only going to use the Web site on your company's network, your network administrator will have to put your Web site files on the company Web server.

Saving Documents as HTML Files

StarOffice allows you to save your text documents as HTML documents very easily within Writer.

TO SAVE A WRITER DOCUMENT IN HTML FORMAT

1   Create a new text document or open an existing Writer document.

2   Choose File, Save As to open the Save As dialog box.

3   Type a new file name for the Writer file (if you want the HTML file to have a different name than the one currently being used for the file).

4   Use the navigation buttons on the Save As dialog box to specify the directory that you wish to save the HTML file in.

5   Click the File type drop-down box and select the HTML (StarOffice Writer) file format.

6   Click the Save button to save the file. StarOffice automatically creates the appropriate HTML code from your text document. Notice that the document on the taskbar now has an HTML symbol instead of the Writer symbol.

TO VIEW A WRITER HTML FILE

You can view a HTML document that you create in Writer with the StarOffice Web browser.

1   Choose File, Open to display the Open dialog box.

2   Use the navigation buttons to locate the HTML file that you wish to view.

3   Select the file in the Open dialog box.

4   Click the Open button.

The HTML file will be opened in the StarOffice Web browser window.

Creating Web Pages with AutoPilot Templates

StarOffice provides AutoPilot templates to help create Web pages and other common documents. The AutoPilot asks you questions and provides you with spaces to fill in the answers. After you provide the information, it creates the HTML document that you requested. Without getting too in depth with the all changes you can make to forms (you will need the StarOffice Base book for that), this section walks you through creating a Web page contact form and making some minor modifications to it. (And for the form to actually *do* anything, you will need to write some CGI, but that is beyond the scope of this book.)

To Create a Web Page Contact Form

1   Choose File, AutoPilot, Web Page to create a new HTML document and open the AutoPilot Web Page: Template dialog box (see Figure 13.1). Notice that in the background the Standard HTML page appears.

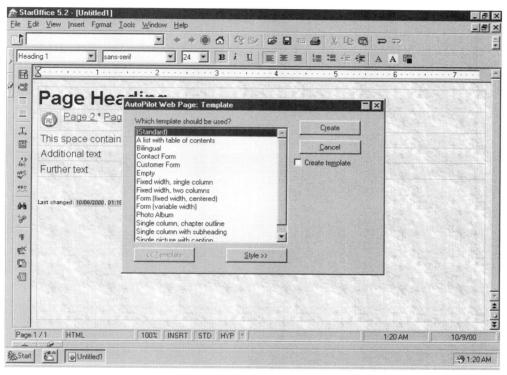

Figure 13.1   You can choose whatever type of Web page template you prefer.

2   Choose the template you want to use from the list, for example, Contact Form. The template will automatically apply to the HTML document in the background.

3   Click the Style button to select from a list of available styles, for example, SUN Look. The style will automatically apply to the HTML document in the background. If you dislike the look, select another style from the list.

NOTE   Select the Create template option on the dialog box if you would like the Web page to be created as a template that you can modify and use as the foundation for multiple HTML pages. Keep in mind that you can always use the AutoPilot to re-create any Web page template.

4   Click the Create button to begin editing the HTML document or template.

For example, perhaps you don't need the "Company" option on your Contact form, but you do need a "Dr." option. Also remember this contact form will be filled out by individuals who visit your Web site, so consider all the possibilities before you finalize your HTML document.

5   Click the Form Controls button on the Main toolbar; click and drag the Form Controls toolbar so that you can use it to modify your HTML document (see Figure 13.2).

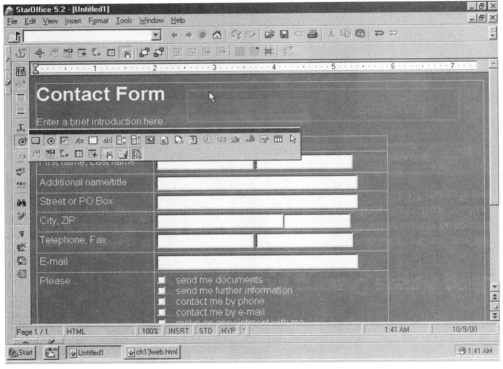

Figure 13.2   Click and drag the Form Controls toolbar onto your desktop.

6   Click the mouse pointer directly in the document and delete the text "Company", and delete the option button as well (using the <Backspace> key). You could also click to select the option button and press <Delete> to remove it.

7   Type "Ms.", add two spaces, and type "Dr."; these will be two more options for selection on the contact form.

8   Click the Select button on the toolbar and click directly on one of the other option buttons already on the contact form. You could also click the

Option button on the toolbar and draw the option button. However, why not copy and paste instead of trying to make the option buttons the exact same size?

NOTE   Be careful copying option or radio buttons within Web pages that are to be used as forms. Because of the CGI code, you might wind up with multiple buttons that use the same internal name in your HTML code. You should be fine when the buttons are all next to each other, and users have to choose only 1 option amongst them, but it might not be fine if you were copying buttons from one set of radio buttons into another, or if you were creating checkboxes or some other kind of control. This would most likely cause problems in the CGI code used to send information to the server.

9   Press <Ctrl+C> to copy the option button, move the pointer to right before the "Ms.", and press <Ctrl+V> to paste the option button. Repeat this to place an option button before the "Dr." as well (see Figure 13.3).

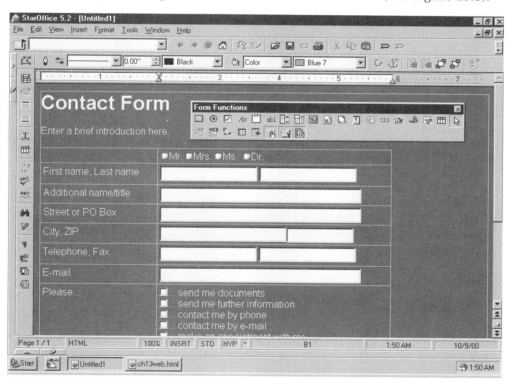

Figure 13.3   Create new options on your contact form using the Form Controls toolbar.

10   Scroll down to the bottom of the contact form and right-click the Reset
      button; we want it to say "Clear" instead. Choose Control from the short-
      cut menu to open the button Properties dialog box.

11   Type to rename the Name of the button control; make sure you rename
      the Label as well (this is the text that you will actually see in the form).
      Click the X Close button to save the changes and apply them to the form
      control (see Figure 13.4).

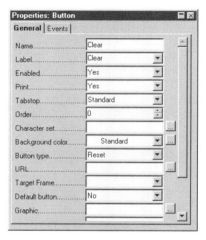

Figure 13.4   Change button control
properties that are on your form.

12   Choose File, Save to open the Save As dialog box. The File type defaults
      to HTML, so all you need to do is indicate the file location and File name,
      and click the Save button.

      If you didn't choose the Create template option on the original AutoPilot
      Web Page: Template dialog box (refer back to Figure 13.1), and want to
      save your HTML document as a template, you can always select Star-
      Writer/Web 5.0 Template as the File type before you save the file.

NOTE   You can make many more form control modifications than
mentioned here; I just wanted to give you a feel for some of the things
you could do to make your AutoPilot Web Pages more personalized.

NOTE   If you don't want to create a Web page using the AutoPilot,
you can always choose File, New, HTML Document and begin
creating your document from scratch.

Inserting Hyperlinks

You can type a hyperlink directly into your document whenever you are in HYP or SEL mode. HYP mode allows you to type in the hyperlink and click on it immediately to display the page in your default Web browser. SEL mode allows you to edit and format hyperlink text, but does not make the hyperlink "live." To make it clickable, switch to HYP mode by clicking on the SEL button in the status bar.

Web page URLs and email addresses display by default as hyperlinks in Writer; they appear by default as underlined blue text (see Figure 13.5) that you can click on to immediately access the URL or create an email (see Figure 13.6 and 13.7 respectively). You might need to refer to the section in Chapter 10, "Sending a Document as Email," if when creating an email you receive a message indicating that you need to create an Outbox.

> **NOTE** If you haven't recently saved the current document, writer will prompt you to save the file.

Figure 13.5 Type in a URL to immediately insert the hyperlink.

Figure 13.6   The URL hyperlink automatically opens your default browser within StarOffice.

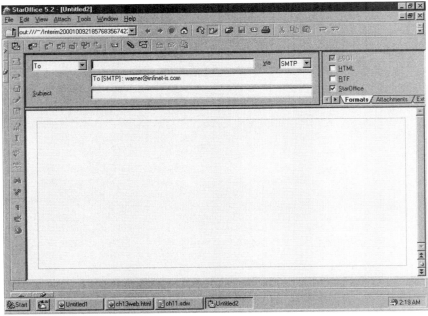

Figure 13.7   The email hyperlink automatically opens your default email application in StarOffice.

TO INSERT HYPERLINKS

To gain more control over the hyperlinks you insert in your documents, you can use the Hyperlink dialog box.

1   Choose Insert, Hyperlink to open the Hyperlink dialog box.

2   Click on the type of hyperlink you would like to insert into your document:

   • Internet—Links directly to a URL.
   • Mail & News—Links directly to an email address or newsgroup.
   • Document—Links directly to another document (not within the same document; to create a link within a document, refer to the section "Inserting Cross References" from Chapter 11).
   • New document—Allows you to create a new file to link to.

   Notice that all types of links have the same Further settings options, as follows:

   • Frame—Designate a target frame in your document where the document will be loaded (your document must already include a frame). Keep in mind that these are Web frames, not Writer frames or floating frames.
   • Form—Determine whether the hyperlink will appear as a button or as text.
   • Events—This button opens the Assign Macro dialog box in which you can assign events their own macro program codes.
   • Note—Text that displays on the button or hyperlink text. If you selected text before you chose Insert, Hyperlink, that text will appear here. If you don't enter text, Writer defaults to inserting the link address.
   • Name—Assign anchor text, which enables you to jump to the hyperlink from another location.

3   Click the Internet option and review the settings (see Figure 13.8):

   • Hyperlink type—Select whether the link is to the Internet (World Wide Web), an FTP directory, or Telnet.
   • Target—Type the target URL into this field.
   • WWW Browser—Click this button to open your default browser and load the URL; you can then copy the URL from the Load URL onto the clipboard and paste it into the Target field.
   • Target—Click this button to open the Target in Document window.

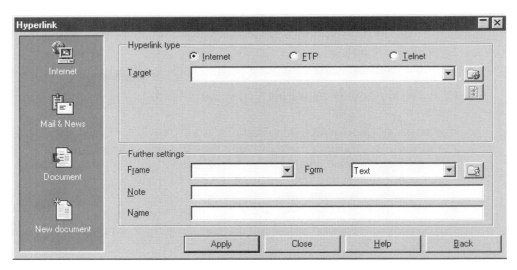

Figure 13.8   The Internet hyperlink settings.

4   Click the Mail & News option and review the settings (see Figure 13.9):

•Mail & News—Select whether the link is an E-mail or News link.

•Receiver—Type the complete URL to the link (for example, mailto:name@domain.com or news.group.server.com). You can click the Addressbook link if you want to copy an address.

•Subject—Type a subject for the RE: field in an email (this doesn't apply to a news link).

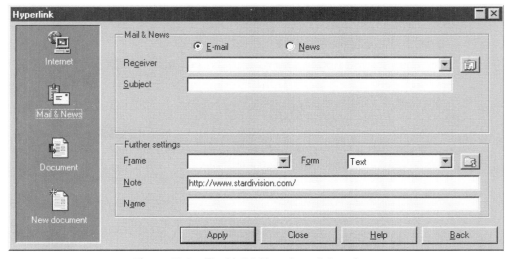

Figure 13.9   The Mail & News hyperlink settings.

5 Click the Document option to review the settings (see Figure 13.10). Indicate the Document Path for the link and a Target for the hyperlink in your document.

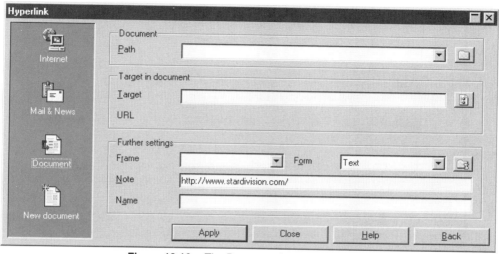

Figure 13.10 The Document hyperlink settings.

6 Click the New document option to review the settings (see Figure 13.11). Indicate whether you want to edit the new document now or later. Indicate the File name, File type, and you can click the Select Path button to locate the path in a window.

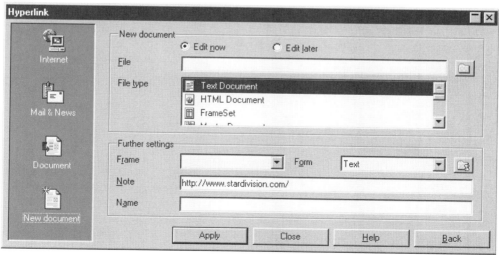

Figure 13.11 The New document hyperlink settings.

7   Click the Apply button to save your changes and return to the document. If you want to reset the original options (since the last Apply), click the Back button.

The hyperlinks you applied to the document are now active; click on the links to activate the appropriate source application.

Controlling Links

If you want to edit the link text that appears in your document, switch to SEL mode and edit the link text. If you prefer to edit the hyperlink type or settings, switch to SEL mode, place the cursor somewhere in the hyperlink text, and choose Edit, Hyperlink (or you can click and drag to select the hyperlink in HYP mode). The appropriate Hyperlink dialog box will open so that you can make your changes and apply them to the document.

If, for example, you delete a file that you have a link to, you will get an error message when you try to link to the file. Conversely, you can delete the link without affecting the data in the destination file.

Also, links between documents are automatically updated whenever you open or switch to the target document. Sometimes, however, you might not want links to be updated right away. For example, if you use many linked objects, updating significantly slows down the response time of an application. Likewise, if you are doing a lot of editing, you might want to wait until you have finished the editing, and then simultaneously update all the links in the target document.

You can also easily change the source of a link. Changing the source is useful if new data becomes available in a different file, or even in the same file; you can change the source without having to delete the linked object and link a new object.

Sharing Data Across Different Applications

Sometimes you may need to open files that have been created in another application. Likewise, you may want to be able to open a Writer file using a different application. Writer is able to open and save files in a wide variety of file formats. When you open a file created in a different file format, Writer simply converts the data to the Writer format, so you can easily use all Writer commands and options. When you save the file, you have the option of saving it in its original format or in Writer format. When you save a file in a different file format, Writer converts the file so that you can open it and edit it in the other application.

Working with Other StarOffice Applications

When working in StarOffice, you are don't really open and close each application individually; rather, you access the features of the menus, commands, and toolbars of the corresponding application within StarOffice desktop.

You can easily move among different StarOffice applications that are already open. To move between them press <Ctrl+Tab>. In addition, you can copy, cut, and paste text and objects between the applications with <Ctrl+C> for copy, <Ctrl+X> for cut, and <Ctrl+V> for paste.

Using Writer's Drawing Tools

Within Writer, you can use the Draw Functions toolbar to insert drawing objects into your documents. Simply click the Show Draw Functions button on the Main toolbar, and click and drag the toolbar to use while working in your document (see Figure 13.12).

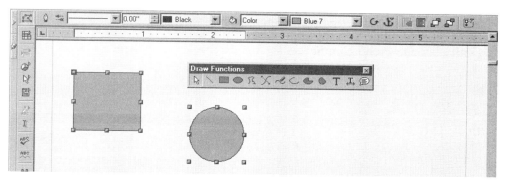

Figure 13.12 You can use the Draw Functions toolbar to add objects to your documents.

Before you modify, move, or size lines and objects, you must be able to select the lines or objects. A selected line or object displays with the sizing handles you have seen displayed through this lesson. Sizing handles appear on each side and corner of an object and at the endpoints of lines. Here are some things to remember when selecting objects:

- To select a single line or object, click it.
- To select more than one line or object, click the first object, hold down the <Shift> key and click each additional item as you hold down the key.
- To select a group of adjacent objects, click the Selection button on the Draw Functions toolbar and drag a rectangle (selection box) around the objects

you want to select. When you release the mouse button, all objects within the rectangle have sizing handles and the selection box disappears. If you prefer these selected objects to always act together as if they were one object, right-click on the selected objects and choose Group, Group from the shortcut menu.

- If you accidentally select an item that you didn't intend to, hold down the <Shift> key, click the object to remove the sizing handles, and deselect the object.

TO POSITION DRAW OBJECTS

By default, drawing objects are inserted as *floating objects*, which means that they can be positioned anywhere on a page, overlapping each other as well as document text. You can easily move a drawing object by dragging it to a new location. A floating object is an object that is placed in the graphics layer of a document so that it can be positioned on top of document text. An inline object is an object that is placed in the text layer of a document. There are other ways to position objects in a document as well. You can rotate them around an axis, or flip them horizontally or vertically.

As you may remember from Chapter 8, "Working with Frames, Graphics, and Objects", you can overlap (layer) objects in a document. In some cases, you can simply drag one object on top of another, or drag one out from behind another. You can also use menu commands to change the order in which objects are layered.

TO FORMAT DRAW OBJECTS

You can enhance the appearance of the Draw Functions by changing the line style, adding color or fills, or adding effects such as 3-D formatting or shadows.

Feel free to experiment with the other formatting options on the Draw Object bar, including the line style and line thickness, area fills, colors, rotation options, anchoring options, and positioning options. If you don't like an effect, simply choose Edit, Undo (or click the Undo button on the Function bar). You can also access other formatting options for draw objects by using the Format menu commands.

You can select colors and styles *before* you draw an object; this will make the settings the default (each object drawn there after will have the same settings). Simply set the line style or color and then select the Draw tool you want to use.

Inserting Files

You can insert many different kinds of files into your Writer documents. For example, you can insert another Writer document or even a text file from another application.

TO INSERT FILES

1 Choose Insert, Files to open the Insert dialog box.

2 Locate the File name or click the File type drop-down list box if you want to specify a certain file to insert.

3 Click the Insert button, and the text and elements from the file will be inserted into the document.

NOTE When you insert files, it is not a hyperlink to a file (see the section "To Insert Hyperlinks"), nor are you inserting the file into a frame (see Chapter 8). These two options, in contrast to simply inserting files, allow automatic updates to file changes within the document.

Using the Gallery

The Gallery provides numerous objects that you can use in your documents. In conjunction with the Beamer, you can quickly drag and drop objects directly to your document.

TO USE THE GALLERY

1 Choose View, Beamer to display the Beamer area.

2 Click the Show button to display the Explorer, and select the Explorer group.

3 Click the + to the left of Gallery to display all the elements available to you in the Explorer.

4 Click on an object in the Beamer and drag it directly into your document; when you release the mouse button, the object will be inserted (see Figure 13.13).

You can manipulate the object like any other object in a document (refer to Chapter 8 for more information on formatting objects).

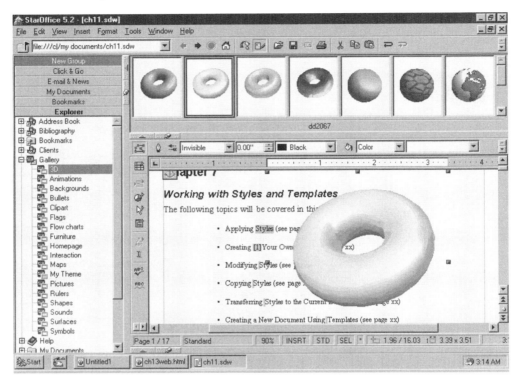

Figure 13.13   Drag and drop the Gallery objects from the Beamer to your document.

Using the Explorer

You can use the Explorer to locate and organize files. If you drag and drop files from the Explorer window into your document, you are creating a link to the information. In conjunction with the Beamer, you can even add hyperlinks to specific files.

TO USE THE EXPLORER TO CREATE HYPERLINKS

1   Choose View, Beamer to display the Beamer area.

2   Click the Show button to display the Explorer, and select the Explorer group.

3   Open the Explorer and choose, for example, the Links within your Book-marks folder. The links display in the Beamer area (see Figure 13.14).

4   Click on a link and drag it to your document, and a hyperlink will auto-matically be created. Depending on your default browser settings it also might try to dial your Internet connection and display the hyperlinked page.

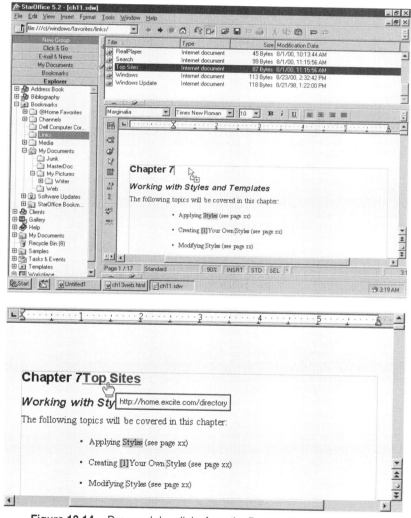

Figure 13.14   Drag and drop links from the Beamer to your document.

Customizing the
Writer Environment

Customizing General Options

When you open the Options dialog box for the first time (by choosing Tools, Options), you will see the User Data register. If you open it again, you will see the last active register.

When you customize the StarOffice options, you can define general StarOffice settings (see Figure 14.1). Most of these settings will apply to all StarOffice applications, but are listed here for when working in StarOffice Writer.

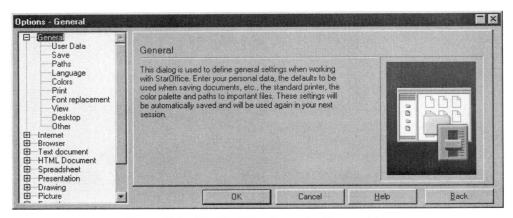

Figure 14.1   The StarOffice General settings register.

NOTE   If you change your mind about a setting, you can click Back to reset it to the default, but this only works if you have not clicked the OK button yet. You must click the Back button on each register that you changed before you clicked the OK button; they will not all simultaneously default to the previous settings unless you click the Cancel button.

TO UPDATE THE USER DATA INFORMATION

1   Choose Tools, Options to open the Options window; click on General and select the User Data register.

2   Type in the user data or update the information in the Address text boxes.

3   Click the OK button to accept the changes and return to your StarOffice Writer text document.

TO ALTER DOCUMENT SAVE OPTIONS

You might use this option if you want to encourage your colleagues to store relevant data about their documents, such as titles and subjects.

1   Choose Tools, Options to open the Options window; click on General and select the Save register.

2   Choose from the available Save options:

- •Edit document properties before saving—Will open the document Properties dialog box automatically every time you save.
- •Always create backup copy—Will create a document with the filename.BAK extension every time you save the filename.SDW normally. You can open the .BAK files in Writer if the original file becomes corrupt.
- •AutoSave every *xx* Minutes—Will automatically save your document every time your documents have been open for *xx* number of minutes. The Prompt to Save option will activate; you can select this option so that you are prompted about the save (in case you prefer not to save in some instances). Keep in mind that resaving a document eliminates the previous version and locks in any changes you might not yet be sure about.

3   Choose from the available Restore editing view options:

- •Document view—Will restore the last document view when you closed and restarted StarOffice. This means that if you saved and closed your document with the cursor on page 4, second paragraph, third character over, this exact location will automatically display the next time you open the document.
- •Open windows—Will restore the window arrangements you were using when you closed and restarted StarOffice.
- •Open documents—Will restore the documents that were currently open when you closed and restarted StarOffice.

4   Choose to Save graphics as Normal (graphics only compressed if they are 4 and 8 bit pixel data), Compressed (pixel graphics will be compressed in a special StarOffice format), or in their Original format (no compression).

5   Choose whether you want to Save URLs relative to the particular File system and the Internet.

6   Choose the Number of steps you can Undo using the Undo button or Edit, Undo command; the default is 20.

7   Click the OK button to accept the changes and return to your StarOffice Writer text document.

TO ALTER THE DEFAULT PATH OPTIONS

It can be convenient to save your documents to a specific path that corresponds to a structure on your system. For example, you can have your Document templates default to a different folder location.

1   Choose Tools, Options to open the Options window; click on General and select the Paths register.

2   Choose the Type of StarOffice feature in which you want to alter the file Path.

3   Click the Edit button; depending on the StarOffice feature, you can choose to change the default path or add or delete additional paths in the Select Path(s) dialog boxes.

4   Click the OK button to accept the changes and return to your StarOffice Writer text document.

TO ALTER THE LANGUAGE OPTIONS

This register allows you to define the properties of the spellcheck and hyphenation options.

1   Choose Tools, Options to open the Options window; click on General and select the Language register.

2   Choose from the following Check spelling options:

   • All caps—Include upper case words in spellcheck (for example, URL); disabled by default. The advantage is a more thorough spellcheck; the disadvantage is potentially more false positives, for example, the flagging of names.
   • Words with numbers—Check the spelling of words that contain numbers (for example, R2D2); disabled by default.
   • Case sensitive—Check the correct use of capitalization (for example, AutoText); enabled by default.
   • Check special regions—Check to include regions like headers, footers, tables, and frames; enabled by default.
   • All languages—Check words for matches with foreign language spellings; disabled by default.

3   Choose the AutoSpellcheck option to Check spelling as you type and whether you prefer it to Don't mark errors. This option is turned on by default.

4   Choose whether you want to utilize the German spelling rules that *preceded* the recent German language reforms, which remain a matter of controversy in Germany. For more than you ever wanted to know about this, see: http://german.about.com/homework/german/library/blreform.htm.

5   Select which Custom dictionaries to use; you can edit, add, or delete a dictionary using the buttons to the right of the list box.

6   Choose from the available Hyphenation rules:

   •Number of Characters per syllable before hyphen (defaults to 2).
   •Number of Characters per syllable after hyphen (defaults to 2).
   •Select Automatic hyphenation (disabled by default).
   •Hyphenate special regions by default (for example, tables, headers, and footers).

7   Choose the desired language from the Default language drop-down list box.

8   Click the OK button to accept the changes and return to your StarOffice Writer text document.

TO ADD, MODIFY, EDIT, OR DELETE COLORS

This register allows you to select a specific color from the color palette; or complete the color palette with an indefinite number of color variations.

1   Choose Tools, Options to open the Options window; click on General and select the Colors register.

2   Choose from the following options:

   •To add—Type in a Name, choose the Color sample data for RGB (red, green, blue) or CMYK (cyan, magenta, yellow, magenta), then click Add.
   •To modify—Select the color from the Standard colors display on the left, make the appropriate changes, then click Modify.
   •To edit—Select the color from the Standard colors display on the left, click the Edit button, make the appropriate changes on the Color chart, click OK, then click Modify if you want to replace the color.
   •To delete—Select the color from the Standard colors display on the left, and then click Delete.

3   Click the OK button to accept the changes and return to your StarOffice Writer text document.

TO SET PRINT WARNINGS

1   Choose Tools, Options to open the Options window; click on General and select the Print register.

2   Choose whether or not you want a Warning to display if the Paper size and/or the Paper orientation are wrong according to the document requirements.

3   Click the OK button to accept the changes and return to your StarOffice Writer text document.

TO ESTABLISH REPLACEMENT DISPLAY FONTS

This register allows you to influence the font display available in StarOffice. The font substitution does not change your documents, it changes the current computer environment.

1   Choose Tools, Options to open the Options window; click on General and select the Font replacement register.

2   Click the Apply replacement table option to activate the font replacement options.

3   Select the font from the Font drop-down list box and the replacement font in the Replace with drop-down list box.

4   Click the green checkmark to apply the settings to the replacement table.

    If you click on a setting in the replacement table, the Delete button will activate in case you want to remove a setting from the replacement table.

5   Click the OK button to accept the changes and return to your StarOffice Writer text document. The settings will immediately be active.

TO ALTER THE DESKTOP VIEW OPTIONS

This register allows you to change different settings that will alter the view of the elements on your desktop, for example, buttons, tabs, mouse controls, and so on.

1   Choose Tools, Options to open the Options window; click on General and select the View register.

2   Choose from the available Display options:
    • Logo—Choose whether to display the application logo when you start a StarOffice application.
    • Look & Feel—Allows you to adapt StarOffice's look and feel to resemble that of your current operating system's graphical user interface.
    • Window Drag—Specifies whether the contents of a window remain visible when you drag the window.

•Scaling—Allows you to alter the scaling percentage of the fonts within dialog boxes.

3   Select whether you want to have Large buttons and/or Flat buttons.

4   Choose the Mouse positioning drop-down list box to indicate whether you want the mouse pointer to have No automatic positioning, move to the Default button in a dialog box, or move to the Dialog center (center of the active dialog box).

5   Choose from the following Options:

•Menu follows mouse pointer—Must be selected to choose menu commands using the mouse pointer; if not selected you will have to click on each individual command to expand a submenu.

•Single line tab controls—Select this option to display tabs tabbed dialog boxes in a single line, not multiple lines. If there are too many tabs, a small arrow will appear at the far right of the tabs, indicating that more tabs are available to view.

•Colored tab controls—Displays colored tabs in dialog boxes.

•Preview in fonts list—Displays the current font settings in the actual font corresponding to the font name in the Font list text box.

•Inactive menu items—Choose this option to make all deactivated menu items display.

•Font history—Specifies whether the Font list displays the fonts recently used in the document at the top of the Font list.

6   Click the OK button to accept the changes and return to your StarOffice Writer text document.

TO ALTER THE DESKTOP OPTIONS

This register defines the basic settings for your desktop icons, for example, positioning, spacing, and other options.

1   Choose Tools, Options to open the Options window; click on General and select the Desktop register.

2   Choose to allow the Positioning of icons to be Free (anywhere you place or drag them), Snap to grid (align with an invisible grid), or to Auto-Arrange (arrange automatically).

3   Choose the Horizontal and Vertical Icon Spacing with the appropriate spin box.

4   Choose from the available options:

•Context-sensitive beamer control—Resets the Beamer view when you switch between two types of documents, for example, a database table displayed when working with a Writer form letter mail merge and the Gallery of objects displayed when working in an Impress presentation.

- •Restore expand state—Opens the folder structure to how it was displayed when you last used StarOffice.
- •Show folders in Web view—Displays all the folders in your system that contain an HTML file. They may be viewed accordingly:

  folder.so—StarOffice Writer/Web depicts the Web view.

  folder.htt—Microsoft Internet Explorer is the Web view.

  folder.htm or folder.html—The default Web browser in StarOffice displays the Web view.

5   Click the OK button to accept the changes and return to your StarOffice Writer text document.

TO ALTER OTHER GENERAL OPTIONS

This register allows you to alter additional settings like language selection, 3-D display, and to configure the Help Agent functions.

1   Choose Tools, Options to open the Options window; click on General and select the Other register.

2   Select if you would like the Help Agent to Start automatically and/or Reset to default start settings.

3   Select if you want to Show Tips (display tips automatically) and/or Reset Tip List (reset the tips over again).

4   Select the year to begin the Year (two digits) range.

5   Choose the 3D View options:

- •Use OpenGL—3D graphics from Draw and Impress will display using OpenGL-compatible video cards or drivers.
- •Optimized output—Optimizes the OpenGL 3D graphics language.
- •Use Dithering—Allows more colors to display with fewer colors available.
- •Object refresh during interaction—Objects are fully visible (not just an outline) when working with objects.

6   Choose the Help Agent options:

- •Start automatically—Automatically opens the Help Agent when you start working with a new or complex StarOffice feature. For example, if you have never created a table before, when you choose Insert, Table, the Help Agent will open (selected by default).
- •Reset to default start settings—Restore the Help Agent settings that were originally installed with StarOffice (not selected by default).

7   Choose the Tips options:

- •Show Tips—Displays a tip every time the StarOffice application is started (selected by default).
- •Reset Tip List—Displays the same first tip each time you start StarOffice; otherwise, if not selected (which is the default), the tip will be different each time you start the StarOffice application.

8   Click the OK button to accept the changes and return to your StarOffice Writer text document.

Customizing Text Document Options

This is where you can define settings specific to Writer Text documents (see Figure 14.2). Some of these settings will apply to other StarOffice applications, but are listed here for those times you are primarily working in StarOffice Writer.

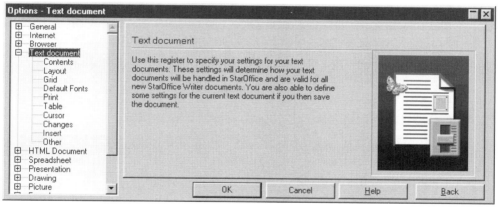

Figure 14.2   The StarOffice Text document settings register.

NOTE   If you change your mind about a setting, you can click Back to reset it to the default, but this only works if you have not clicked the OK button yet. You must click the Back button on each register that you changed before you clicked the OK button; they will not all simultaneously default to the previous settings unless you click the Cancel button.

TO DISPLAY DOCUMENT CONTENTS, HIGHLIGHTING, AND NONPRINTING CHARACTERS

This register determines the default settings for the display of document contents; for example, the display of window elements, nonprinting characters, and/or the highlighting of certain fields.

1   Choose Tools, Options to open the Options window; click on Text document and select the Contents register.

2   Choose to select or deselect the available Display options: Graphics and objects, Tables, Drawings and controls, Field codes, Notes. Deselecting these options will hide the specific element from display.

3   Choose to select or deselect from the available Highlighting options: Index entries, Indexes, Footnotes, Fields. Deselecting these options will turn off the gray highlighting the element would normally display.

4   Choose to select or deselect from the available nonprinting characters options: Paragraph end, Optional hyphens, Spaces, Protected spaces, Tabs, Breaks, Hidden text, Hidden paragraphs. Selecting these options will display characters regarding the specific elements in the document.

5   Click the OK button to accept the changes and return to your StarOffice Writer text document.

TO ALTER DOCUMENT DISPLAY LINES AND WINDOW CONTROLS

1   Choose Tools, Options to open the Options window; click on Text document and select the Layout register.

2   Choose from the following Lines options:

   • Text, Table, and Section boundaries—Determines whether a thin line displays around the text margins, around cells in a table, or between sections (all selected by default).
   • Guides—Determines whether to display guides around frames when moving them (not selected by default).
   • Simple control points—Determines whether to display the sizing handles as non-3D squares on objects (not selected by default).
   • Large control points—Determines whether to display bigger sizing handles on objects (not selected by default). Choose this option if you find yourself having trouble grabbing onto the default control points.

3   Choose from the following Window options:

   • Horizontal and Vertical scroll—Specifies whether to display the horizontal and vertical scroll bars (both selected by default).
   • Horizontal and Vertical ruler—Specifies whether to display the horizontal and vertical rulers (only Horizontal by default).

- •Smooth scroll—Regulates the scroll speed of using the mouse to select text (not selected by default).

4   Click the OK button to accept the changes and return to your StarOffice Writer text document.

TO ALTER THE UNITS OF MEASURE IN A DOCUMENT

1   Choose Tools, Options to open the Options window; click on Text document and select the Layout register.

2   Select the Meas. Units drop-down list box and choose either Millimeter, Centimeter, Inch (the default), Pica (the vertical measurement typically used in desktop publishing and professional printing), or Point (the horizontal measurement typically used in desktop publishing and professional printing).

3   Click the OK button to accept the changes and return to your StarOffice Writer text document.

The Ruler will automatically change to display the alternative measurement unit and all dialog boxes that contain measurement values.

TO ALTER THE SIZE OF TAB STOPS

1   Choose Tools, Options to open the Options window; click on Text document and select the Layout register.

2   Click the Tab stops spin box controls to increase or decrease the size of the tab stops. The tab stop is 1/2" by default—when you press the <Tab> key in your document, the cursor moves over 1/2" unless the tabs have been changed within the document or altered on this options window.

3   Click the OK button to accept the changes and return to your StarOffice Writer text document.

The Ruler will automatically change to display the alternative tab stop size.

TO ALTER THE GRID OPTIONS

This register sets a grid that you can configure on your document pages. The grid helps you define the exact position of your objects; you can also set it to snap objects to the grid.

1   Choose Tools, Options to open the Options window; click on Text document and select the Grid register.

2   Choose from the following options:

- Snap to grid—Specifies whether you prefer objects to align with a grid automatically (not selected by default).
- Visible grid—Specifies whether a grid should display when working with objects (not selected by default).
- Grid X and Y axis—Defines the size between vertical and horizontal grid points; by default, Resolution 0.50" and Subdivision 1 point.
- Synchronize axes—Specifies whether the Grid X and Grid Y values change symmetrically (selected by default).

3   Click the OK button to accept the changes and return to your StarOffice Writer text document.

TO ALTER THE DEFAULT FONTS

This register allows you to set the default fonts in your documents, which also defines the default fonts for predefined templates.

1   Choose Tools, Options to open the Options window; click on Text document and select the Fonts register.

2   Make changes to any of the following default font settings: Standard (the Standard style text), Heading (any text styled as a heading), List (bulleted and numbered lists), Caption (frame, object, and table captions), and Index (all index elements).

3   Click the Current document only option if you prefer the selected Default fonts to apply only to the current document. If you have other documents open, or if you open additional documents later, the new options you select will not apply to those documents.

4   Click the Default button if you want to return to all of Writer's original default fonts settings.

5   Click the OK button to accept the changes and return to your StarOffice Writer text document.

TO ALTER WHAT WILL AND WON'T PRINT

1   Choose Tools, Options to open the Options window; click on Text document and select the Print register.

2   Choose from the various contents that will print—Graphics, Tables, Drawings, Controls, and Backgrounds all print by default. Only Print black is not selected by default, in case you have a different color applied to your text.

3   Choose how you want the Pages to print—All Left and Right pages print by default; Reversed will reverse the printing order, and Brochure will

print the document as a brochure (two pages will appear on one printed page—these can be folded to create a brochure, like a gift card).

4   Choose how you want to display Notes in your document—None (print no notes at all), Notes only (print only the notes), End of document (notes print at the end of the document), or End of page (notes print at the end of each page).

5   Click the Create single print jobs Output option if you prefer each print job to begin on a new sheet of paper, even on a duplex printer.

6   Select the Fax drop-down list to choose the fax modem to use if you have fax software installed and you want to be able to fax/print directly from the document.

7   Click the Paper tray From printer setup option to ensure the printer will define the paper source.

8   Click the OK button to accept the changes and return to your StarOffice Writer text document.

TO ALTER ROW AND COLUMN EFFECTS IN TABLES

This register lets you specify the default settings for columns and rows and set the standard values for adjusting tables.

1   Choose Tools, Options to open the Options window; click on Text document and select the Table register.

2   Alter the Shift Row and Column spin boxes to alter the value used in the event a table row or column is moved.

3   Alter the Insert Row and Column spin boxes to alter the value used in the event a table row or column is inserted.

4   Select the Effect option to determine the relative effect of changes to rows, columns, and the entire table.

5   Click the OK button to accept the changes and return to your StarOffice Writer text document.

TO ALTER THE DIRECT CURSOR

This register lets you determine how text is inserted in your document at the click position of the direct cursor.

1   Choose Tools, Options to open the Options window; click on Text document and select the Cursor register.

2   Click the Direct cursor option to activate it within your documents.

3   Choose from the Insert options:

- •Paragraph alignment—Sets the paragraph alignment option where the direct cursor was clicked in the document.
- •Left paragraph margin—Sets the left indent at the horizontal position of where the direct cursor was clicked in the document.
- •Tabs—Inserts the appropriate number of tabs into the document leading up to the where the direct cursor was clicked in the document.
- •Tabs and spaces—Inserts the appropriate number of tabs and spaces into the document leading up to the where the direct cursor was clicked in the document.

4   Select the Color drop-down list box for the direct cursor indicator you see on screen.

5   Click the OK button to accept the changes and return to your StarOffice Writer text document.

TO ALTER TEXT DISPLAY AND LINE CHANGES

1   Choose Tools, Options to open the Options window; click on Text document and select the Changes register.

2   To control how additions to the document are displayed, click the Insert option and select from the various Attributes and Color drop-down list boxes; the changes will display in the Example area. By default, inserted text is underlined and the color displays according to the author, so each person's additions will appear in a different color.

3   To control how deletions from the document are displayed, click the Delete option and select from the various Attributes and Color drop-down list boxes; the changes will display in the Example area. By default, deleted text shows as strikethrough and the color displays according to the author, so each person's deletions will appear in a different color.

4   To display how changes to document attributes (for example, italics) display, select from the various Attributes and Color drop-down list boxes; the changes will display in the Example area. By default, changed text is bold and the color is black.

5   To help reviewers quickly locate changes, Writer places a vertical black line, called a Mark, in the outer margin of any line with a change. To specify a different location, choose the new location from the Mark drop-down box. To change the Mark's color, choose from the Color drop-down box.

6   Click the OK button to accept the changes and return to your StarOffice Writer text document.

TO SET AUTOMATIC CAPTIONS TO OBJECTS

1   Choose Tools, Options to open the Options window; click on Text document and select the Insert register.

2   Click the Captions Automatic option (not selected by default).

3   Click the Object selection button and indicate which caption options and settings you want automatically created from the Caption dialog box that opens.

4   Click the OK button and the next time you create a new object in the selection, a caption will automatically accompany it.

TO ALTER TABLE DEFAULTS

1   Choose Tools, Options to open the Options window; click on Text document and select the Insert register.

2   Choose from the Tables options:

   • Header—Creates all new tables with headers; enabled by default. When using AutoFormatting, Writer will automatically apply a header style to it.

   • Repeat header—Anytime a new table is created, it will allow repeat headers on a new page if the table flows to multiple pages; enabled by default.

   • Don't split—Prevents tables from splitting due to page breaks; disabled by default.

   • Border—Adds solid black line border to all table cells; enabled by default.

3   Choose from the Insert in tables options:

   • Number recognition—Automatically recognizes numbers in tables, right-aligning them, and saving them in number format so they may be used in calculations. This feature is enabled by default.

   • Number format recognition—Determines whether or not numbers entered into a cell must have a particular format —otherwise it will be in error (this is a default). For example, if the cell format is set to Date, then entering 1.1 will be interpreted as a date, not a number.

   • Alignment—If you clear this checkbox, even when Writer recognizes a number, it leaves the number aligned as text, instead of right-aligning it. This feature is enabled by default.

4   Click the OK button to accept the changes and return to your StarOffice Writer text document.

To Update Links, Fields, and Charts Automatically

This register allows you to specify if you want to automatically update the links in your text document. In addition, you can set spacing parameters to guarantee the compatibility of paragraphs, tables, and table spacing with Microsoft Word documents.

1   Choose Tools, Options to open the Options window; click on Text document and select the Other register.

2   Choose to Update links: Always, On request (by choosing Tools, Update, Update All), or Never. Select the Current document only if you don't want this to apply to all documents.

3   Choose whether to automatically Update fields and automatically Update charts. These are separate check boxes, so you can choose to automatically update fields but not charts, or vice versa. Select the Current document only if you don't want this to apply to all documents.

4   Choose from the Compatibility options when importing Microsoft Word documents:

   • Add paragraph and table spacing to start of pages—The spacing in StarOffice Writer documents is defined differently than in Microsoft Word documents. If you set above and below spacings between two paragraphs, the spacing will be added in Microsoft Word documents; whereas StarOffice Writer uses the largest one.

   • Add paragraph and table spacing to start of pages—This setting allows for spacings above the paragraph at the beginning of a page. The paragraph spacing to the top will be applied at the beginning of a page or column, if positioned on the first page of the document (also applicable with page breaks). When you import a Microsoft Word document, the distances is automatically added when converting to StarOffice.

NOTE   The Compatibility section on this dialog box also allows you to choose the Add spacing between paragraphs and tables in the current document option and the Add paragraph and table spacing to start of pages option.

5   Click the OK button to accept the changes and return to your StarOffice Writer text document.

Configuring Menus

You can customize menus in your applications as you prefer. You can define new menus and commands (for example, by adding a macro as a command from the StarOffice BASIC Macros Category list), rename existing menus and commands, and even change the order of your menus and commands. You can also save your custom menu configuration as a file and reload it anytime you want. Keep in mind that you cannot change shortcut/context menus (menus selected by right-clicking).

Choose Tools, Configure to open the Configuration dialog box and click the Menu tab (see Figure 14.3). The menu structure displays the menu name on the left and its respective function on the right. The tilde (~) to the left of the letter indicates the keyboard command (in conjunction with pressing the <Alt> key) that selects the menu (known as the menu command accelerator). The left-most level displays the title of each menu command and the subsequent levels display the menu commands and sub-menu commands.

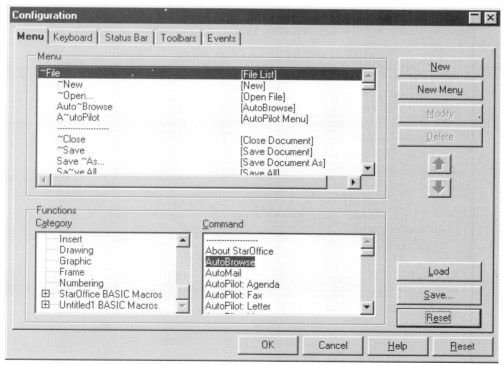

Figure 14.3   The Menu tab of the Configuration dialog box.

TO CONFIRM MENU CONFIGURATION CHANGES

It is important that you read the following options concerning the buttons on the bottom right of the Menu tab before you perform any of the menu additions, modifications, and deletions in the next sections. This is because you can inadvertently make changes that will be hard to unmake:

- Click the Reset button directly below the Save button (not the one to the right of the Help button), if you decide that you don't want to keep the changes to the Configuration Menu tab. All current changes in the active dialog will be irretrievably lost. The menu configuration since the last time you clicked the Save button will reappear, even if you clicked the OK button and returned to the document (and exited and reopened StarOffice).

- Click the Save button to open the Save Menu Configuration dialog box to save the configuration settings. Note that if you save the newly created menu configuration as <u>soffice.cfg</u>, the program-specific configuration file is overwritten. You can select the active configuration file by clicking the Load button.

- Click the Load button to access the Load Menu Configuration dialog box. A specific configuration will be active until it is replaced by a new one— perhaps one that you will create in the next few sections.

TO CHANGE A MENU NAME

1   Choose Tools, Configure to open the Configuration dialog box and click the Menu tab.

2   Click directly on the menu item name and wait for the name to be highlighted. This may take a few moments, or more. Only the name will be selected, as opposed to the entire row.

> **NOTE**   Menu names appear flush left in the Menu scroll box, and command names appear indented. Also, the tildes represent keyboard shortcut hot buttons.

3   Edit the name in a text box and press <Enter>.

4   Click the Save button to make the changes permanent and click the OK button. Refer to the section "To Confirm Menu Configuration Changes" to make sure this is what you want to do.

TO CHANGE A MENU'S STRUCTURE

1   Choose Tools, Configure to open the Configuration dialog box and click the Menu tab.

2   Select a menu item that you want to move to a different location.

3   Click and drag the item to a new location in the Menu list. A horizontal line displays where the menu item will be inserted when you release the mouse button.

4   Click the Save button to make the changes permanent and click the OK button. Refer to the section "To Confirm Menu Configuration Changes" to make sure this is what you want to do.

TO MOVE AN EXISTING MENU COMMAND

1   Choose Tools, Configure to open the Configuration dialog box and click the Menu tab.

2   Select the menu item you want to move.

3   Click the Upward arrow to move a menu item upwards in the menu list (only one menu position at a time).

4   Click the Downward arrow to move a menu item downwards in the menu list (only one menu position at a time).

    You can also alter the structure of the menus, for example, by moving a command from the Window menu to the Help menu. You can also drag and drop menu items to move them to a different location in your menu structure.

5   Click the Save button to make the changes permanent and click the OK button. Refer to the section "To Confirm Menu Configuration Changes" to make sure this is what you want to do.

TO DELETE AN EXISTING MENU ITEM

1   Choose Tools, Configure to open the Configuration dialog box and click the Menu tab.

2   Select the menu item you want to delete. Notice that the main hierarchical menu items (for example, ~File) cannot be deleted.

3   Click Delete to remove the selected element or elements without a previous conformation.

4   Click the Save button to make the changes permanent and click the OK button. Refer to the section "To Confirm Menu Configuration Changes" to make sure this is what you want to do.

TO MODIFY AN EXISTING MENU ITEM

1   Choose Tools, Configure to open the Configuration dialog box and click the Menu tab.

2   Select the menu item you want to modify. Notice that the main hierarchical menu items (for example, ~File) cannot be selected for modification.

3   Click the desired Category and Command from the Functions area. The Function list boxes show the program areas and associated functions:

Category—Where you can select the category containing the function you want to assign to a menu item (for example, the Documents category).

Command—Where you can select the command you want to assign to a menu item (for example, the Close Document command within the Documents category).

You can use the dotted line (the uppermost entry in the Command field) to insert a subdivision into a menu.

4   Click the Modify button to apply the change to the Menu list.

5   Click the Save button to make the changes permanent and click the OK button. Refer to the section "To Confirm Menu Configuration Changes" to make sure this is what you want to do.

TO CREATE A NEW MENU (TO THE RIGHT OF HELP)

You cannot create a new menu between the current default menus or anywhere to the left of the Help menu. You can break the menus in half, but you don't want to do this because it can make the menus confusing.

1   Choose Tools, Configure to open the Configuration dialog box and click the Menu tab.

2   Double-click on all the highest level menus in the hierarchy to condense the menu list, or scroll to the bottom of the list.

3   Click the New Menu button to insert "Menu" into the menu list with a menu subdivision bar below it.

4   Rename the menu by clicking on it and waiting for the highlighting; this indicates that you can type in a new name (see Figure 14.4). Don't forget to place the (~) before to the left of the letter you want to indicate the keyboard command.

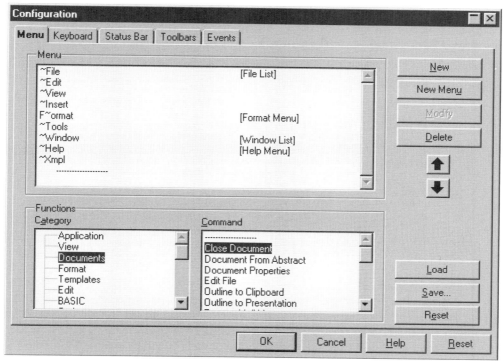

Figure 14.4   You can add a new top-level menu to your applications.

5   At this point, you have a new menu; now you can add commands to it. Click the desired Category and Command from the Functions area. The Function list boxes show the program areas and associated functions:

Category—Where you can select the category containing the function you want to assign to a menu item (for example, the Documents category).

Command—Where you can select the command you want to assign to a menu item (for example, the Close Document command within the Documents category).

6   Click the New button to insert the new menu command you have selected. Repeat steps 5 and 6 for each menu command you want added to your new first-level menu. You can rename the menus and move them around as you prefer.

7   Click the Save button to make the changes permanent and click the OK button. Refer to the section "To Confirm Menu Configuration Changes" to make sure this is what you want to do.

TO ASSIGN A NEW FUNCTION TO A MENU ITEM

This set of steps shows you how to add a new command function to a menu, whether it be a default menu or a new menu you have created.

1   Choose Tools, Configure to open the Configuration dialog box and click the Menu tab.

2   Select the current menu item in the list and select the desired function in the Functions area.

3   Click the Modify button to assign the new function to the menu item.

4   Click the Save button to make the changes permanent and click the OK button. Refer to the section "To Confirm Menu Configuration Changes" to make sure this is what you want to do.

Configuring the Keyboard

Keyboard commands allow you to quickly access commands, functions, and macros in your documents without having to follow the menu structures to access the action you want to perform. You can customize the keyboard commands in your applications as you prefer. You can assign commands and macros to keys or key combinations, and even reassign existing keyboard commands. You can also save your custom keyboard configuration as a file and reload it anytime you want. This is convenient if you have documents in which you have specific keyboard commands assigned, that you wouldn't use in most of your other documents.

Choose Tools, Configure to open the Configuration dialog box and click the Keyboard tab (see Figure 14.5). Use the Category, Command, and Key list boxes to select a command to apply to a key or key combination.

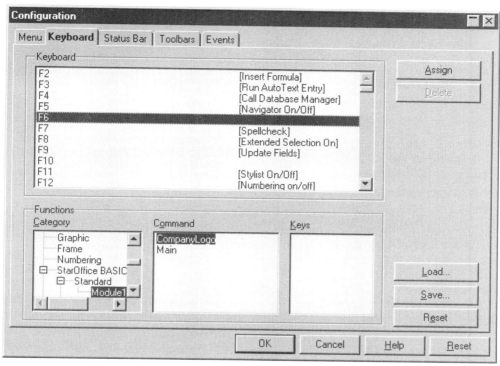

Figure 14.5   The Keyboard tab of the Configuration dialog box.

TO CONFIRM KEYBOARD CONFIGURATION CHANGES

It is important that you read the following options concerning the buttons on the bottom right of the Keyboard tab before you perform any of the keyboard additions, modifications, and deletions in the next sections:

- Click the Reset button directly below the Save button (not the one to the right of the Help button), if you decide that you don't want to keep the changes to the Configuration Keyboard tab. All current changes in the active dialog will be irretrievably lost. The keyboard configuration since the last time you clicked the Save button will reappear, even if you clicked the OK button and returned to the document (and exited and reopened StarOffice).

- Click the Save button to open the Save Keyboard Configuration dialog box to save the configuration settings. Note that if you save the newly created keyboard configuration as <u>soffice.cfg</u>, the program-specific configuration file is overwritten. You can select the active configuration file by clicking the Load button.

- Click the Load button to access the Load Keyboard Configuration dialog box. A specific configuration will be active until it is replaced by a new one—perhaps one that you will create in the next few sections.

To Assign or Reassign a Keyboard Configuration

You can quickly assign or even reassign a keyboard configuration to specific keys on your keyboard.

1   Choose Tools, Configure to open the Configuration dialog box and click the Keyboard tab.

2   Select the Keyboard configuration from the list (for example, <F6>, <F10>, <Ctrl+Shift+W>, and so on).

   If the keyboard configuration is already assigned, it will have an associated command (for example, [Insert Formula]) or macro (for example, [CompanyLogo(Standard.Module1)]) listed in brackets on the right.

3   Click the desired Category and Command from the Functions area. The Function list boxes show the program areas and associated functions:

   Category—Where you can select the category containing the function you want to assign to a keyboard shortcut (for example, the Documents category).

   Command—Where you can select the command you want to assign to a keyboard shortcut (for example, the Close Document command within the Documents category).

   Keys—If there is a keyboard function assigned, it will display in this list.

4   Click the Delete button if you want to delete a keyboard function and reassign it.

5   Click the Save button to make the changes permanent and click the OK button. Refer to the section "To Confirm Keyboard Configuration Changes" to make sure this is what you want to do.

NOTE   If you choose to reassign a key or key combination that has already been assigned, you will not see a message box asking you to confirm your reassignment; Writer will simply reassign the command. The same is true if you select a key or key combination and click the Delete button.

Configuring the Status Bar

The Status bar is along the bottom of the desktop, right above the Task bar. The Status bar can display the current page number, page style, page scale, insert mode, selection mode, hyperlinks in active or edit mode, whether changes to a document have been saved, and information about the active document. Choose Tools, Configure to open the Configuration dialog box and click the Status Bar tab (see Figure 14.6).

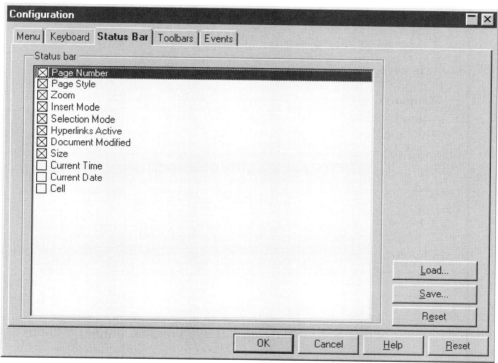

Figure 14.6 The Status Bar tab of the Configuration dialog box.

Select the following check boxes to indicate the information you would like to display in the status bar:

- Page Number—Displays the current page out of the total number of pages.
- Page Style—Displays the current template name, for example, Standard.
- Zoom—Displays the percentage of your document that is viewable in the document window. Refer to the section "To Enter Text Into a Document" in Chapter 1 for more information.

- Insert Mode—Displays whether you are in insert (INSRT) or overtype (OVER) mode, and allows you toggle between modes by clicking on them in the status bar. This checkbox is checked by default. Refer to the section "To Use Overtype and Insert Mode" in Chapter 2 for more information.

- Selection Mode—Displays the Standard (STD), Extended Selection (EXT), or Additional Selection (ADD) modes. This checkbox is checked by default. Refer to the section "To Select Text" in Chapter 3 for more information.

- Hyperlinks Active—Displays whether you are in hyperlink mode (HYP) where you can click on a link in the document to access the Web or a linked document, or, selection mode (SEL) where the links aren't active (meaning, you cannot click on the link to directly access the Web or a linked document). This checkbox is checked by default.

- Document Modified—If you have modified your document and not saved it since the previous save (or at all), an asterisk (*) will display. This checkbox is checked by default.

- Size—Displays the size and dimensions of frames, objects, and graphics selected in your document. This checkbox is checked by default.

- Current Time—Displays today's time. This checkbox is cleared by default.

- Current Date—Displays today's date. This checkbox is cleared by default.

- Cell—Displays the cell address location if the cursor is in a table. This checkbox is cleared by default.

> **NOTE**   The Cell and Size fields are displayed in the same area on the Status Bar, which is to the right of the Document Modified field and to the left of the Current Time field.

To Confirm Status Bar Configuration Changes

It is important that you read the following options concerning the buttons on the bottom right of the Status bar tab before you confirm the selection or deselection any of the Status Bar options:

- Click the Reset button directly below the Save button (not the one to the right of the Help button), if you decide that you don't want to keep the changes to the Configuration Status Bar tab. All current changes in the active dialog will be irretrievably lost. The Status Bar configuration since the last time you clicked the Save button will reappear, even if you clicked the OK button and returned to the document (and exited and reopened StarOffice).

- Click the Save button to open the Save Status Bar Configuration dialog box to save the configuration settings. Note that if you save the newly created Status Bar configuration as soffice.cfg, the program-specific configuration file is overwritten. You can select the active configuration file by clicking the Load button.

- Click the Load button to access the Load Status Bar Configuration dialog box. A specific configuration will be active until it is replaced by a new one—perhaps one that you will create in the next few sections.

Configuring Toolbars

You can customize toolbars in your applications as you like. For example, if you find that you don't use the Reload and Edit File buttons on the Function bar, you can remove them. You can define new toolbars and buttons (for example, by adding a macro as a button from the StarOffice BASIC Macros Category list), rename existing toolbars and buttons, and even change the order of your toolbars and buttons. You can also save your custom toolbar configuration as a file and reload it anytime you want.

Choose Tools, Configure to open the Configuration dialog box and click the Toolbars tab (see Figure 14.7). All the available toolbars are listed in conjunction with the Function Bar, Object Bar, Main Toolbar, and Navigation Bar.

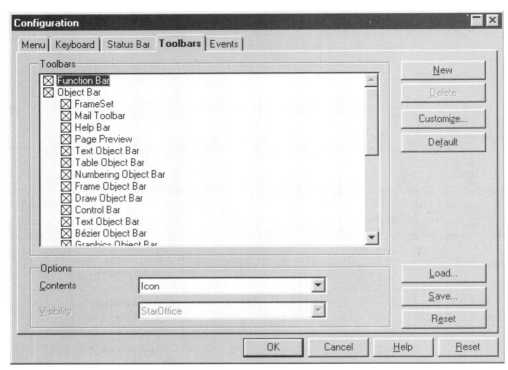

Figure 14.7   The Toolbars tab of the Configuration dialog box.

TO CONFIRM TOOLBAR CONFIGURATION CHANGES

It is important that you read the following options concerning the buttons on the bottom right of the Toolbars tab before you perform any of the toolbar additions, modifications, and deletions in the next sections:

- Click the Reset button directly below the Save button (not the one to the right of the Help button), if you decide that you don't want to keep the changes to the Configuration Toolbar tab. All current changes in the active dialog will be irretrievably lost. The toolbar configuration since the last time you clicked the Save button will reappear, even if you clicked the OK button and returned to the document (and exited and reopened StarOffice).

- Click the Save button to open the Save Toolbar Configuration dialog box to save the configuration settings. Note that if you save the newly created toolbar configuration as soffice.cfg, the program-specific configuration file is overwritten. You can select the active configuration file by clicking the Load button.

- Click the Load button to access the Load Toolbar Configuration dialog box. A specific configuration will be active until it is replaced by a new one— perhaps that you will create in the next few sections.

TO DISPLAY OR HIDE A TOOLBAR BY DEFAULT

You can indicate whether you want a specific toolbar to automatically display by default. This is different than displaying and hiding the Function Bar, Object Bar, and Main Toolbar using the View menu.

1   Choose Tools, Configure to open the Configuration dialog box and click the Toolbar tab.

     You can also right-click directly on the toolbar to activate the shortcut menu, and select Configure. This will open the dialog box and highlight the exact toolbar name.

2   Click on the check box to the left of the toolbar name. If the checkbox is not selected, the toolbar won't display by default, even if the toolbar would normally appear when a command activates the toolbar. The Function Bar, Object Bar, and Main Toolbar can always be activated using the View, Toolbars submenu; but, if you deactivate a context-sensitive menu (for example, the Table Object Bar, which displays as the active Object bar when working with tables), it will not appear until you reactivate it specifically on this dialog box.

3   Click the Save button to make the changes permanent and click the OK button. Refer to the section "To Confirm Toolbar Configuration Changes" to make sure this is what you want to do.

TO CHANGE A TOOLBAR NAME

The most common instance of when you would want to change a toolbar name, is if you wanted to change the name of one that you already created or you were changing the desktop for a particular user.

1   Choose Tools, Configure to open the Configuration dialog box and click the Toolbar tab.

     You can also right-click directly on the toolbar to activate the shortcut menu, and select Configure. This will open the dialog box to the toolbar you clicked on.

2   Click directly on the toolbar name and wait for the name to be highlighted. You may have to wait a few moments. Only the name will be selected, as opposed to the entire row.

3   Edit the name in a text box and press <Enter>.

4   Click the Save button to make the changes permanent and click the OK button. Refer to the section "To Confirm Toolbar Configuration Changes" to make sure this is what you want to do.

TO DISPLAY OR HIDE TOOLBAR BUTTONS

1   Right-click directly on the toolbar to activate the shortcut menu, and select Visible Buttons. This will display the buttons available on the toolbar.

2   Click a button command. If there is a checkmark to the left of the command, it is displayed; if there is not a checkmark, the button won't display.

You must perform steps 1 and 2 each time you want to add or remove a button on a toolbar.

TO CREATE A NEW TOOLBAR AND ADD BUTTONS

1   Choose Tools, Configure to open the Configuration dialog box and click the Toolbar tab.

2   Click the New button to insert "User-defined no.1" to the end of the toolbar list.

You can always select this new toolbar and click the Delete button if you decide you don't want to create a new toolbar, although you cannot delete the four main toolbars within StarOffice Writer.

3   Rename the toolbar by clicking on it; wait a few moments for the cursor to the right of the highlighted name to blink. Then, you can type in a new name (for example, Macros).

4   Select the following from the Options area (see Figure 14.8):

•Contents—Click this drop-down list box to select whether buttons on the toolbar will display an Icon, Text, or Icon & Text (for example, choose Icon).
•Visibility—Click this drop-down list box to select when the toolbar will display on the desktop (for example, choose StarWriter for it to be visible all the time, like the Function and Object Bars).

If you chose the StarWriter option, notice that the new, blank toolbar will appear on screen once you move to step 5 (also refer to the callout on Figure 14.9). Otherwise, it will appear when activated by the action you chose in the Visibility list.

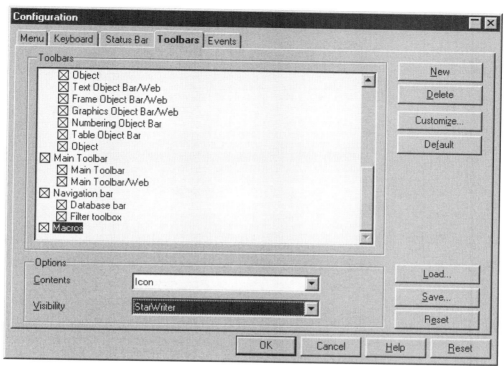

Figure 14.8   You can create a new toolbar and indicate how and where it will appear on screen.

5   Now that you have created a new toolbar, you can add buttons to it. Click the Customize button to open the Customize Toolbars dialog box (see Figure 14.9).

New Macro Toolbar

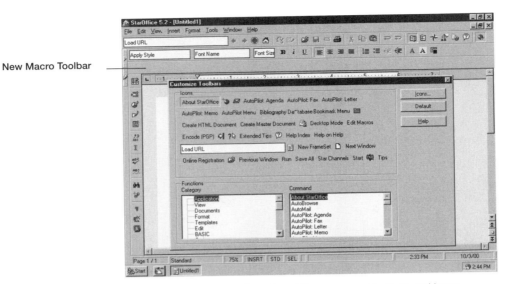

Figure 14.9   You can customize your toolbars by adding command buttons and icons.

6   Click the desired Category and Command from the Functions area. The Function list boxes show the program areas and associated functions:

Category—Where you can select the category containing the function you want to assign to a toolbar [for example, select a macro from the StarOffice BASIC Macros (Standard, Module1)].

Command—Where you can select the command you want to assign to a toolbar (for example, the CompanyLogo macro you created in Chapter 12).

7   Click the Icons button to open the Customize Buttons dialog box (see Figure 14.10). You can click the up and down arrows to move through the Buttons list.

Notice the Command you selected in step 6 is listed in the Function text box. If you change the text in this text box, the new text is what will appear when you move the mouse pointer over the button and a Help Tip appears. Click the OK button to return to the Customize Toolbars dialog box; now move the mouse pointer over the new icon and review the Help Tip name.

Selected Icon

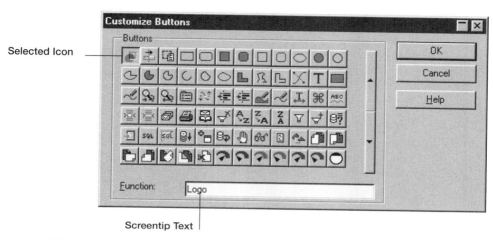

Screentip Text

Figure 14.10   You can select icons for your buttons and alter the Help Tip text.

8   Click directly on the new button you added an icon to (step 7) and drag and drop it on the new toolbar you created (steps 2 through 4). Refer to Figure 14.11. This will place the button on your toolbar immediately, while leaving the Customize Toolbars dialog box open to select more buttons, if you prefer (simply repeat step 6).

NOTE   You could also drag and drop a button in the Customize Toolbars dialog box to any of the other toolbars visible on the desktop.

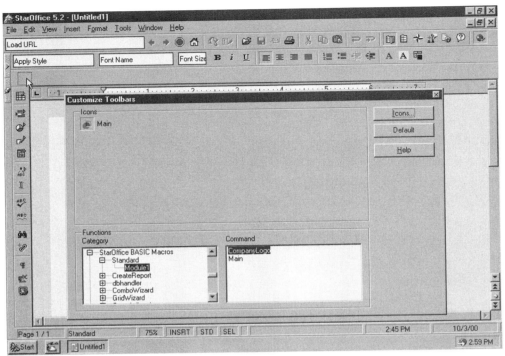

Figure 14.11   You can drag and drop buttons directly onto the desired toolbar.

9   Click the X Close button on the Customize Toolbars dialog box to return
to the text document.

The new toolbar configuration will automatically be saved to your sof-
fice.cfg configuration file. You can always choose Tools, Configure to open
the Configuration dialog box, click the Toolbar tab, and click the Reset
button, which will reset your StarOffice Writer toolbars back to their
original settings.

TO MODIFY EXISTING TOOLBAR BUTTONS

The following procedures can be performed in StarOffice Writer on any toolbar
that is on screen:

• To delete a toolbar button, press <Alt> and click and drag it off the toolbar.
• To move a toolbar button to a new position on the same toolbar or on a
  different toolbar, press <Alt> and click and drag the icon to the new
  position.

- To insert a button grouping line before a toolbar button, press <Alt> and click and drag the icon to the right (drag the icon to the left to remove a button grouping line).

Configuring Events

This is where you assign macros to run upon specific events (for example, when you create a new document). The macro will automatically run each time the selected event occurs.

Choose Tools, Configure to open the Configuration dialog box and click the Events tab (see Figure 14.12).

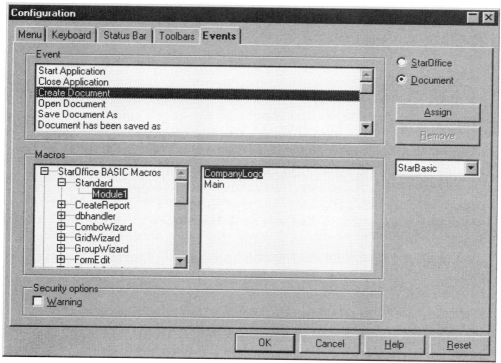

Figure 14.12   The Events tab of the Configuration dialog box.

The following is a list of the list boxes, options, and buttons available to you for configuring events:

- Event—Select the specific event that you want to assign a macro.

- StarOffice—Select this option to run the macro every time the selected event occurs, regardless of the document type (only applicable to global macros). Macros that are linked to a specific document will only run if the corresponding document is open.

- Document—Select this option if you only want the assigned macro to run when the document containing the macro is open.

- Macros—The left list box displays all available libraries and modules for your stored macros. You can click on a plus sign to expand the lower levels, or click on a minus sign to hide the lower levels. The different macros are structured in two groups, as indicated by the two main entries in the list. One displays the documents that contain macros (for example, Untitled1 BASIC Macros if you just opened a new text document), and the other shows global macros in the application that apply to any and all documents (for example, StarOffice BASIC Macros). The right list box displays the respective macros assigned to the module selected in the left list box.

- Programming language—Click this drop-down list and choose either to integrate StarOffice Basic, JavaScript or StarOffice Script macros. If you select the JavaScript options, a text box will appear in which you can type your script directly.

- Security options—Select the Warning check box if you want a message to appear before each event-triggered macro runs.

- Assign—Click this button to assign the selected macro to the selected event; the macro information will be written to the right of the event entry.

- Remove—Click this button to clear the macro assigned to the selected entry; no warning message will appear confirming this action.

Click the Reset button at the bottom of the dialog box if you decide that you don't want to keep the changes to the Configuration Events tab. All current changes in the active dialog will be irretrievably lost. The event assignments since the last time you clicked the OK button will reappear. Otherwise, click the OK button to save the event settings.

Writer Shortcut Keys

This appendix contains keys and key combinations that will help you quickly perform specific commands and functions within StarOffice Writer.

KEYS	FUNCTION
<Ctrl+A>	Selects everything in the document
<Ctrl+B>	Bolds text
<Ctrl+Shift+B>	Subscripts text
<Ctrl+C>	Copies the selected items
<Ctrl+D>	Double underlines text
<Ctrl+E>	Centers text
<Ctrl+Shift+E>	Opens and moves focus to the Explorer

\<Ctrl+F\>	Opens the Find & Replace dialog box
\<Ctrl+Shift+F\>	Searches for the least entered search term
\<Ctrl+I\>	Italicizes text
\<Ctrl+Shift+I\>	Toggles the Integrated Desktop/Window View
\<Ctrl+J\>	Justifies the paragraph or selection
\<Ctrl+Shift+J\>	Toggles the view between Full screen mode/normal mode
\<Ctrl+L\>	Aligns the paragraph or selection to the left
\<Ctrl+N\>	Displays the New document dialog box to create a new document
\<Ctrl+O\>	Displays the Open dialog box where you can choose a document to open
\<Ctrl+P\>	Displays the Print dialog box where you can choose settings and print the current document
\<Ctrl+Shift+P\>	Superscripts text
\<Crtl+Q\>	Exits the application
\<Ctrl+Shift+Q\>	Interrupts a macro
\<Ctrl+R\>	Aligns the paragraph or selection to the right
\<Ctrl+S\>	Saves the current document
\<Ctrl+Shift+S\>	Displays the Special Character dialog box when in the Find & Replace dialog box

<Ctrl+U>	Underlines the text
<Ctrl+V>	Inserts (pastes) the recent cut or copied information from the clipboard
<Ctrl+X>	Cuts the selected elements
<Ctrl+Y>	Opens the Style Catalog
<Ctrl+Z>	Undoes the previous action
<Ctrl+1>	Applies single line spacing
<Ctrl+2>	Applies double line spacing
<Ctrl+5>	Applies 1.5 line spacing
<Ctrl++>	Must use the "+" in the calculator part of the keyboard at the far right; calculates the selected area (for example, 3487+3456); the result is copied to the clipboard and must be inserted into the document from the clipboard
<Ctrl+->	Inserts optional hyphens; a word will not be hyphenated if it has this indicator as the first character
<Ctrl+Spacebar>	Inserts a protected space; not wrapped at the end of a line and not expanded if the text is justified
<Shift+Enter>	Inserts a line break without paragraph change
<Ctrl+Enter>	Inserts a hard page break
<Ctrl+Shift+Enter>	Inserts a column break in multicolumn texts
<Alt+Enter>	Inserts a new paragraph directly before or after a section

<Arrow Left>	Moves the cursor to the left
<Shift+Arrow Left>	Selects from the cursor to the left
<Ctrl+Arrow Left>	Moves to the beginning of the word
<Ctrl+Shift+Arrow Left>	Selects to the left; word by word
<Arrow Right>	Moves the cursor to the right
<Shift+Arrow Right>	Selects from the cursor to the right
<Ctrl+Arrow Right>	Moves to the end of the word to the right
<Ctrl+Shift+Arrow Right>	Selects to the right; word by word
<Arrow Up>	Moves the cursor up one line
<Ctrl+Arrow Up>	Moves the entire paragraph up one paragraph
<Shift+Arrow Up>	Continues the selection up by one line
<Arrow Down>	Moves the cursor down one line
<Shift+Arrow Down>	Continues the selection down by one line
<Ctrl+Arrow Down>	Moves the entire paragraph down one paragraph
<Home>	Moves the cursor to the beginning of the line
<Shift+Home>	Moves the cursor to the beginning of the line and selects it

\<End\>	Moves the cursor to the end of the line
\<Shift+End\>	Moves the cursor to the end of the line and selects it
\<Ctrl+End\>	Moves the cursor to the start of the document
\<Ctrl+Shift+End\>	Selects text to the start of the document
\<Ctrl+End\>	Moves the cursor to the end of the document
\<Ctrl+Shift+End\>	Selects text to the end of the document
\<Ctrl+PageUp\>	Switches the cursor between text and header
\<Ctrl+PageDown\>	Switches the cursor between text and footer
\<Insert\>	Toggles Insert mode on and off
\<PageUp\>	Moves the viewable screen page up
\<Shift+PageUp\>	Moves the highlighted selection up the screen page with the current selection
\<PageDown\>	Moves the viewable screen page down
\<Shift+PageDown\>	Moves the highlighted selection down the screen page with the current selection
\<Ctrl+Delete\>	Deletes text to the end of the word (or if there in punctuation, like an apostrophe, it will delete to the punctuation)
\<Ctrl+Backspace\>	Deletes text to the beginning of the word (or if there in punctuation, like an apostrophe, it will delete to the punctuation)

<Ctrl+Shift+Delete>	Deletes text to the end of the sentence (and deletes forward to any punctuation at the beginning of the next sentence)
<Ctrl+Shift+Back-space>	Deletes text to the beginning of the sentence (and deletes back to any punctuation at the end of the previous sentence)
<Ctrl+Tab>	Moves to the next open document; or to the next suggestion when using Automatic Word Completion
<Ctrl+Shift+Tab>	Moves to the previous open document; or to the previous suggestion when using Automatic Word Completion
<Alt+O>	Accepts a word marked as unknown or incorrect in the given input row (word), when using the Spellchecker
<Ctrl+Double-click>	Docks or undocks the Navigator, Stylist, or another window
<F1>	Displays the Help Agent
<Shift+F1>	Changes the cursor to a pointer and question mark, which can be moved over commands and buttons for context Help
<F2>	Activates the Formula Bar
<Ctrl+F2>	Activates the Fields dialog box
<F3>	Completes an AutoText entry
<Ctrl+F3>	Edit an AutoText entry
<F4>	Opens the Beamer (if there is a database active, for example, when performing a form letter mail merge)
<Ctrl+F4>	Closes the current task and prompts you if you want to save the document

\<Alt+F4\>	Exits the application and prompts you if you want to save the documents you are working in
\<F5\>	Toggles the Navigator on and off
\<Shift+F5\>	Moves to next frame (text box)
\<Ctrl+Shift+F5\>	Activates the Navigator
\<F7\>	Activates the Spellchecker
\<Ctrl+F7\>	Activates the Thesaurus
\<F8\>	Activates the Extended Selection (EXT) mode in the Status bar
\<Ctrl+F8\>	Toggles the Field shadings on and off
\<Shift+F8\>	Activates the Additional Selection (ADD) mode in the Status bar
\<F9\>	Updates fields in the document
\<Ctrl+F9\>	Shows fields in the document
\<Ctrl+Shift+F9\>	Updates input fields
\<F10\>	Selects the Menu (works like \<Alt\>)
\<Ctrl+F10\>	Toggles Nonprinting Characters on and off
\<F11\>	Toggles the Stylist on and off
\<Shift+F11\>	Activates the Create Style dialog box

<Ctrl+Shift+F11>	Updates a style in the document
<F12>	Toggles paragraph numbering on and off
<Ctrl+F12>	Activates the Insert Table dialog box
<Shift+F12>	Toggles paragraph bullets on and off
<Ctrl+Shift+F12>	Toggles paragraph Numbering and Bullets off

Index

 *Solutions from experts you know and trust.*

Articles | Free Library | eBooks | Expert Q & A | Training | Career Center | Downloads | MyInformIT

Login | Register | About InformIT

Topics
Operating Systems
Web Development
Programming
Networking
Certification
and more...

Expert Access

Free Content

www.informit.com

✓ Free, in-depth articles and supplements

✓ Master the skills you need, when you need them

✓ Choose from industry leading books, ebooks, and training products

✓ Get answers when you need them - from live experts or InformIT's comprehensive library

✓ Achieve industry certification and advance your career

Visit  today
and get great content
from PH
PTR